Sydney George Fisher

The Evolution of the Constitution of the United States,

showing that it is a development of progressive history and not an isolated document struck off at a given time or an imitation of English or Dutch forms of government

Sydney George Fisher

The Evolution of the Constitution of the United States,
showing that it is a development of progressive history and not an isolated document struck off at a given time or an imitation of English or Dutch forms of government

ISBN/EAN: 9783337301118

Printed in Europe, USA, Canada, Australia, Japan

Cover: Foto ©Suzi / pixelio.de

More available books at **www.hansebooks.com**

The Evolution of the Constitution of the United States

Showing that it is a Development of Progressive
History and not an Isolated Document
Struck Off at a Given Time or
an Imitation of English
or Dutch Forms of
Government

By

Sydney George Fisher

Philadelphia
J. B. Lippincott Company
Mdcccxcvii

Copyright, 1897,
BY
J. B. Lippincott Company.

Preface

HISTORIES of the Constitution usually describe the labors of its framers in the Convention of 1787 and the contests of political parties over the adoption of the instrument by the requisite number of States in the following year, together with such changes or developments as have taken place since that time. The works which have touched on its sources or origin have treated it as invented by the convention which framed it, or have sought in England or other European countries for forms of government which were like it or might have suggested its various provisions.

Having for a long time been convinced that the Constitution is neither an invention nor an imitation, but almost exclusively a native product of slow and gradual growth, I have in this book undertaken to trace back, through previous American documents in colonial times, every material clause of it. These documents are very numerous, and consist of twenty-nine colonial charters and constitutions, seventeen Revolutionary constitutions, and twenty-three plans of union,—in all, sixty-nine different forms of government which were either in actual or in attempted operation in America during a period of about two hundred years, from 1584 to 1787. These constituted the school of thought, the experiments, and

Preface

the training which in the end produced the national government under which we now live.

The time of two hundred years was sufficiently long, and the sixty-nine different forms of government were certainly numerous and varied enough, to bring about the final result; and they account for the final result in a more clear, complete, and satisfactory manner than any of the theories of sudden inspiration or imitation of England or Holland that have been broached.

In order to show the evolution in all its details, I have divided two of the chapters into sections. Each section traces back a clause of the Constitution through all the previous documents, with quotations from each document showing the gradual development, the experience that was acquired, or the experiments that were made. This has made necessary a great deal of small print, and sometimes rather long quotations from the old documents, which were very verbose. But the reader has it all before him, and can, in most instances, see at a glance the nature of the development without any laborious search through the sixty-nine documents. I have also tried to lessen his efforts, wherever I could, by comments and summaries.

Besides this detailed analysis, there are chapters giving a general view of the growth and discussing the supposed resemblances to European forms of government. The last chapter deals with Mr. Campbell's theory that part of the Constitution and many other American institutions were derived from Holland.

PHILADELPHIA, February, 1897.

Contents

CHAPTER I.
CONFUSED IDEAS AS TO THE ORIGIN OF THE CONSTITUTION . . PAGE 11

CHAPTER II.
THE COLONIAL CHARTERS AND CONSTITUTIONS 26

CHAPTER III.
THE CONSTITUTIONS OF 1776 70

CHAPTER IV.
THE ENGLISH SOURCES OF THE CONSTITUTION 90

CHAPTER V.
THE EVOLUTION FROM THE COLONIAL CHARTERS SHOWN IN DETAIL 105

CHAPTER VI.
THE EVOLUTION OF FEDERALISM 215

CHAPTER VII.
THE EVOLUTION OF FEDERALISM SHOWN IN DETAIL 267

Contents

CHAPTER VIII.

CLAUSES OF THE CONSTITUTION WHICH WERE OF SHORT DEVELOPMENT 310

CHAPTER IX.

DUTCH SOURCES 315

APPENDIX.

CONSTITUTION OF THE UNITED STATES 375

Documents in the Evolution from the Colonial Charters

1. Sir Walter Raleigh's Charter, 1584.
2. Virginia Charter, 1606.
3. Virginia Charter, 1609.
4. Virginia Charter, 1611–12.
5. New England Charter, 1620.
6. Grant of New Hampshire, 1629.
7. Massachusetts Charter, 1629.
8. Maryland Charter, 1632.
9. Grant of New Hampshire, 1635.
10. Fundamental Orders of Connecticut, 1638.
11. Grant of Maine, 1639.
12. Connecticut Charter, 1662.
13. Charter of Carolina, 1663.
14. Rhode Island Charter, 1663.
15. Grant to the Duke of York, 1664.
16. Concessions of East Jersey, 1665.
17. Charter of Carolina, 1665.
18. Locke's Carolina Constitution, 1669.
19. Grant to the Duke of York, 1674.
20. Concessions of West Jersey, 1677.
21. Commission for New Hampshire, 1680.
22. Pennsylvania Charter, 1681.
23. Pennsylvania Frame of April 2, 1683.
24. Pennsylvania Frame, 1683.
25. Massachusetts Charter, 1691.
26. Pennsylvania Frame, 1696.
27. Pennsylvania Charter of Privileges, 1701.
28. Explanatory Massachusetts Charter, 1726.
29. Georgia Charter, 1732.

Documents in the Evolution

30. New Hampshire Constitution, begun December 21, 1775; finished January 5, 1776.
31. South Carolina Constitution, adopted March 26, 1776.
32. Virginia Constitution, begun May 6, 1776; adopted June 29, 1776.
33. New Jersey Constitution, begun May 26, 1776; adopted July 3, 1776.
34. Delaware Constitution, begun August 27, 1776; adopted September 21, 1776.
35. Pennsylvania Constitution, begun July 15, 1776; adopted September 28, 1776.
36. Maryland Constitution, begun August 14, 1776; finished November 11, 1776.
37. North Carolina Constitution, begun November 12, 1776; finished December 18, 1776.
38. Georgia Constitution, begun October 1, 1776; finished February 5, 1777.
39. New York Constitution, begun July 10, 1776; finished April 20, 1777.
40. Vermont Constitution, begun July 2, 1777; finished July 8, 1777.
41. Rejected Massachusetts Constitution, 1778.
42. South Carolina Constitution, passed as an act of assembly March 19, 1778; went into effect November, 1778.
43. Rejected New Hampshire Constitution, 1778.
44. Massachusetts Constitution, begun September 1, 1779; finished March 2, 1780.
45. New Hampshire Constitution, begun June 12, 1781; finished October 31, 1783; adopted June 2, 1784.
46. Vermont Constitution, 1786.

The Constitution, 1787.

Documents in the Evolution of Federalism

1. New England Confederation of 1643.
2. Commission of Council for Foreign Plantations, 1660.
3. William Penn's Plan of Union, 1696.
4. Report of Board of Trade on union of New York with other colonies, 1696.
5. D'Avenant's Plan of 1698.
6. A Virginian's Plan, in "An Essay on the Government of the English Plantations on the Continent of America," 1701.
7. Livingston's Plan, 1701.
8. Earl of Stair's Proposals, 1721.
9. Plan of the Lords of Trade, 1721.
10. Daniel Coxe's Plan, in "A Description of the English Province of Carolina," 1722.
11. Kennedy's Plan, 1751.
12. Franklin's Plan, 1754.
13. Richard Peters's Plan, 1754.
14. Hutchinson's Plan, 1754.
15. Plan of the Lords of Trade, 1754.
16. Dr. Samuel Johnson's Plan, 1760.
17. Galloway's Plan, 1774.
18. Franklin's Articles of Confederation, 1775.
19. The Articles of Confederation, 1778.
20. Drayton's Articles of Confederation, 1778.
21. Webster's Sketches of American Policy, 1785.
22. Randolph's Plan, 1787.
23. Pinckney's Plan, 1787.
The Constitution, 1787.

The Evolution of the Constitution of the United States

CHAPTER I.

CONFUSED IDEAS AS TO THE ORIGIN OF THE CONSTITUTION.

To set men thinking and incite them to conduct investigations of their own is often more important than to persuade and convince them. No words of Mr. Gladstone have been so much considered by the American people, and none have aroused them to so much research, as those in which he said that "as the British Constitution is the most subtle organism which has proceeded from progressive history, so the American Constitution is the most wonderful work ever struck off at a given time by the brain and purpose of man."

At first glance there seems to be a compliment in the striking, clear-cut language of the great English statesman, and if the phrase had been applied to some nations—the French, for example—they would probably continue to think it complimentary. But along with the first impression of a compliment the Anglo-Saxon instinct of Americans received an impression which it

Evolution of the Constitution

resented. Our people were at first pleased, but the next moment they were irritated at the thought that their government had been made off-hand.

They have the reputation of being smart and quick, —smarter and quicker than their cousins the British,— and they rather like to be told so. But when you tell them that they were smart and quick in creating a political institution you touch another and far deeper feeling. You cut them off from their past; and veneration for their past, even their far-distant past, is a passion which, though often secretly nourished, fills a large part of their lives. And so it has come to pass that, of all the sentences the Liberal leader of England ever wrote, there is none which Americans have been so anxious to refute as the one in which he doubtless thought he was saying what would be most surely acceptable to them.

Soon after his assertion became generally known, dissent from it began to appear, here and there, in addresses and newspaper and magazine articles, and now there are whole books on the subject, all laboring to show that the Constitution was not "struck off at a given time," but that its source and lines of development stretch far back into the past.

Unfortunately, these learned gentlemen who trace the sources of the Constitution do not agree with one another. In fact, there is a most extraordinary and even ridiculous contradiction in the sources they assign. Mr. Bryce, in his great work, "The American Commonwealth," finds the sources in the British government of King, Lords, and Commons, and he is followed by

Confused Ideas as to its Origin

Taylor, Stevens, and others, with variations of the same general opinion; while Foster, in his recent work on the Constitution, seems somewhat inclined to go back to Mr. Gladstone's view. But Mr. Campbell, in his "Puritan in Holland, England, and America," denies all English sources, and gives our institutions an origin in Holland.

When we look further into the general subject of the sources of American institutions, municipal as well as constitutional, we find the same tendency to assign queer foreign origins. The New England township system, according to some learned people, is of German origin. The New England town, they say, especially in colonial times, with its common land and self-government, almost exactly resembled the old Teutonic village.

Between the occurrence of these two resemblances centuries of time elapsed when such towns were unknown to the race and forgotten by it. But a few centuries are a mere trifle to a man who has detected one of these mystical resemblances. By a little skilful language, a "doubtless" or a "perhaps" or an ingenious hypothesis, he will easily jump æons of time and oceans of space. Only let him find in Mexico or Yucatan a building or some pottery with an outline like something in Persia, and five thousand years and three thousand miles of ocean are nothing. He will put volcanoes under the water and raise islands, and then an ancient continent, until he has made history to suit him.

Every generation seems to have its crop of these extraordinary suggestions and hypotheses, which their advocates soon extend beyond their proper sphere of mere

Evolution of the Constitution

suggestions and insist that they are certainties. For many years after the Revolution it was supposed that some of the American Indians were descended from a lost tribe of Welshmen who came to this continent under a leader called Madoc. Remains of burial mounds and ancient customs were found, which the learned insisted were very like remains in Wales, and they heaped up the suggestions until they had what they thought was proof. Fortunately, the craze had passed away when the tribe of Modoc Indians became prominent soon after the Civil War, or we might have had it continued indefinitely.

During the same period many people believed that all our Indians were descendants of the lost tribes of Israel. They found many resemblances, and the one which impressed them most was that some of the Indians had cities of refuge like the Israelites. Cooper satirized these people in his novel "Oak Openings," in which there is a character who proves the connection by the passage in the Psalms, "God shall wound the head of his enemies, and the hairy scalp of such a one as goeth on still in his wickedness." But these ancient fancies are hardly any worse than Mr. Campbell's notion that our American institutions, including the New England town system, are derived from Holland.

I admit that there is great fascination in these speculations, and I admit that there may possibly be something more than fascination in the theory of the recurrence of ideas and institutions at long intervals in the history of a race. That passage in Du Chaillu's "Viking Age" in which he asserts that the Norsemen, the ances-

Confused Ideas as to its Origin

tors of the English and Americans, had a federal government like that of the United States, is certainly most interesting and impressive:

"Every Herad was independent of the Fylki in its local affairs, and every Fylki was independent one from the other, each having self-government. When the affairs of the country required the presence of all the people, then the boendr of the Herads and Fylki met together at a general Thing, called Allsherjar Thing (Thing of all the hosts), and all had to abide by the decision taken . . . The closest approach to this ancient form of government is that of the United States."

But before we resort to these far-fetched and romantic speculations we should exhaust the nearer and more accurate method, and this is what the writers on the sources of the American Constitution have failed to do. Taking the Constitution as it was framed in 1787, they immediately look for something in Europe from which they assume it must have been copied, instead of tracing its origin backward from itself through the two hundred years of the colonial period.

If I find on American soil the footprints of a man, and wish to discover whence he came, I surely ought not to assume at once that he is a foreigner and take the next steamer for England or Holland to see if I can find footprints over there that are like his. It would be better, it seems to me, to start backward on his trail from the very spot where I find it; for it may be that he is a native, and I may be able to follow his tracks for hundreds of miles in this country, and, when I come to his house, find that he and his ancestors have been living there for many generations. In any event, I should follow back his track until it ends on the sea-shore, and after that search for him in other countries.

This is, I believe, the only sound, legitimate, and scientific way to trace the origin of a public document or institution. We must go back, step by step, in the direct line of ancestry, and keep in that line until it ends. There must be no jumping, no wanderings aside, and no searching for vague resemblances in the world at large.

If the writers on the sources of the Constitution had followed this plan there would, I think, be less disagreement among them, or at least not the extraordinary contradiction which we now find. The contradiction follows naturally enough from their method; for as soon as they leave the direct line of growth and begin to search for resemblances everywhere they will find plenty of them. Human nature is in a general way much the same all the world over, and human beings have been laboring for many centuries and encountering the same problems and conditions in one country as in another. Within recent years vast quantities of historical details of almost every country have been published, and a man who has a fancy for some particular nation can easily frame a specious argument to show how other nations have apparently copied from it.

There have been instances of direct and literal imitation; but they are comparatively rare, and very rare among the Anglo-Saxon race. The instances where one nation has been influenced in a general way by what it knows of the workings of institutions in another

Confused Ideas as to its Origin

nation are more numerous; but in these instances there is not what would properly be called an imitation or a taking. Very often the institutions of the foreign country are considered as an example of what should not be done. Some of the provisions of our own Constitution were influenced in this way by what were supposed to be evils in the English system.

In other cases a nation, having to solve a problem which has troubled it for many years, works out in time what seems to be a solution, and is the more convinced that it will prove successful because something like it has been adopted by another country. The foreign institutions are used in these instances argumentatively, and are not imitated in the true sense of the word, because the nation has an experience of its own with which it is working, and it uses the foreign institution merely to reinforce its own ideas.

For example, in colonial times our people were very familiar with the veto power in the colonial governors, and also in the king. The governors could, in many instances, veto the laws of the assemblies immediately on their passage, and the same laws had to be submitted to the king, who had a certain number of years, usually about five, to examine them, and at the end of that time, if he disapproved, he could annul them. These vetoes of governors and king were absolute. They killed the laws, and there was no arrangement for passing the laws over their veto by a two-thirds vote. But the people suffered so much inconvenience from these absolute vetoes that when they came to make their own State constitutions in the Revolution they usually gave their governors no veto power at all, until at last New York hit upon the plan of a modified veto, which could be overcome by a two-thirds vote of the legislature; and when the National Constitution was framed this same modified veto was given to the President. It is certainly not an imitation of the veto power of the English king, for it was developed solely out of American experience of the evils of the king's absolute veto.

The United States Senate is, as we shall see, a gradual development from the Governor's Council of colonial times, which was first a mere advisory council of the governor, afterwards a part of the legislature sitting with the assembly, then a second house of legislature sitting apart from the assembly, as an upper house; sometimes appointed by the governor, sometimes elected by the people, until it gradually became an elective body, with the idea that its members represented certain districts of land, usually the counties. It had developed thus far when the National Constitution was framed, and it was adopted in that instrument so as to equalize the States and prevent the larger ones from oppressing the smaller ones. This was accomplished by giving each State two Senators, so that large and small were alike. The language in the Constitution describing the functions of the Senate was framed principally by John Dickinson, who at that time represented Delaware,—one of the smaller States of the Union,—which had suffered in colonial times from too much control by Pennsylvania.

The Senate as it exists to-day is therefore primarily the result of our own experience. But some writers insist on seeing in it an imitation of the British House

Confused Ideas as to its Origin

of Lords, and Mr. Campbell, finding that the States-General of the Netherland Republic was composed of representatives of states and that each state had only one vote, and that the framers of our Constitution were familiar with Netherland institutions, jumps to the conclusion that the United States Senate was a Dutch importation.

If it really had been an imitation from the Dutch, there would be some evidence of it in the debates of the Constitutional Convention. The Dutch resemblance would have been urged by some as a reason in its favor and by others as a reason against it. Afterwards, when the Constitution was before the people for adoption and closely discussed and criticised in numerous pamphlets and newspapers, the Dutch imitation, if there had been one, would have been surely referred to either by friends or by enemies. But Mr. Campbell cites no evidence of this sort, and, as a matter of fact, there is none.

The sources of our Constitution are to be found in the colonial period of about two hundred years which preceded the framing of the Constitution, in 1787. Literally, the time began with Sir Walter Raleigh's charter of 1584, which makes a period of two hundred and three years. Those two hundred years were ample for formation and growth, and they cannot be safely skipped. But writers have thus far dismissed them, or summarized them in a sentence or two, and rushed off to Europe to look for foreign sources.

It must be confessed that the supposed foreign sources make easier and more interesting work. The material is all at hand, has been well analyzed and arranged by

Evolution of the Constitution

eminent scholars, and all educated people are more or less familiar with it. But our colonial history is an unknown land of scattered material,—long, wordy documents difficult to read,—and has been so neglected, and the little research that has been made in it so stupidly done, that most people instinctively avoid it. There is supposed to be little or nothing in it, and a habit has grown up of believing that all of value or interest in our history began with the Revolution.

But that despised colonial period contains all our beginnings; and not only our beginnings, but a large part of our maturity; for at the time the Constitution was framed, in 1787, our people had had a vast experience in constitution-making,—greater and more varied, I am inclined to think, than any other people of the world. They had been living under charters from the Crown,—constitutions of their own making,—and some of them without either charters or constitutions, for nearly two centuries, and during the Revolution they had nearly all made new constitutions, under which they had been living for ten or more years.

In fact, our experience of constitution-making and constitution-working previous to 1787 covered a much longer period than our experience since that year. Our modern experience has dealt with larger populations and vaster problems, but it covers a period of less than one hundred and ten years, while the previous experience was of two hundred years, and was more varied, experimental, and elementary.

When Massachusetts sent her delegates, in the year 1787, to frame the National Constitution, she had had

Confused Ideas as to its Origin

over a hundred and fifty years' experience of constitution-tinkering. During that time she had lived under two charters, a constitution, and an *interregnum*, when she had neither charter nor constitution and was under the direct rule of the Crown. Her first charter was so liberal that she had enjoyed for fifty years what was in effect independence. She elected her own governors, coined her own money, and was not obliged to send her laws to England for approval. Her second charter was just the reverse, and gave her a taste of something very near to despotism. During the Revolution she made for herself a constitution which was rejected by her people, but before the Revolution closed she made another, which was accepted. She had had a double experience of constitution-making during the seven years of the Revolution, and, taken all in all, a very severe and long preparation for her part in the national document of 1787.

Virginia had had very much the same experience and training, and for a longer period of time. Pennsylvania had been living for more than ten years under a constitution which she had made for herself in 1776,—a most bungling instrument, with which the majority of her people were heartily disgusted. Previous to that she had been living under an excellent constitution of her own making for seventy-five years, before which she had lived under several constitutions, or frames, as they were then usually called, none of them successful.

Other colonies had had greater or less experience, and it was certainly all very varied. When we consider that the delegates came to the Convention of 1787 with all this experience in their minds, each with the experience of his own colony and what he had heard of the experience of the other colonies, we begin to feel the truth of my main proposition,—that it is to the colonial period we must look for the immediate and most evident sources of the National Constitution, and that the National Constitution when framed, in 1787, instead of being a contrast to the British Constitution and "struck off at a given time," was, even when judged as a purely American production, more than a hundred years old.

The colonial sources of the Constitution are, first of all, the charters of government, which were framed not by the colonists themselves, but for them by the officers and ministers of the British Crown. It is easy enough to give the details of these. We have them all in Poore's admirable collection. They are very trying to read, because, like other documents of that time, each of them, though many pages long, is supposed to be one sentence from beginning to end. The clerks who draughted them were paid by the line, and their ingeniously involved language almost compels one to believe the assertion in Kid's "Social Evolution" that the modern brain is inferior to the ancient. But their immense verbosity conceals usually only a few very simple arrangements of government. They were the foundation and beginning of our constitutional experience.

The second source of our experience is comprised in the constitutions, or frames as they were often called, which were made by the colonists themselves, with little or no dictation from the Crown. Some of these, as in Pennsylvania, rested on an authority given by the Crown

Confused Ideas as to its Origin

to the people to make such a government as they could agree upon with their feudal proprietor. The first constitution of Connecticut, however, was made by the people of their own accord, without any outside influence. These native constitutions might naturally be expected to differ very radically from the royal charters. But in matters of government and political forms there was very little difference, and both charters and constitutions seem to have been influenced by the same process of evolution.

The third class of sources is the actual working and experience under these charters and constitutions, and under the governments which sprang up or were established by the Crown when a colony was without either charter or constitution. In this class we find the same evolution at work, and the practical experience under these governments reinforced the ideas developed by the written documents.

The fourth class of sources comprises what I shall call the Revolutionary constitutions, or constitutions of the year 1776. I call them constitutions of 1776 because most of them were made in that year. They were all the result of a resolution of the Continental Congress passed in 1775, calling on each of the commonwealths, that were then still colonies, to abolish their charters, constitutions, or whatever sort of colonial government they had, and adopt new constitutions suited to the movement for independence.

It was a resolution which at the time it was passed was considered of great importance. The people were wavering and hesitating to join the movement for inde-

Evolution of the Constitution

pendence because they retained a lingering sentiment for the old order of things, the order under which they had lived and prospered for more than a hundred years, and which had given them pretty much all the experience they possessed of civil rights and government. This sentiment was generally believed to be wrapped up in the old charters and colonial constitutions, and if they could be broken the sentiment, it was said, would lose more than half its strength.

It was certainly in many respects a wise resolution from the point of view of those who passed it. It has not been much noticed by writers on the sources of the Constitution, but it was the indirect source of more constitutional experience to the American people than anything else that can be named. It was obeyed by all the colonies except Connecticut and Rhode Island, whose charter governments were so liberal and gave so much essential independence that they were already substantially American. Connecticut continued to live under her old royal charter down to the year 1818, and Rhode Island down to the year 1842.

Under the inspiration of this resolution the majority of the commonwealths that eleven years afterward made the National Constitution rushed into an active experience in constitution-making in the years 1776 and 1777; and they had an opportunity to test the constitutions thus made for ten years before they were called upon to frame the national document.

Of the seventeen constitutions of 1776, eight were put in operation in the year 1776, three in 1777, and one in 1778. Massachusetts framed a constitution in

Confused Ideas as to its Origin

1778 which was rejected by her people, and another in 1779 which was adopted March 2, 1780. New Hampshire, which had adopted a constitution in 1776, framed another in 1779 which was rejected, and another in 1784 which was adopted. But even in the instances of Massachusetts and New Hampshire, where the experience was prolonged and difficult, the constitutions had been in actual working for several years before the assembling of the National Convention of 1787. Vermont adopted a new constitution in 1786, the year before the assembling of the Convention, but it differed very slightly from her constitution of 1777, which was a copy of the Pennsylvania constitution of 1776.

When we read all these constitutions of 1776 together, in the light of our present knowledge, we see at once that they bear a most curious but immature resemblance to the National Constitution. They are full of blunders, untried experiments, well-tried experiments, individual suggestions good and bad, old colonial traditions and experience, strange remnants of aristocratic feeling, and all the natural characteristics of apprentices free for the first time to slash about at will with their master's tools and materials. And the most striking part of all is that when we read them in chronological order we find them developing step by step, and that those which took longest in making, like the constitution of Massachusetts, most nearly resemble the National Constitution.

CHAPTER II.

THE COLONIAL CHARTERS AND CONSTITUTIONS.

(1584 to 1732.)

THESE old documents, when carefully studied in chronological order, show a steady development towards the forms of the National Constitution of 1787. The earliest of them was Sir Walter Raleigh's charter of 1584. This charter was the first step in English colonization in America, and, in a certain sense, the first American written constitution. It authorizes Sir Walter to discover and settle heathen lands, without mentioning any particular continent or part of the world. But it was intended to encourage colonization in North America, and the five unsuccessful voyages made under it were all directed to that continent.

Sir Walter and his heirs and assigns are to be the absolute owners of any lands they settle. He is to have "full power and authority to correct, punish, pardon, govern, and rule" in every way for six years the people who shall come to him or who shall live within two hundred leagues of him. His absolute power during those six years is given in the fullest manner, and the only exceptions to it are that his laws must conform "as near as conveniently may be" to the laws of England, and if he robs any British subjects or the subjects of any prince at peace with Great Britain he must make resti-

Colonial Charters and Constitutions

tution, under penalty of being declared out of the allegiance and protection of his country and "free for all princes and others to pursue with hostility."

The first notion, therefore, which the English had of colonization and government in America was to give the absolute ownership of the land to a single individual, and let him govern it with absolute power for six years. The object was evidently by high reward to encourage some daring spirit to attempt the enterprise, and if he should be successful for six years a more orderly government of the colony could be provided.

The more orderly government appears in the next document, known as the first charter of Virginia, granted in the year 1606. Sir Walter's efforts under his charter of 1584 had been wholly unsuccessful, and no settlement was established. But he gave the name Virginia to the whole country between the present States of Maine and Georgia, so that the next charter could at least be less vague than his had been. We find it, indeed, describing with considerable exactness the country it granted as extending from latitude 34° N. to latitude 45° N. This huge tract was to be divided between two colonies, the first of which was to settle somewhere between Georgia and Pennsylvania and the second between Pennsylvania and Maine.

The absolutism given to a single proprietor in Sir Walter's charter is abandoned in this charter, and in place of it the same absolute power is divided between the king and a council. The government is to consist of a council of thirteen persons in London and a council of the same number in each of the two colonies.

Evolution of the Constitution

Each council in the colonies was to govern its people according to such laws and instructions as the Crown should give, and these instructions were to provide for the appointing and removal of members of each council. But to each council was distinctly given the right to defend its colony by war on sea and land and establish a coin to pass current in trade. The London council was to have a general oversight of both the colonies, but its powers were of the vaguest kind. This charter was, however, a great advance on Sir Walter's. The law-making power was taken from the single proprietor and reserved to the king, and the administration of the laws was given to a more or less numerous council.

The power to make war and coin money was of a decidedly political nature, and shows a conscious shaping of the beginnings of a commonwealth. But the charter did not resemble any part of the British Constitution of that period. So far as it resembles anything it is more like the arrangement of the old English trading corporations. They were very apt to have the governing power in the hands of a set of individuals, called a council or some such name. Afterwards there was a head, called president or governor, with a council to assist him, and in time the corporation government by president, board of directors, and stockholders was developed as we have it to-day.

Thus, the charter of the famous Grocers' Company, granted in 1429, places the whole power and government in three or four individuals called wardens. They are to govern; and apparently, so far as the charter

Colonial Charters and Constitutions

speaks, the members—or stockholders, as we should now call them—have no vote, and there is no head or president. The charter of the Merchant Adventurers, granted in 1505, shows a development by allowing the adventurers to meet and elect a governor or governors and also "four-and-twenty assistants to the said governor or governors." This term "assistants" was afterwards, as we shall see, used in the Massachusetts charter of 1629, showing very clearly how our American forms of government originated in the trading charters.*

The first Virginia charter is evidently framed on some

---

*An interesting account of some of these old companies can now be found in Gawston and Keane's "Early Chartered Companies." They were all, in their forms of government, very much like the early charters of the colonies in America. They were the beginning of the great English colonial system, and were for the encouragement of trade, exploration, and settlement in foreign countries. They were necessary as the most convenient method of concentrating capital and energy, because private individuals could not bear the great expense of contending with the pirates, who had to be fought with heavy armaments or bought off with expensive presents. These necessities of warfare first suggested the giving of governmental powers, which were rather novel functions for traders. The chronological order of the creation of these companies is significant: Merchant Adventurers, 1505; Russia Company (for trade towards Russia), 1554; Eastland Company (also for trade to Russia), 1579; Turkey Company (for trade to the Mediterranean), 1581; Marocco Company, 1585; First Guinea Company, 1588; East India Company, 1599; Guiana Company, 1609; Bermuda Company, 1612; Second Guinea Company, 1631; China Company, 1635; Third Guinea Company, 1662; Canary Company, 1665; Hudson's Bay Company, 1670; Fourth Guinea Company, 1672.

such model. Its draughtsmen naturally followed some of the forms to which they were accustomed in organizing ordinary enterprises of business, and, as this one was to found a settlement in a new country, they threw in the political rights to coin money and to defend the settlement by waging war. They were soon to become convinced that a full-fledged corporation was the best form of government for establishing a colony.

Three years after, in 1609, another charter was issued for Virginia, which professes to be an enlargement and improvement on the first one. It is less vague. Experience had been acquired, and more details and more definite arrangements could be ventured upon. The striking part is that it creates an out-and-out corporation modelled on the trading companies of the time, with the usual expressions giving a common seal, perpetual succession, and the right to hold real estate and to implead and be impleaded.

A settlement had been effected in 1607, on the James River, within the territory of the first colony; but nothing had been accomplished within the domain of the second colony. The second colony was therefore abandoned, and the first colony incorporated under the name of "The Treasurer and Company of Adventurers and Planters of the City of London for the First Colony in Virginia." A trading company was the natural form for the enterprise to take, for these rather reckless adventurers who were going to Virginia had no political project in their minds, and were not bent on carrying out any particular political theory. They were in search of gold or wealth in any form they could find it, and for that purpose the king was allowing them to enter on a tract of land in his wilderness domain.

Their quest was a business one; and so they were incorporated as a business company, with one or two rough provisions added to enable them to live together in the wilderness. They were a trading company which might also have to fight savages or pirates or the king's enemies, and might also have to control and punish unruly men among their own number. They were very much like the Hudson's Bay Company and the East India Company, whose charters show this same peculiarity of an ordinary trading charter changed slightly so as to enable its members to contend with wild nature and wild men.

The first charter of Virginia named no officer as head of the undertaking. But now we have the treasurer as head, and the charter of incorporation goes on to provide that there shall be two councils as in the former charter, one resident in England and the other resident in the colony. The council in England is to appoint a governor and other officers and make laws for the colony, and the council and treasurer are to be elected by the members of the company. The council, treasurer, and members of the company collectively are given a sort of general police power to correct, punish, and pardon offences, and the governor is given the right to make use of martial law when occasion requires it.

Here we have some decided governmental powers worked out under the forms of a trading corporation. A definite governor or executive is provided for the first time; and the pardoning power appears also for the first

Evolution of the Constitution

time given to the collective legislative body of the whole company as well as to the governor and other officials, and not to the governor alone, as in later developments. The right of the company to elect the treasurer and council is also a considerable advance; and the absolutism of the two previous charters has disappeared.

In 1611–12 another charter added a further development, and gave to the treasurer and members of the company the right to hold general courts or meetings, and to make laws, appoint officers, arrange the manner of government, and elect persons to the council. Here we have the power of making laws and appointing officers taken away from the council and given to the whole body of the members of the company,—a definite move towards more popular government within the forms of a trading corporation. The council is relegated to the position of a sort of executive body to manage the affairs of the company from day to day, and we shall soon see it become the governor's council. There is also a provision allowing the company to admit as members aliens, or persons not liege subjects of the British Crown, which is evidently a move towards the right possessed by all political governments to naturalize foreigners.

Thus far the American form of government as developed out of a corporation seems to be a council and head of the company called treasurer, a governor, and the members of the company meeting in a body to legislate. But under the condition of affairs in Virginia the governor became more and more of an important person, and the colony was soon ruled by governors with a strong and even violent hand,—a method which

Colonial Charters and Constitutions

was doubtless well suited to the restless and unruly spirits of the adventurers. One of the governors controlled them by martial law, which the charter allowed to be used in case of necessity.

Meantime there was great contention in England among the members of the company as to what was the proper form of government for the colony. In 1619, under the powers they had to make laws, they adopted a new political organization, evidently the result of experience and thought. The governor was to have a council to assist him as the executive of the colony, and the members of the company in the colony were to elect representatives to a little legislative assembly called the "house of burgesses." Thus the right of all the members to meet and enact laws, having become obviously inconvenient, was transferred to delegates.

Here we have the germ of all our American governments and of the National Constitution. It is simply a slight extension of the forms of the old trading corporation to suit the conditions in Virginia. The Massachusetts charter of 1629, which was modelled on the Virginia charters and gave the law-making power to the whole body of the freemen or members of the company, was developed by custom into the same form that prevailed in Virginia. The members of the company found it inconvenient to meet all together, and they transferred their law-making power to a smaller body of delegates.

This simple type of governor and council for the executive and a single house of legislature was not copied from the British form of government, but was developed

Evolution of the Constitution

by circumstances and necessities from the trading company. It remained the fundamental form of government in the colonies for more than a hundred years, constantly putting forth branches and growths which resembled nothing in England, but resembled very strongly what afterwards became parts of our National Constitution. We shall follow the details of all these growths and gradually see the governor's council expand into the Senate of the United States.

The Virginia charters were dissolved in 1623, and from that time until the Revolution the colony had no charter or written constitution. The form of government, however, of governor's council and single house of legislature survived, and showed the same kind of development that we shall find in the other colonies. The governor acquired the veto power on legislation, the right to pardon criminals, the right to appoint to office, and the command of the militia. His council showed a decided tendency to develop into a second or upper house of the legislature. In 1680 they ceased to sit with the burgesses, and, as time went on, acquired more and more legislative functions.

There was the same confusion of the departments of government as we shall notice in the other colonies. The governor was not only an executive officer, but a judicial officer as well, and acted as chancellor and chief justice. He also had the power, which we shall find in some other colonies, of adjourning the legislature at his pleasure. The constitution of Virginia became one of custom and laws passed from time to time, the result of what had been done under the charters, of

Colonial Charters and Constitutions

what had been done without them, of what had been done by the Crown and the royal governors, and of what the popular party by resistance could win for itself.

"The Agreement between the Settlers at New Plymouth" might be our next document, as it was made in 1620. But, although much sentimental praise has been lavished upon it by some writers, it is not a charter, nor, properly, a constitution, and still less a frame of government. It was drawn up on the "Mayflower" by the Pilgrim Fathers before they landed on the coast of Massachusetts, and is only about a dozen or fifteen lines of print to the effect that its signers solemnly and mutually combine themselves into a body politic to be governed by laws afterwards to be prepared. There are no details, there is no frame of government of any sort, nor is an officer of any kind named. It is merely such a simple agreement as any ship-load of people of any race about to land on a wild coast might prepare. It is an agreement to make a government in the future, rather than the government itself.

We shall pass it, therefore, and take up the charter of New England, which was granted in the same year,— 1620. This document reveals a curious reaction; in fact, a return to the absolutism of the Virginia charter of 1606. A council of forty persons is created, which is to be a corporation and to continue its existence by elections among its own members. It is to elect one of its members to be president and preside over its meetings, and has in every respect the fullest power to appoint the governor and all other officers and to make all laws which shall be thought necessary.

Evolution of the Constitution

The reason for this return to absolutism may have been that New England was at that time unsettled and all attempts to establish a permanent colony there had failed. The climate was cold and the country barren and unattractive. A council with full power might be able to encourage the beginnings of settlements, for they could work in their own way without interference.

But still, even amidst this absolutism, there are signs of advance. The corporation is called a "body politicque and corporate," showing a consciousness that these corporations were becoming something more than mere trading companies. A new kind of corporation was being developed, which was neither a private nor a municipal corporation, but a political corporation. The grant of judicial power is also more liberal than any that has appeared hitherto. Instead of the cautious permission of the Virginia charter of 1611–12, which allowed the council merely to punish crimes, we find the New England council given full judicial authority in civil as well as in criminal cases.

When they came to making laws and a government for New England under their absolute authority the council were evidently influenced by the advance free government had already made in Virginia. Two years after they received their charter they published a pamphlet entitled "A Brief Relation of the Discovery and Plantation of New England," which was intended to encourage settlers and described the sort of government the council had decided to adopt. The government was modelled on the Virginia type, and consisted of a governor and council and a general assembly of depu-

Colonial Charters and Constitutions

ties elected by the counties, baronies, and hundreds into which the county was divided. A slight tendency to advance is shown in the provision that there should be a treasurer for finance, a marshal for arms and war, a master of ordnance for ammunition and artillery, and an admiral for all marine affairs. The president and council in England were to order the assembling of the general assembly and "give life to the laws," which probably meant a veto power.

The next charter in order is that of Massachusetts, granted in 1629. It also has the characteristics of a corporation, and, like the last one, calls the company a body "corporate and politique." In the sort of government created by it the Virginia charter of 1611–12 is followed quite closely, with a slight development. There were to be a governor, a deputy governor, and eighteen assistants, or governor's council, all—including the governor and deputy—to be elected by the freemen or members of the company, who, together with these officers whom they elected, were to make the laws. This is nothing more than an ordinary trading-company government, in many respects like those of modern times. The freemen—that is to say, those that were made free of the company, as the expression was in those times—were the members or stockholders, as we should now call them. They elected the assistants, who corresponded to the modern board of directors or trustees, and the governor corresponded to the modern president.

Very quickly, however, the freemen, finding it inconvenient to meet in a body to transact the company's business, elected delegates to represent them, and thus, as in Virginia, a legislature was formed,—the outgrowth simply of an inconvenience in administering the powers of a trading company. Again, we have, as in Virginia, the typical colonial government,—governor, governor's council, and a single house of legislature.

The charter had given the power of making laws to the governor, assistants, and all the freemen assembled together. This was a confusion of executive and legislative functions, natural and proper enough perhaps in a trading company. When the legislature was developed out of the inconvenience of the freemen all meeting together, the same confusion continued. The legislature, the assistants, and the governor sat together to make laws; and after a time the assistants sat as a separate body.

This mingling of the distinct departments of government was common in all the colonies, and was the natural result of a development from trading companies. It continued all through the colonial period, and at times grew worse, for the judicial function was often added to the executive and sometimes to the legislative. Its unsoundness and inconvenience were at last realized, and in the constitutions of 1776 efforts were made to correct it. Several of those constitutions announce with great emphasis the principle that the legislative, judicial, and executive departments must never be confused and never exercised by the same persons. In the National Constitution no such principle is stated, because it had become fixed and settled, and it was necessary only to act upon it. The national document certainly made all those departments entirely distinct, and the evolution on this point was complete.

In the Massachusetts charter, as in the Virginia charter, there is no copying of the forms of the British government. There is no double legislature, no House of Lords and House of Commons to act as checks on each other. Some would say that the assistants, or governor's council, were like the English Privy Council of the king. But the king's Privy Council did not sit with the English House of Commons, and was not elected by the people, as the assistants were. The assistants were an executive, legislative, and judicial body, acting as magistrates, laying down rules and regulations in the absence of a meeting of the freemen or their delegates, and giving advice to the governor,—performing, in short, very much the same functions that a corporation board of directors would now perform under the same circumstances.

The persons who influenced the draughting of the Massachusetts charter were, first of all, the Puritans, who wanted it, and, secondly, the officers of the Crown, whose duty was merely to see that the rights of the British government were protected. The Crown officers had no wish to create a political government in the American wilderness, and least of all to create it for such persons as the Puritans, who had already made themselves so troublesome by political agitation. It would be better to limit such reckless and fanatical men within the form of a trading charter rather than give them a government which in either model or dignity could be compared to that of Great Britain. The Puritans, on the other hand, would have been the last persons to want a government on such a model; for they were hostile to the British government, and had little or no sympathy for its monarchical and aristocratic forms.

They succeeded admirably in getting all they wanted within the forms of a corporation. There was no provision, as in subsequent charters, requiring their laws to be submitted to the Crown for approval. They could elect their governor and all other officers. In fact, the charter proved to be so liberal that the Puritans set up under it what was in effect almost an independent state.

We must next dispose of some charters which were of a peculiar character and show but little development. The first is that of Maryland, granted in 1632. It was a proprietary grant, or conveyance of a great tract of land, making Lord Baltimore the feudal lord and owner; and in these proprietary grants the Crown usually gave its favorite the privilege of creating any sort of government he and his colonists could agree upon. This was a considerable advance on the absolutism of the proprietary grant to Sir Walter Raleigh, who could govern without consulting his colonists at all.

Lord Baltimore was allowed to make laws "with the advice and consent" of the freemen, or a majority of them or their delegates. He was also to have the privilege of appointing judges and various other officers, and of pardoning criminals. These powers of appointing and pardoning were afterwards a common attribute of colonial governors, and show a slight development. There was also some advancement shown in the power given Lord Baltimore to establish courts of law for both

Colonial Charters and Constitutions

criminal and civil cases. The previous charters had given only criminal jurisdiction.

There was a curious provision allowing the proprietor to make laws without the consent of the freemen in any sudden emergency when they could not be called together in time. This privilege, which was also given to William Penn in the Pennsylvania charter, and to the proprietors of the Carolina charters of 1663 and 1665, was seldom if ever exercised. It was so close to despotism that the mere mention of it would arouse the indignation of the people. Penn threatened to use it, or, rather, reminded the people that he could use it, and seriously injured his popularity.

We may also at this point dismiss the Pennsylvania charter of 1681, which, so far as a form of government was concerned, was the same as Maryland's. The two proprietary charters of the Carolinas—one in 1663 and the other in 1665—and the grant of Maine in 1639 may be dismissed in the same way. They gave the proprietor the same rights as the Maryland charter. The two proprietary grants of New Hampshire—one in 1629 and the other in 1635—were very bald and crude, simply giving John Mason the right to make a government, and if the people thought it was wrong they could appeal to the council of the New England Company that made the grant. The grants to the Duke of York, one in 1664 and the other in 1674, were mere gifts of absolute power, like Sir Walter Raleigh's charter of 1584.

The fundamental orders of Connecticut of 1638 come next in order after the Maryland charter of 1632. These orders, as they are called, form a constitution which is exceedingly interesting, because it is the first constitution made upon American soil without any interference or influence from the British Crown. The Connecticut people who made it had migrated from the Massachusetts colony and settled themselves about the site of the present town of Hartford. They were outside of the jurisdiction of Massachusetts. In fact, they were not within the limits of any colony, and had no title except a title of mere occupancy to the land on which they settled. They drew up the fundamental orders by mutual agreement and understanding among themselves, and we should naturally expect it to be a document somewhat resembling the Massachusetts government and at the same time without any of the trammels of corporation forms or Crown influence.

It is curiously worded, and begins wrong end foremost. The duties of the legislature are described before we are told that there is to be a legislature at all. But as we read on it seems that the people of the towns were to send deputies to an assembly which was called the general court. This general court had two stated meetings a year,—one in April, called the court of election, at which a governor and other public officers were to be chosen, and another in September, for passing laws and transacting general business.

The magistrates were apparently a governor's council, like the assistants in Massachusetts. In fact, the Massachusetts assistants were often spoken of as magistrates. The governor was to summon the general court a month before the time of the meeting, and, "if the governor and the greater part of the magistrates see cause upon any special occasion to call a general court, they may give order to the secretary so to do within fourteen days' warning." This power to call the legislature together in an emergency was afterwards given to the president in the National Constitution.

When the general court met it was to be composed of the deputies and also the governor and at least four of the magistrates. There were to be six magistrates elected by the whole body of the freemen, and they were given judicial power. But apparently the governor was to be elected by the general court.

That this instrument was in the main a copy of the government of Massachusetts as it had developed under the charter is quite evident. We have the governor and his council of assistants or magistrates, a house of deputies elected by the people, and governor, magistrates, and deputies all sit together as a single-branch legislature. The only difference is that the governor seems to be elected by the general court instead of by the people, and this is easily accounted for when we find that for a short time in Massachusetts the right to elect the governor was surrendered by the freemen.

Even when left to themselves, therefore, and uninfluenced by the Crown, the colonists seem to have followed the forms already in existence as developed from the trading-company charters.

Only one or two other points in the Connecticut fundamentals deserve mention. The magistrates are distinctly given the power to sit as a court or as separate courts of law. They were to be guided by the laws as established from time to time, and, when there were no laws, by the word of God, and this was a familiar custom in Massachusetts. The Connecticut governor was to preside over the general court, and could not adjourn it without its consent. But the most striking advance is a clause giving the general court the power of impeaching public officers, and this is the first appearance of the power of impeachment.

In 1643 the inhabitants of Rhode Island were given a patent which allowed them to rule themselves by such form of government as the majority should find suitable to their condition. As this patent contains no special form of government and is merely a license to make any government that shall be suitable to the majority, it need not be discussed further than to say that it was an obvious step towards referring all political power to the people. The government established under it was modelled on those that already existed in Massachusetts and Virginia, and consisted of a governor, governor's council, and assembly elected by the people.

Our next charter belongs to Connecticut, and may be considered at the same time with the charter of Rhode Island, for the two were only a year apart, being granted respectively in 1662 and 1663, and are almost precisely alike. They are also like the Massachusetts charter, and a slight advance upon it.

The Connecticut people had come from Massachusetts, and when they sent Winthrop to England as their agent to obtain a charter he naturally followed the Massachusetts model, and the Crown officers seem to have had no objection. It was so liberal in its terms that it always has been somewhat of a wonder how it was obtained, and stories have been told of the influence exercised by Winthrop with a ring which his father had received from Charles I. At any rate, Charles II. and his ministers seem to have been in an easy mood, and not so stringent in their ideas of colonial rule as they afterwards became. The charter suited the Connecticut people so well that they refused to abolish or alter it in the Revolution, and lived under it until the year 1818. It may therefore be regarded as very American and in many respects a native product.

It is very general in its provisions for government, is still in the corporation form, and calls the company it creates a body "corporate and politick." The freemen were to elect the governor, deputy governor, and twelve assistants; and the assistants were, of course, intended to be a governor's council. So far it is just like the charter of Massachusetts.

The Massachusetts charter, it will be remembered, provided that all the members of the company were to meet together in a body to legislate, and this, being found inconvenient, was changed by custom and a house of delegates created. The Connecticut charter, however, creates this house of delegates at once. In other words, it copied the Massachusetts form of government as it had developed up to the year 1662, and so far was an advance on the forms of the old trading corporations. It also advanced by giving the name general assembly to the governor, assistants, and house of deputies, when they all met together to enact laws,— a name which became very common, and is still retained in some of our States.

Evolution of the Constitution

The general assembly was given the power to punish crimes and offences, and also the power to pardon. In the colonial governments the pardoning power was sometimes given to the executive department and sometimes to the legislative, until, as we near the National Constitution, it becomes a fixed prerogative of the executive.

Besides the general power to make laws, this general assembly was distinctly given the right to create and organize general courts of justice, both civil and criminal. This right had been given for the first time to Lord Baltimore in the Maryland charter of 1632. One might suppose that it would be implied in the power to make laws. But evidently there was a doubt on this subject, and the existence of this doubt shows how government was developing out of the forms of the trading corporations.

To create courts which shall enforce rules of conduct by seizing the property of citizens in some cases, and seizing their persons in other cases and condemning them to imprisonment or death, is a very important power, and one of high prerogative. It is not, and never has been, the usual incident of a business corporation. It might possibly be implied as part of the necessary powers of a corporation which was to undertake the unusual task of settling and planting a wilderness. But evidently it was thought better, as these colonial planting and trading corporations became more and more like real governments, to give somebody in them the distinct and express power of creating courts of justice. The failure to make this matter clear in the Pennsylvania constitution of 1701 afterwards led to a

Colonial Charters and Constitutions

very bitter dispute whether the governor or the assembly had the right to institute courts.

As the Rhode Island charter was granted the year after that of Connecticut and contains the same provisions of government, it is not necessary to enlarge on it in detail. It was obtained by a Baptist minister, Rev. John Clarke, who, like Winthrop of Connecticut, went over to England as agent. He naturally followed the easiest course, and obtained a charter like the one just granted to Connecticut, which at that time, in New England, was generally believed to be the best instrument of government.

Thus we have in the year 1663 three specimens of the most advanced form of American government. It is allowable to call them American, and not English, because the Massachusetts government was to a large extent a growth on the soil, and had added to itself the house of delegates, which was not provided for in the charter as drawn in England. The other two had copied this development and added to it an advance of their own in distinctly saying that the general assembly should have the power to create courts of justice. Moreover, it is to be observed that, as these two were obtained by agents who went from the colonies to England, they may be said to have been draughted by American influence, the result of American experience, and they were not the mere theorizing of Crown officers or of persons who had never lived in America.

It should be noticed that in none of these governments was the legislature composed of an upper and a lower house acting as a check on each other. The

Evolution of the Constitution

legislature was to consist principally of representatives elected by the people. The governor's assistants, or council, were to sit with them, not as a separate body to act as a check, but as a part of them. There were as yet no veto power and no pardoning power in the governor, and no detailed description of his relation to the legislature or of the legislature's relation to him. There was not the slightest resemblance to the British government of King, Commons, and House of Lords. All I see, and all I think any one can see, is an English business corporation altered a little to suit unusual circumstances,—the circumstances of planting and trade instead of trade alone,—and by experience in those circumstances somewhat developed and enlarged in the direction of a true political government.

Two or three years after these charters of Connecticut and Rhode Island another frame of government was prepared for the colonies, and this was the "Concessions and Agreements of the Proprietors of East Jersey," of 1665. This instrument was not a royal charter, and in the making of it the Crown officers had no influence. It was prepared by the proprietors of the province according to their own ideas, and it is interesting to observe that it accepts the form of government as developed in Virginia and New England under the royal charters, and adds some developments and improvements.

There is to be a governor, with a council of from six to twelve, "with whose advice and consent" he is to govern; a house of deputies, elected by the people; and governor, council, and deputies are to sit together in making laws, and be called the general assembly; and

Colonial Charters and Constitutions

the assembly is to have the right to establish courts of law. So far the New England type is strictly followed. Then comes an advance, and some details are added, showing a conscious framing of more complete government.

The assembly is told that it may appoint its own time of meeting and adjourn when it pleases. This same power of adjourning at pleasure had been given to the assembly by the Fundamental Orders of Connecticut in 1638, but it was so much of an advance that it was not followed in the Connecticut charter of 1662 or in the Rhode Island charter of 1663. Even in these Concessions of East Jersey of 1665 it was found to be ahead of time, and had to be set back.

Other increased details of power follow. The assembly was to decide what should be its quorum, levy taxes, lay out ports and towns, divide the country into counties and districts, naturalize foreigners, establish forts and arm them, and organize the militia. The governor and his council were to appoint the judges of the courts and see that they and all other officers did their duty; also to appoint military officers, to command the militia, and to reprieve criminals until the case could be heard by the proprietors, with whom rested the pardoning power.

Here we have a large and detailed development of both legislative and executive authority, taking American government a long way out of the old forms of trading corporations; and we also find that the proprietors retained the privilege of rejecting all bills passed by the general assembly, which was a veto power like that of Lord Baltimore in the Maryland charter of 1632.

Evolution of the Constitution

This somewhat excessive development was the result of the constitution being framed not by the people who were to live under it or by regularly constituted officers of the Crown, but by a few men of good education and advanced ideas, who were free to theorize a little and carry out favorite principles. Whenever men of this sort draughted an American constitution we usually find an abnormal development, in some cases so abnormal as to produce reaction.

In the present instance of the constitution of East Jersey an amendment was made in 1672 taking away from the assembly the right to control its own adjournments and giving that control to the governor and his council. But two years afterwards, in 1674, the development went on, and we have an instance of an attempt to create a double-branch legislature. The governor and council were no longer to sit with and vote with the deputies, but to sit by themselves and have a veto on everything passed by the deputies.

This constitution of East Jersey and the constitution of West Jersey, to be noticed hereafter, were abrogated in 1702, when both provinces were surrendered to the Crown. After that the Jerseys were ruled as one colony by governors appointed by the king, without charter or constitution, the people always protesting that they still retained all their rights under the old proprietary Concessions.

About four years after the "Concessions and Agreements of the Proprietors of East Jersey" another charter appears, which seems to have been almost exclusively the work of one man. This was the famous constitu-

Colonial Charters and Constitutions

tion of John Locke, in 1669. It was prepared for the government of the Carolinas and only partially put in operation. It was never successful, and was abrogated in 1693.

It was not made by the people themselves or by practical men who were politicians or lawyers, but by a philosopher who was idealizing. Nevertheless, it is valuable as showing development, for Locke, although a philosopher, was also a human being, influenced by the opinion of his time, and he had read all the charters and constitutions of his day and knew the problems to be solved. In fact, he foresaw one of the problems of the future in a very remarkable way. He emancipated himself completely from the forms of a trading corporation and attempted to create an out-and-out American political government.

He began in the most scientific manner by dividing the province into counties, and the counties into seigniories, baronies, and precincts, and the precincts into colonies. The head, or governor, was to be called the palatine. There were to be lords proprietors, landgraves, and caziques; also admirals, chamberlains, chancellors, high stewards, chief justices, and treasurers. No lawyers were to be allowed, nor could any one plead for a fee. Not satisfied with making the constitution and laws secure by the absence of lawyers, he provided that there should be no comments or expositions of any kind on the constitution or statutes, so that they might always remain clear and easy to understand. The constitution was never to be altered in any way, and, that it might not be gradually and imperceptibly altered by laws, all laws were to become inoperative one hundred years after their passage.

But in the midst of all these extraordinary provisions we begin to see some light when we find him providing for a registry of deeds and mortgages in each precinct. A similar registry had been provided for in the Concessions of East Jersey. He also provided for the collection of vital statistics, and a little closer attention reveals a double-branch legislature. His grand council was a separate legislative body, whose function was to propose measures for the lower house, or parliament, as it was called, and nothing could be proposed in this parliament unless it had passed the grand council. This was the first appearance in American written constitutions of a double-branch legislature, and it was followed in 1774 in the amendment to the Concessions of East Jersey.

The plan of giving the upper house the sole power of originating legislation was some years afterwards introduced into Pennsylvania by William Penn. But it was very unpopular, subversive of the ordinary political rights of Englishmen, and finally defeated by the people.

Besides the attempt to form a double legislature, this constitution of Locke gives an elaborate sort of veto on legislation to the palatine and his court and some of the lords proprietors. Leaving out what was the result of Locke's individual and peculiar views, this constitution adds something to the development reached in the document last considered of East Jersey, while in the main it follows it quite closely.

But Locke foresaw in a curious way that the great

Colonial Charters and Constitutions

difficulty with these written constitutions would be in devising some body or department which should prevent infringements and prevent the passage of unconstitutional laws. This problem was afterwards attempted to be solved in some of the constitutions of 1776 by creating a board of censors, whose duty it should be to prevent infringements and expose them when committed. Since then the Supreme Court of the United States and the courts of last resort in each State have become the guardians of constitutional integrity. But the only method Locke could think of besides limiting the life of all laws to a hundred years was to intervene a delay and reconsideration between the passage of a suspected law by the parliament and its approval by the palatine. His provision on this point is so curious that it is worth quoting in full. The suspected act could be protested for unconstitutionality :

"And in such case, after full and free debate, the several estates shall retire into four separate chambers,—the palatine and proprietors into one, the landgraves into another, the caziques into another, and those chosen by the precincts into a fourth,—and if the major part of any of the four estates shall vote that the law is not agreeable to this establishment and these fundamental constitutions of the government, then it shall pass no farther, but be as if it had never been proposed."

Next after Locke's attempt at constitution-making comes the "Concessions and Agreements of the Proprietors of West Jersey," which appeared in 1677. It begins by appointing commissioners who are to govern the colony by instructions received from the proprietors until other commissioners are elected by the inhabitants, and these commissioners elected by the inhabitants are to govern until a general assembly is elected. Then comes "The Charter or Fundamental Laws Agreed Upon."

It is quite likely that the draughtsmen of these fundamental laws had been reading Locke's constitution, for they begin by trying to invent a method of preventing unconstitutional legislation. The constitution must not be violated by the assembly, they say, and any assemblyman moving anything unconstitutional shall, on proof of seven eye-witnesses, be proceeded against as a traitor. Then follow a few provisions about trial by jury which at the time of the Revolution would have been included under the head of what was usually called a "Bill of Rights." These bills of rights were generally affixed, in some form or other, to all the constitutions of 1776, and this constitution of West Jersey shows the beginning of them in American governmental documents.

The remaining provisions for West Jersey are, however, very meagre. A registry of deeds is provided, as in Locke's constitution and in the Concessions of East Jersey. The assembly may fix its own quorum, adjourn as it pleases, erect courts of law, appoint judges, and lay out towns and counties. No governor is provided, but the assembly is to elect ten commissioners, who are to be the executive. Certainly this was a very crude instrument,—of slight advance, and in some respects a reaction. The same fate befell it as befell the Concessions of East Jersey. It was surrendered and abrogated when the two provinces became one colony under direct royal government in 1702.

Colonial Charters and Constitutions

New Hampshire's charter comes next, and this also shows only a slight development. It was, however, not properly a charter, but a mere royal commission granted in 1680 for the purpose of governing the province during the king's pleasure. At first New Hampshire had been a proprietary colony under John Mason; but the proprietorship was not successful, and the settlers sought the protection of Massachusetts in 1641, and remained under her tutelage until 1675.

The royal commission of 1680, though not a charter, is professedly a method of government, and shows in a rough way some of the general ideas that were in all the colonial governments. The president and his council were to be the executive of the province, control the militia, encourage good living and virtue, and also act as a court of justice,—a very gross confusion of the departments. There was to be a house of representatives to make the laws, and the president and council had an absolute veto power.

Here it is evident we have the Massachusetts, Connecticut, and Rhode Island charters over again with a slight development. The governor or president, with his council, is given the veto power, which had not before been given in New England.

The president and council are also given the power of commanding the militia. This power was not distinctly given in the Massachusetts charter, or in either of the other two New England charters which were modelled on it, though, like the power to create courts of law, it might doubtless have been implied. But now we find it, as in the East Jersey Concession, distinctly given to a definite department as the power to create courts was, as already shown, distinctly given. The addition of these two powers, which also appear in a crude way in the Jersey constitutions, shows a gradual working out of the details of a regular government. In subsequent frames of government we find them given with more or less detail all the way down to the National Constitution, where they appear in their most mature form.

But the most interesting part of the New Hampshire commission is a clause directing the president to recommend to the general assembly such acts, laws, and ordinances as may tend to establish the people in obedience to the king's authority, preserve due peace and good government, protect them from their enemies, and enable them to raise taxes for the support of government. This was certainly something in the nature of a president's message, an idea afterwards worked out in the New York constitution of 1777 and adopted in the National Constitution.

Our next document, the Pennsylvania frame of 1682–83, is more mature than the commission for New Hampshire. It preserves the forms as developed out of the trading charters of Virginia and New England, and adds to them some striking developments. It is especially worthy of notice because it is the second advanced frame of government that was made exclusively on American soil. The Connecticut Fundamental Orders of 1638 is the first document of this sort, as already shown, but it merely copied the Massachusetts form, with a slight advance upon it. The Pennsylvania frame,

Colonial Charters and Constitutions

as being more fully developed, is more significant and interesting. It was made by William Penn and his colonists under that clause in the grant to Penn which allowed him to make laws "by and with the advice, assent, and approbation of the freemen." The clause did not tell him that he and the freemen might make a constitution; it simply said laws; and it shows the instincts of the race that Penn and his people inferred that under this they must first of all make an organic law, a fundamental order, or, more briefly, a constitution.

There was no royal influence affecting the making of this constitution. No officer of the Crown was present, or had a right to be present. Both Penn and his people were standing on the soil of Pennsylvania, and could do as they pleased. That, under the circumstances, they framed a government which followed the line of development in other colonies, and advanced on it a little, shows that the royal charters heretofore discussed were not entirely the result of mere Crown influence, but were largely what the colonists themselves desired and had suggested.

The constitution begins with a preamble on the nature of government which has been generally supposed to contain Penn's own ideas on the subject. Government, he said, was of divine origin and a part of religion. There were many theories of it current; but the actual practice was a different and also a very difficult matter, because the government must be suited to its people and locality. This was certainly very Saxon; and then he adds a sentence which has been often quoted:

Evolution of the Constitution

"Any government is free to the people under it (whatever be the frame) where the laws rule and the people are a party to those laws, and more than this is tyranny, oligarchy, or confusion."

Governments, he went on, depended on men rather than men on governments; and an ill-framed government in good hands might be quite successful. After all, the great end was "to support power in reverence with the people, and to secure the people from the abuse of power."

All this was much better theorizing than anything Locke had said in his constitution. Penn was one of the most accomplished men of his time, and, though not a metaphysician, was as competent as Locke to draw up an ideal political dream. But he started on the established forms, and, while he made some important developments, kept well within legitimate lines and swerved comparatively little from the normal.

As we read along in his constitution we find a governor, a governor's council, and an assembly of the people, just as in the constitutions developed in New England and East Jersey. The people were to elect the council, as in the New England charters, and it is called the provincial council.

The variations on the New England type were, first of all, that the council was to be very large and contain seventy-two members. In the other colonies the assistants or council were seldom more than ten or twenty in number. This enlargement of the council shows at once a tendency to develop it into an upper house of the legislature, and this is confirmed when we find that the council is to originate all legislation, and that the assembly is merely to accept or reject the proposals of the council. In this idea of developing the council into an upper legislative house of such importance that the lower house would be completely dwarfed and insignificant, Penn seems to have been influenced by Locke's constitution.

It may be added that this sudden attempt to develop a second house and develop it excessively was very much in advance of the time. Not only was Penn's whole arrangement in this respect changed and the legislative department put back in its normal colonial state, but Pennsylvania continued to have a single-branch legislature until long after the Revolution.

In developing the council so excessively Penn naturally gave to it the power to create courts of law, which in the other governments was usually given to the general assembly. He also gave to it the power to enter judgments on impeachments,—that is to say, the right to try impeachments,—which were to be originated and prosecuted by the assembly, or lower house. Previously the right to remove officials had been given in a general way to the general assembly by the Fundamental Orders of Connecticut of 1638, the charter of Connecticut of 1662, and the charter of Rhode Island of 1663, and apparently the general assembly was to try as well as to charge and accuse the culprit. The word impeachment was not used, and it is found in this Pennsylvania frame of 1683 for the first time.

In this frame the dividing up of the work of impeachment as it appears in the National Constitution is found for the first time. The general assembly was to bring

Evolution of the Constitution

the impeachment, and the council was to try it and decide on guilt or acquittal. It was the natural result of the provision for a double legislature, and shows the gradual working out of a more detailed political form. When double legislatures were finally adopted in the Revolution this arrangement for impeachment accompanied them and was reproduced in the National Constitution.

The executive part of Penn's government was worked out with considerable detail. The governor and his council were to have care of the peace and safety, lay out towns, model public buildings, inspect the treasury, and establish schools. The governor was to preside at the council meetings and have a treble vote. This treble vote was probably some pet idea of Penn's.

But the most striking part about this description of executive duties is a sentence which sums them up in a general way:

"The governor and provincial council shall take care that all laws (statutes and ordinances which shall at any time be made within the said province) be duly and diligently executed."

This clause, shortened by omitting the part in parenthesis, which is mere surplusage, was adopted with little or no change in the constitutions of 1776, and finally appeared in the National Constitution as a summing up of the executive duties of the President in the phrase, "He shall take care that the laws be faithfully executed."

The germ of this clause had appeared in the Massachusetts charter of 1629, in a sentence which said not that any particular person or department should execute the laws, but simply that all the laws should be "duly

Colonial Charters and Constitutions

observed, kept, performed, and put in execution." The Maryland charter of 1632 assigned to Lord Baltimore the duty of executing the laws, and in the Fundamental Orders of Connecticut of 1638 and the Concessions of East Jersey of 1665 the duty is assigned to the governor. The first step out of corporation forms was to say, with more words than were necessary, that all the laws should be kept, performed, and executed. The next step was to assign their execution to a particular department, still using more words than were necessary. The duty and the person to perform it being now defined, we find in the constitutions of 1776 that the language for expressing it is much abbreviated, until in the National Constitution it reaches complete condensation in the simple phrase, which covers everything, "He shall take care that the laws be faithfully executed."

There was also an interesting clause providing a way for amending the constitution. It could be done by the consent of the governor and six parts in seven of the council and assembly. Locke had provided that his constitution should never be altered, and other charters and constitutions had been silent on the subject, though, of course, it was generally understood that they could be changed by the authority that had made them. But this provision in Penn's constitution was the first appearance in American governments of any definite way of amending. It was repeated with various changes in the constitutions of 1776, until the way now found in the National Constitution was reached.

Annexed to Penn's frame are "Laws Agreed upon in England," many of which are what afterwards became known as bill-of-rights provisions, such as fair trial by jury, process to be in English, fees and fines to be moderate. We have already observed the first bill of rights of this kind starting in the Concessions of West Jersey, and the bill we find in Penn's frame is simply a development, with a few provisions added.

Penn's frame was amended, a few months after it was passed, by reducing the provincial council from seventy-two to eighteen members, and by adding that the governor must act "by and with the advice and consent of" the provincial council,—peculiar words, which have appeared several times, which seem to have been used in old trading-corporation charters, for they can be found in the charter of the Grocers' Company granted in 1429, and which, after being repeated all through the colonial charters and the constitutions of 1776, took their place in the National Constitution.

We must now consider the next charter in chronological order,—the second Massachusetts charter of 1691. The Puritans had created under their first charter a government so free and independent, and had assumed so many of the attributes of sovereignty, coining their own money and cutting the cross out of the English ensign, that they needed looking after. Soon after Charles II. came to the throne he became convinced that all the colonies required a little overhauling, Massachusetts most of all. It would be well, he thought, to hold dissenters like the Puritans with a somewhat stronger hand. Proceedings were begun to annul the Massachusetts charter, and they were consummated June 18, 1684.

Colonial Charters and Constitutions

For some years Massachusetts had no charter, and was under direct royal rule, with a governor appointed by the Crown. But in 1691 Mary and William granted a new charter, which embodied some of the developments we have seen in the other colonies. The people appear to have had some voice in shaping it, for they had their agents in England.

This charter of 1691 provided that there should be a governor, a deputy governor, and a secretary, all appointed by the Crown, and not elected by the people as in the old charter. The people were allowed to elect the members of a legislature called the house of freeholders. There were to be twenty-eight assistants elected by the general assembly, which was to consist of the governor, the assistants, and the house of freeholders, all sitting together.

The twenty-eight assistants were the most interesting feature of the government, for they were to be chosen to represent different localities of the colony, very much as senators are now chosen under our National Constitution. The province of Massachusetts, under this charter of 1691, was a union of the old province of that name with New Plymouth, Maine, and the land between the Sagadahoc River and Nova Scotia; and it is very significant that each of these divisions is given its representatives in the council, or assistants, as they were called, which afterwards developed into the Senate of the national government and represented the States. The union under the Massachusetts charter was a union of provinces which had been formerly, in a certain sense, distinct sovereignties, as the States which formed the

Evolution of the Constitution

Union under the National Constitution had been distinct sovereignties. It is certainly remarkable that the Massachusetts union should have foreshadowed the National Union in its method of giving representation to the provinces of which it was composed.

It is another instance to show how the natural conditions in America were of their own inherent force, and without imitation, constantly tending towards the form of government that was finally reached. It shows, also, that, in the forms which were gradually adopted, there was no thought of imitating anything in the British Constitution. The framers of the Massachusetts charter, in advancing the governor's council to the function of representing the separate provinces of a union, were certainly not imitating the House of Lords, for that body had no such function. They were merely conforming to natural conditions, using what had already proved itself suitable for certain purposes, and adapting means to ends in a very practical manner.

The confusion of legislative, executive, and judicial functions was rather worse than usual in this Massachusetts charter, for not only were the governor and the assistants part of the general assembly, but the governor and assistants were also to act as a court to probate wills and grant letters of administration.

By another provision, the governor, "with the advice and consent of" the assistants, appointed judges, sheriffs, marshals, and other officers, which was an appointing power similar to that of the President and Senate under the Constitution. The governor had also an absolute veto on all the bills passed by the general court.

Colonial Charters and Constitutions

The veto power is now clearly established in American governments. While showing one remarkable advance, this charter also contained the most important and best-tested provisions of previous experience.

There was one provision, however, of a peculiar character, and the result of the more stringent policy of colonial control which Charles II. had started. The governor had power to dissolve the assembly whenever he chose. By an amendment to the charter in 1726 the representatives could adjourn from day to day, and for a period of two days, but not longer without the consent of the governor. This power of the governors over the popular assemblies seems to have existed after the year 1701 in most of the colonies except Pennsylvania, and was always bitterly resented by the people. But in the end it proved to be a source of constitutional development; for their long experience with it led to a very careful framing of the powers of the President over Congress.

We now come to two frames of government in Pennsylvania which may be considered together,—the frame of 1696, usually known as Markham's frame, and the Charter of Privileges of 1701, usually known as the constitution of 1701. The frame of 1696 is noticeable chiefly for its reactionary tendency. It reduced to a normal condition Penn's frame of 1683, which, as we have seen, was excessively developed,—developed, in fact, far beyond any other colonial constitution.

The frame of 1696 was made by Governor Markham and the people during Penn's absence, and was to remain in force unless Penn should object to it. The principal feature of it was that the right to originate legislation was taken away from the council and given to the assembly. Thus this strange idea of creating an upper house which alone could originate laws, which had been a mere freak of Locke's and Penn's, was done away with forever in American governments.

A few years after this frame of Markham's Penn returned to the province, and in 1701, after much consultation with the people and repeated discussions and meetings, gave them the constitution of 1701, always regarded in Pennsylvania as a very good one, and under it the people lived until the Revolution.

It also was reactionary, and, as often happens when there has been excessive action, the reaction was excessive. Penn had attempted in his first frame to develop the council into a second house of legislature, and developed it too much. In the constitution of 1701 he went to the other extreme and abolished the council altogether. There was to be merely a governor appointed by himself and an assembly elected by the people.

The assembly was allowed to control its own adjournments without interference from the governor,—a right of which the Pennsylvanians were always very proud,— and they maintained it unimpaired down to the Revolution.

The assembly was also allowed to impeach officials and have all the power of an assembly according to the rights of freeborn subjects of England. In after-years, in its contests with the governor, the assembly relied on this clause to give it all the privileges of the British

Colonial Charters and Constitutions

House of Commons. Some of the members became very learned in English parliamentary history, and their minutes are full of evidences of it.

Some new bill-of-rights provisions appear in this constitution, and some of the privileges given to the assembly were also distinct developments and became permanently embodied in American constitutional forms. The assembly was told that it could choose its own speaker and officers and "be judge of the qualifications and elections of its own members." This right and the very words in which it was given were repeated in the constitutions of 1776 and appeared in the National Constitution.

Penn's excessive reaction in abolishing the council was corrected in a curious way, which shows how natural that body was to the colonial governments. The constitution did not provide for the election or appointment of a council, but a council was incidentally referred to in a clause which said that no person should be obliged to answer before the governor and council, or in any other place than an ordinary court of justice, unless appeals to the governor and council should be established by law.

It is difficult to understand why this strange side-reference to a council should have been put in unless it was the result of carelessness and haste in having the constitution quickly adopted on the eve of Penn's hurried return to England. At any rate, it was not long before Penn began appointing a council to assist the governor, and his heirs continued the practice. The assembly from time to time protested, and appealed to the constitution

Evolution of the Constitution

as not authorizing a council in any way. But the council was always appointed, and maintained its position as a *de facto* if not a *de jure* part of the government.

It acquired in time almost the same function as an upper house of legislature, because it would advise the governor to veto the bills of the assembly, and the governor was under instructions from the proprietors to be guided by the council. This, the assembly always declared, was an outrageous violation of its rights, because the constitution provided for only a single legislative body, and by the instructions to the governor and the appointment of the council a second house of legislature, unknown to the constitution, was forced upon the people. But it all shows how inevitable was the development towards a second house.

Our last charter is that of Georgia, granted in 1732. We should naturally expect it to show remarkable developments, but, owing to peculiar circumstances, it does not. It differed from all the other colonial charters and constitutions, and was neither the charter of a trading company nor the constitution of a people, but a charitable trust or eleemosynary corporation. General Oglethorpe and some other good people wished to relieve the debtor prisons of England, and adopted the plan, by no means yet obsolete in Europe, of dumping their contents on America.

A grant of land was obtained, and the company was called the "Trustees for Establishing the Colony of Georgia in America." The trustees were in the first instance to appoint the common council, and as vacancies occurred in this council, by death or resignation, the members of the company could elect persons to fill them. The members of the company were to make rules and laws, to be approved by the Crown. The common council was to carry on the business affairs of the company and appoint judges, treasurers, secretaries, governors, and such other officers as should be found necessary, and to apportion land among the debtors, but not to any members of the company.

There is always some contribution towards development in the crudest and most reactionary document; so in this one we find the first attempt to separate the departments of government in a clause providing that no person holding an office of profit under the corporation should be a member of the corporation.

The corporation was to remain in existence twenty-one years, and in that time could establish courts of law. But the command of the militia was given to the governor of South Carolina. At the expiration of the twenty-one years such form of government could be established as the Crown should think best.

The scheme was not successful, and when the twenty-one years expired the trustees were glad to surrender. Soon after 1751 the Crown organized a government which resembled those of the other colonies, which have been already described. There were a governor, a council,—which seems to have sat as an upper house,—and an assembly, and the governor and council sat together as a court of chancery and admiralty.

CHAPTER III.

THE CONSTITUTIONS OF 1776.

THE Georgia charter of 1732, discussed in the preceding chapter, may very well be omitted from our consideration, for it was not in the line of development of the other governments. Its peculiar feature of creating a charity organization sets it completely aside.

This gives us the Pennsylvania constitution of 1701 as the last written frame of government that appeared in colonial times. The three Pennsylvania constitutions taken together,—of 1683, of 1696, and of 1701,—with their amendments, and the Massachusetts charter of 1691, constitute the most advanced colonial forms, and show the nearest approach in the colonial period towards the final goal of the national document.

By about the year 1700 the colonial governments seem to have all reached a stage of development which was sufficient for practical purposes. They had partially emerged out of the trading-company forms, and usually consisted of a governor, a governor's council, and a single-branch legislature, with a tendency on the part of the council to develop into an upper house of legislature, and one or two of the colonies had an upper house. Besides this, several of them had a few of the bill-of-rights provisions, which were afterwards much extended, and most of them had peculiar arrangements

The Constitutions of 1776

or peculiarly worded sentences, which afterwards appeared in the National Constitution.

This development was sufficient for the needs of the time, and in the seventy-five years that passed between the year 1700 and the outbreak of the Revolution there was little or no advancement that can be traced in documents or writings. No doubt the colonists discussed the subject, for while some of the colonies, like Connecticut and Rhode Island, which elected their own governors, were well content, others, like Massachusetts, which were under royal governors, saw many things in their forms of government that they would have liked to change. It was in this long period of apparent silence and inaction that it was gradually seen that the confusion of departments which prevailed in all the governments was a mistake.

But it was not until the year 1776, when all the colonies except Rhode Island and Connecticut set actively to work to make new constitutions for themselves, entirely free from any influence from the Crown, that there was developed any intensity of thought upon the subject. In that year there was certainly a great school of constitution-making at work, and the comparison of ideas and conflict of opinion were a lesson and discipline in fundamental principles such as have never been known in America in any one year before or since.

Judging by the first constitution which was made at that time, the development in the subject since the year 1700 had been very slight. This first constitution was that of New Hampshire. The work on it was begun December 21, 1775, and finished January 5, 1776. It was finished several months before any of the others were begun. There were no guides for it except the old colonial charters and constitutions, most of which had been made in the previous century, and it is not surprising that we find it a very crude instrument.

The province is still called a colony, and the constitution is to continue in force only "during the present unhappy and unnatural contest with Great Britain." The convention which framed it was elected by the people and called a "Congress." The constitution begins by providing that this Congress is to become the House of Representatives of the new government, and is to choose twelve persons, taking them from different counties, to be a distinct and separate branch of the legislature by the name of a "Council for the Colony."

If, however, the war should last longer than a year, this council was to be elected by the people, each county electing its proportion. The council was to appoint its own president, and both branches of the legislature must agree to every act before it could become a law. Neither branch could adjourn longer than from Saturday to Monday without the consent of the other. Money-bills must originate in the lower house. Both houses together were to appoint all public officers, including the general field officers of the militia. The office of governor was not provided for.

This was certainly, in some respects, a crude instrument. The absence of a governor and the appointment of all public officers by the legislature was barbarous. But still it adopts the idea of a double-branch legislature, which, as we have seen, had been gaining ground all

The Constitutions of 1776

through the colonial period; and, like the Massachusetts charter of 1691, it assigns to the upper branch the function of representing certain localities,—the counties,—in which we see the germ of the United States Senate's representation of States.

The provision that money-bills must originate in the lower house was, of course, familiar English parliamentary law, and was also a principle that had been successfully contended for in the colonial assembly of Pennsylvania, but had never appeared before in an American written frame of government.

The clause which says "neither branch shall adjourn for any longer time than from Saturday until the next Monday without the consent of the other" was repeated in various forms in the other constitutions, until we find it in the National Constitution in the form, "Neither house, during the session of Congress, shall, without the consent of the other, adjourn for more than three days."

South Carolina came next, and her constitution was finished March 26, 1776. This was before any of the others had been begun except New Hampshire: so New Hampshire's document was the only guide, and it was followed quite closely.

The convention, or provincial congress, as it was called, resolved itself into the general assembly, or lower house, of the new government, and, after October 21, 1776, was to be elected by the people. As in New Hampshire, the lower house was at first to choose the upper house, which was to be called the legislative council and be composed of thirteen members.

Here the resemblance to New Hampshire's constitution stops, for South Carolina is to have a governor called "President and Commander-in-Chief;" and this is the first use of the term president to describe the executive in the constitutions of 1776. There are also to be a vice-president, and a privy council composed of the vice-president and six others, three from the assembly and three from the legislative council.

This privy council is to advise the president, when required, and was, no doubt, copied from or suggested by the privy council of the English king. As the governor's council of colonial times had passed into an upper house of legislature, it may have been thought necessary to supply its place by this privy council. It may also have been the mere personal suggestion of William Henry Drayton, who had great influence in the draughting of the constitution.

Some of the later constitutions of 1776 adopted this privy council, and added details for keeping a written register of its advice and opinions which should always be open to inspection. This is, I think, one of the few instances that can be found of a direct imitation of a foreign form; and it is to be observed that it is an imitation that failed. It was tried for a few years in several of the States and then abandoned. In future chapters we shall find other instances of this same fate befalling imitations, and it goes to show that foreign imitations or plagiarisms in constitution-making are not only few, but also usually unsuccessful.

The president, in the South Carolina constitution, was given an absolute veto. He could not, however, adjourn or dissolve the legislature, though he might call

The Constitutions of 1776

them before the time to which they stood adjourned. The advance here is evident, and requires no comment. But the confusion of departments in the vice-president and privy council forming a court of chancery was gross.

Virginia's constitution was finished June 29, 1776,—a few months after South Carolina's. It was made by a convention of forty-five members of the house of burgesses, and has prefixed to it a bill of rights adopted June 12, 1776, the first part of which has the language of the opening paragraph of the Declaration of Independence. The rest of the bill of rights is remarkable as being very full and complete and containing more provisions than had ever appeared before in the colonies. Besides the ordinary bill-of-rights provisions, the bill contains some political maxims, and among these is the first statement in our constitutions of the principle that the legislative, executive, and judicial departments of government should be separate, and that the same persons should never exercise the powers of any two of them.

When we come to the constitution itself, we find it repeats the statement of the necessity of keeping the departments separate. The legislature is to consist of two houses,—a lower house, called the house of delegates, and an upper house, called the senate; and this is the first time the upper house is called a senate. As it was emerging from the condition of a governor's council, it was called, as in the New Hampshire constitution, a legislative council. But now it has become a legislative body in the full sense of the term, and is given an appropriate name. It is also representative of large districts or localities, as in the New Hampshire constitution.

Both the senate and the lower house are given power to choose their own speaker, appoint their own officers, and settle their own rules of proceeding. In subsequent constitutions we find this power given in very much the same words, with the addition that each house is to determine the elections and qualifications of its own members, and these phrases are repeated until they appear in the National Constitution.

All laws are to originate in the lower house, and the senate can only reject or approve, or amend with consent of the lower house. Money-bills, however, cannot be amended by the senate, but can only be rejected or approved. The lower house has the right to impeach, and the impeachments are to be tried not by the senate, but by a court.

This rather excessive privilege of the lower house alone having the right to originate legislation was a mere freak, which was not followed by the other States.

The governor is to be elected by joint ballot of the two houses, and is given the pardoning power, but not the veto power. He cannot adjourn the legislature, but can call them before the time to which they stand adjourned. He has to assist him a privy council of eight, chosen by joint ballot of both houses from their own members or from the people. The council is to choose a president, who shall be the lieutenant-governor, and the proceedings of the council in giving advice to the governor and other matters are to be entered in a book and signed by the members. Any member has the privilege of dissenting from any act of the council and entering his dissent in the book, and the book is to be always open to inspection by the legislature.

Subsequent constitutions in the other States copied this provision for the record-book of the council, and an unsuccessful effort was made to have a council of this sort in the National Constitution. But this imitation of the British privy council failed at every point, and was soon abandoned by the States that had adopted it.

The New Jersey constitution was begun on May 26 and finished July 3, 1776. This was the first of the constitutions of 1776 that was submitted to the people for their approval. The others had all been prepared and put in force by the conventions which framed them.

The New Jersey document was made about contemporaneously with the constitution of Virginia, and shows a strong resemblance to it. The legislature is to have two branches,—an assembly and a legislative council,—and the two branches are to elect the governor by joint ballot, as in Virginia. Both the upper and the lower house can, however, originate legislation, and the upper house is not confined to the mere right of rejecting the bills of the lower house. But the upper house cannot originate a money bill.

It is to be observed that the upper house is called a legislative council, going back to the name it had when it was just emerging from the condition of governor's council. There is also another provision which looks backward. The privy council is composed of three members of the legislative council,—a curious sort of restoration of the legislative council's old function of governor's council.

A method of impeachment, however, is provided which is quite advanced. The lower house is to bring the impeachment, and the upper house is to try it; and this plan was afterwards adopted in the National Constitution.

The governor is to be chancellor and surrogate-general, and the governor and the legislative council are to constitute a court of appeals. The confusion of departments is quite gross, and the doctrine of separation so distinctly announced in Virginia was evidently not yet appreciated in New Jersey.

Delaware's constitution was put in force September 21, 1776, and was closely modelled on those that had preceded it, but added some developments. The executive is called the president, as in the South Carolina constitution, and in several subsequent constitutions of 1776 the same word is used to describe the governor. Afterwards, when the chief magistrate of the United States was named President, the States all went back to the term governor.

In this Delaware constitution the president, with the advice of the privy council, may lay embargoes and prohibit the exportation of goods for a period not exceeding thirty days during a recess of the legislature. This was the first appearance of this provision, and it was often repeated afterwards. There is also in this constitution a method of amendment by five members in seven of the assembly and seven members of the legislative council. This way of amendment was evidently taken from the

The Constitutions of 1776

Pennsylvania colonial constitutions, and was the first appearance of a method of amendment in any of the constitutions of 1776. Each house of the legislature is for the first time given power to expel a member, and the provisions for adjournments show a nearer approach to methods finally adopted in the National Constitution.

The Delaware constitution, however, shows the usual confusion in the appointing of public officers. The president and the general assembly are to appoint the justices of the Supreme Court and the county courts; the president and privy council are to appoint the secretary, attorney-general, and some other officers; and the general assembly is to appoint generals and field officers of the militia and all other officers of the army and navy.

But the president, with the advice and consent of the privy council, may embody the militia and act as captain-general and commander-in-chief of them. In the constitutions of 1776 the governor is commonly described as commander-in-chief of the State forces. Sometimes he is called captain-general and commander-in-chief, and sometimes merely commander-in-chief. In the National Constitution the President is given part of this title, and called commander-in-chief of the army and navy of the United States.

Pennsylvania's constitution was finished September 28, a few days after Delaware's. It began with a bill of political and civil rights made up to some extent from the Declaration of Independence, which had been passed a few months previously. It provides for amendment by vote of the people, and then, strangely enough, clings to the old colonial system of governor, council, and assembly, without any second or upper house of legislature. This failure to fall in with the tendency towards an upper house may possibly have been due to the influence of Franklin, who had a fancy for a single-house legislature. But it was more probably due to the unprogressive element in the population, which at that time had seized the political power in Pennsylvania, and in after-years destroyed the prestige that had made Philadelphia the metropolis of the country.

But Pennsylvania soon got more than enough of a single house, which, having no check upon its action, became very reckless and endangered the liberties of the people. A sort of make-shift for a double house was provided for in compelling every bill to pass two sessions of the assembly before it became a law, but this proved entirely unsuccessful.

The president's council, which was to be known as the Supreme Executive Council, was to consist of twelve members elected from the different counties by the people. The president and council were to appoint public officers, propose business to the assembly, hear impeachments by the assembly with the justices of the Supreme Court, lay embargoes, pardon offences, and "take care that the laws be faithfully executed." This was another retrogression, and a most bungling contrivance. It was an attempt to create a twelve-headed executive with functions taken from the old governor's council of colonial times, and new ones added.

But the most curious part of this constitution was that it provided for a council of censors, two from each

The Constitutions of 1776

city and county, who were to see that the constitution was not violated and that all departments of government did their duty. It was to pass censure when duty was neglected, order impeachments, recommend measures to the legislature, and, when necessary, call a convention to amend the constitution. It was an awkward attempt to prevent unconstitutional legislation. Altogether, this was a most extraordinary constitution, not much of an advance, and caused great dissatisfaction in its working.

After Pennsylvania's constitution was put in force, more than a month passed away before a new one appeared, which was Maryland's, finished November 11, 1776. It begins with a bill of rights which was the most complete and advanced that had up to that time appeared. It announced again the doctrine that the legislative, executive, and judiciary departments should be kept separate. Then followed provisions about freedom of speech, trial by jury, right to petition, right of search, and quartering of troops on the people. In fact, it was so full that it completed the development of bills of rights, and the hundred years that have since elapsed have added little or nothing to it.

When the National Constitution was submitted to the people, great complaints were made that it contained no bill of rights, and when the States finally agreed to adopt it it was with the understanding that a bill of rights should immediately be added by way of amendment. The first eleven amendments to the National Constitution contain this bill of rights, and they are taken, in many instances, word for word from the bill of rights of Maryland. For example, the following clause in the

Evolution of the Constitution

bill of rights of the Maryland constitution is copied verbatim in the eighth amendment to the National Constitution, except that the words "ought not to" are changed to "shall not:"

> "Excessive bail ought not to be required, nor excessive fines imposed, nor cruel and unusual punishments inflicted."

Again, in the Maryland bill of rights we find, "That a well-regulated militia is the proper and natural defence of a free government;" and the second amendment to the National Constitution says, "A well-regulated militia being necessary to the security of a free State, the right of the people to keep and bear arms shall not be infringed." The Maryland bill of rights says, "No soldier ought to be quartered in any house in time of peace without the consent of the owner, and in time of war in such manner only as the legislature shall direct;" and the third amendment to the National Constitution says, "No soldier shall in time of peace be quartered in any house without the consent of the owner, nor in time of war but in a manner to be prescribed by law."

We find also in this Maryland bill of rights several other ideas which were adopted in the National Constitution, such as the prohibition of *ex post facto* laws, of attainder of treason, of the granting of titles of nobility, and of the receiving, by any person in public office, of a present from any foreign prince or state.

In the matter of political government the Maryland constitution provided for a legislature of two branches, a senate and a house of delegates. The forms in previous constitutions were, for the most part, followed;

The Constitutions of 1776

but the lower house was given the right to inquire into complaints and grievances as the grand inquest of the State, to punish for contempt or breach of privilege, and to commit any person to jail for any crime, to remain until discharged by law. The senate, it is interesting to observe, is to be chosen by electors in each county, —very much after the manner adopted in the National Constitution for electing the President.

A month later, December 18, 1776, North Carolina's constitution appeared. It begins with a bill of rights copying many of the provisions that we have just observed in Maryland and forbidding retrospective laws. The only new provision, which was afterwards universally accepted, is that all bills shall be read three times in each house before they become laws, and must be signed by the speakers of both houses. Except for this, there is nothing particularly advanced about this constitution, and it provides no way of amendment.

The Georgia constitution, adopted February 5, 1777, shows no development whatever. In fact, it goes back to the old colonial system of a governor, a governor's council, and a single-branch legislature. The pardoning power is given to the legislature instead of to the governor, and the document is in every way an inferior one.

New York's constitution was adopted April 20, 1777. It had been a long time in making,—in fact, since July 10, 1776. Much difficulty seems to have been experienced with it, and the convention adjourned and readjourned repeatedly, moving about from place to place. In most respects it conformed to previous instruments, but had two striking developments which passed into the National Constitution.

It begins with a long and rather irrelevant preamble, reciting the condition of the country in general and of New York in particular, and then quotes the whole of the Declaration of Independence, of which it highly approves. When we come to the frame of government we find a legislature consisting of an assembly and a senate. The governor or chancellor and the judges of the Supreme Court are to constitute a council to revise all the bills of the legislature before they are passed into laws, so as to prevent hasty legislation. This council is also to have a veto power if they think a bill should not be passed, and this veto power is described in almost the same language as the veto power of the President in the National Constitution:

"And that all bills which have passed the Senate and Assembly shall, before they become laws, be presented to the said council for their revisal and consideration; and if upon such revision and consideration it should appear improper to the said council, or a majority of them, that the said bill should become a law in this State, that they return the same, together with their objections thereto in writing, to the Senate or House of Assembly (in whichsoever the same shall have originated), who shall enter the objections sent down by the council at large in their minutes, and proceed to reconsider the said bill. But if, after such reconsideration, two-thirds of the said Senate or House of Assembly shall, notwithstanding the said objections, agree to pass the same, it shall, together with the objections, be sent to the other branch of the legislature, where it shall also be reconsidered, and, if approved by two-thirds of the members present, shall be a law. And, in order to prevent any unnecessary delays, be it further ordained that if any bill shall not be returned by the council within ten days after it shall have been presented, the same shall be a law, unless the legislature shall, by their adjournment, render a return of the said bill within ten days impracticable; in which case the bill shall be returned on the first day of the meeting of the legislature after the expiration of the said ten days."

The National Constitution, in Section 7 of Article I., after providing that the President, if he approve of a bill, shall sign it, goes on to say,—

"But if not, he shall return it, with his objections, to that house in which it shall have originated, who shall enter the objections at large on their journal and proceed to reconsider it. If after such reconsideration two-thirds of that house shall agree to pass the bill, it shall be sent, together with the objections, to the other house, by which it shall likewise be reconsidered, and, if approved by two-thirds of that house, it shall become a law. . . . If any bill shall not be returned by the President within ten days (Sundays excepted) after it shall have been presented to him, the same shall be a law, in like manner as if he had signed it, unless the congress by their adjournment prevent its return, in which case it shall not be a law."

This shows with great clearness how the modified veto power of the President in the National Constitution was gradually worked out on American soil, and that it was not a copying of the absolute veto power of the British king. The two quotations also show how the National Constitution improved and simplified in language all the provisions it took from previous documents.

The New York governor is also to send to the legislature a message informing it of the condition of the State, and recommending to its consideration matters that he deems important; and this, of course, suggested

Evolution of the Constitution

the similar provision in the National Constitution for the President's message.

These resemblances to the National Constitution are certainly remarkable. But in other respects the New York constitution had nothing in it particularly worthy of notice, except that it provided for voting by ballot as an experiment to see if it was better than *viva voce* voting. The assembly was also once a year to appoint a council of senators to appoint public officers. This was also evidently an experiment. The assembly was to bring impeachments, and the impeachments were to be tried before a court consisting of the president, the senators, the chancellor, and the judges of the Supreme Court.

The constitution of Vermont was adopted July 8, 1777, but it shows no advancement, because it was copied almost word for word from the constitution of Pennsylvania. It followed the Pennsylvania plan of a governor and council, with a single-branch legislature, and even copied the Pennsylvania council of censors.

The rejected constitution of Massachusetts was ordered by the convention to be laid before the people February 28, 1778. Although voted down by the people, it embodied much of the best thought of the time in constitution-drawing. Its legislature was to consist of a senate and a house of representatives, the same names that were afterwards used in the national document, and the senators, twenty-eight in number, were to be chosen from certain districts. The senate and the house were to be distinct bodies, and money-bills could originate only in the house. The governor was president of the senate,

The Constitutions of 1776

commander-in-chief of the militia, and admiral of the navy. He could also grant reprieves for six months, but had not the pardoning power, which was placed in a sort of committee, consisting of the governor, the lieutenant-governor, and the speaker of the house of representatives. The governor could lay embargoes for forty days in a recess of the general court, and he and the senate were to try impeachments which should be prosecuted by the house. There was also a provision, taken from the New York constitution, that the governor should inform the legislature of the condition of the State and recommend matters to its consideration. This rejected constitution disclosed no new developments, but contained most of the best provisions which had been in previous documents.

A new constitution for South Carolina was framed about the same time, and finished March 19, 1778, but did not go into effect until November of that year. It provided for a governor, a senate, and a house of representatives, and was in other respects so well abreast of the times that no comment is required. In fact, the State constitutions had now brought forth about all that they were to contribute to the national document. Their senate and house of representatives, methods of adjournment, impeachment, veto power, and bills-of-rights provisions were almost the same as in the National Constitution.

New Hampshire also at this time framed a new constitution for herself, which was finished June 10, 1778, submitted to the people, and rejected. It was very simple and short. The previous constitution had provided no governor, and this one did not definitely provide a governor, but gave the president of the council some of the usual executive powers. The council was an upper house of the legislature, and elected its own president. Besides this double-branch legislature, one or two other modern improvements were added; but New Hampshire was very backward in constitutional development, and seemed disinclined to make much effort to advance.

The next constitution in order was one which Massachusetts finally persuaded her people to accept in 1780. It was very elaborate and verbose, giving reasons for its provisions, and full of generalities about the sovereignty of the people and the absurdity of hereditary titles, all of which was probably thought necessary to overcome the suspicions of the people and gain their acceptance of the instrument. The governor is given the modified veto power which we found in the constitution of New York, and in other respects this Massachusetts constitution, like the one that was rejected, is fully up to the times. One or two new developments appear,—a provision about the suspension of habeas corpus, and another giving members of the legislature privilege from arrest, both of them very like similar provisions which afterwards appeared in the National Constitution.

New Hampshire, like Massachusetts, having had her constitution of 1778 rejected by the people, made another attempt, and in 1784 secured a new constitution. It requires, however, but little comment, because it was copied from the Massachusetts constitution of 1780. Only one new development appeared,—a pro-

The Constitutions of 1776

vision prohibiting persons accused of crime from being twice tried for the same offence. This afterwards appeared in the National Constitution, and has been almost universally copied in modern State constitutions.

The last constitution of all was a new one for Vermont in 1786. But it was a mere repetition, with slight changes, of her constitution of 1777, which was taken from the Pennsylvania constitution of 1776.

CHAPTER IV.

THE ENGLISH SOURCES OF THE CONSTITUTION.

AFTER reading the assertions of learned writers that our Constitution was modelled on the British government as it existed in 1787, I have sometimes turned to the words of the Constitution to see the resemblance, and have never been able to find it. As one reads along, sentence after sentence, everything seems so un-English and so original and peculiar to our own locality that the mind is forced to the conclusion that it either grew up as a natural product of the soil or was invented off-hand,—struck off at a given time, as Mr. Gladstone says. I recommend to those who believe in the British model theory to adopt this simple plan: Read our Constitution, sentence by sentence, from beginning to end, and see how many sentences they can trace to an origin in the British government.

I do not deny that in a certain sense it is all English. In fact, I have taken considerable pains to show how our Constitution was developed by English colonists out of the forms of English trading corporations through the English colonial charters. Nor will any one deny that our language, literature, laws, and many of our customs and modes of thought, as well as our characteristic instincts and feelings, are of English origin. I would be the last person in the world to dispute the

English Sources

Anglo-Saxon influence in our civilization. But all this is very different from the dogma some wish to establish, that our Constitution was taken or copied from or suggested by the forms of the British government as it existed in 1787. In my opinion, there was no copying, because we were so thoroughly Anglo-Saxon in our instincts and feelings that imitation was excluded. We acted after the manner of our race, and built, stone by stone, out of the natural material and conditions round us.

In the first eleven amendments to the Constitution a number of the provisions about trial by jury and freedom of speech were doubtless evolved from the experience of the race in England. But even these, as already shown, were worked out slowly and re-evolved on American soil. In the body of the Constitution itself—the political frame-work proper—there is little or nothing that can be traced to the forms of the British government as it existed in 1787, or at any other time for hundreds of years previous.

I do not deny that the framers of our Constitution considered and discussed the forms of the British Constitution. But they considered them principally, as the minutes of their debates will show, for the purpose, or at any rate with the result, of avoiding them. They were intelligent men,—a large number of them were college-bred,—and they discussed the forms of government of all countries. They were not unmindful of the example of Holland, the democracies of Greece, the Roman republic and empire, and the free republics of the Middle Ages. They took what light they could

Evolution of the Constitution

from them all; and I think as good an argument could be framed to show that they were guided by what they knew of classic antiquity as could be brought forward to prove that they were guided by the British Constitution.

But the foundation for all their final decisions, the basis which the forms of government in Europe merely illustrated or made more certain, was their own experience of nearly two hundred years with the colonial charters and constitutions and the constitutions of 1776. What they took from England went back through that two hundred years, and then not to the British government, but to the forms of the old trading charters. What had been evolved from the trading charters had been so long with us that it was completely Americanized, and it was valued by the framers of the Constitution for that reason, and because it had been tested by two hundred years of American life.

They did not commit the absurdity of skipping those two hundred years of their history, or of crossing an ocean and entering other countries to copy constitutions. If they had done such a thing it would have been very unlike the Anglo-Saxon race. On the contrary, they did, I think, just what we should expect of that race. They took their own experience as it was up to that date in the place and community for which they were making a frame of government. They made no skips or jumps, but went backward in the past directly from themselves and in their own line, taking for their guide that which was nearest to them and latest developed, provided it had been tested in that line of

English Sources

their own past. The Anglo-Saxon always works in this way, step by step, beginning with what he has and what is directly applicable. He seldom, if ever, obliterates his past or goes aside or afar to seek a new theory, and never invents a brand-new political fabric off-hand.

The East India Company, for example, was first chartered in 1599 under the name of the "Governor and Company of Merchants of London Trading with the East Indies." It had a governor and twenty-four directors. The directors were to elect the governor and all other officers, make laws, punish crimes, and so forth. It was, nevertheless, merely a trading company, with a touch of political power, just like the companies that founded the American colonies which we have been discussing in the previous chapters. Yet out of it has grown, by slow degrees, the present vast and completed political government of India. All this growth was, so to speak, out of itself, like the growth of the trading companies of the American colonies. In 1661 we find Charles II. giving it the high governmental power of making peace or war with any power not Christian, of erecting forts, and exercising criminal and civil jurisdiction through judges, just as we find these same powers gradually given to the American colonies in the colonial charters. In 1677 it was allowed to establish a mint and coin money. And so it went on, adding huge territorial possessions to the British Empire, and becoming more and more of a political power, and yet remaining in form the same old trading corporation, until 1833.

Even then, when its trading attributes were mostly taken from it and all its property was vested in the

Evolution of the Constitution

Crown, the forms of the trading charter still remained, and it governed the vast properties and possessions as trustee for the Crown. It was slowly transformed, not to suit a theory or to imitate anything, but to suit changing circumstances, until, in 1858, it became a recognized department of the British government with one of the secretaries of state in control, instead of the old trading board with its committees on finance, on politics and war, on judicial and legislative interests, and the famous secret committee.

But let us return to our own Constitution and be definite and accurate about it, and accuracy and definiteness is more than can be said for the advocates of the theory that it was copied from the British government. Let us examine its provisions closely, to see what they resemble.

We will begin with the powers of the President, because they are the most simple and striking, and it is said that they were copied from the powers of the British king. Blackstone, in his commentaries on the English law, has five or six chapters devoted to the powers of the king, and it is said that the convention of 1787 selected from these the powers of our President. Mr. Bryce, in his "American Commonwealth," declares that, being guided by the description of the royal power in Blackstone, the framers of our Constitution were misled into taking rather ancient kingly powers for the President, because the description in Blackstone gave the theory of royal power rather than its practice, and its theory was many years behind its practice.

When we read those chapters in Blackstone we find

English Sources

most of them taken up with a description of all sorts of prerogatives and powers, the king's dignity, his sovereignty and pre-eminence, his perpetuity, his privy council, his right to appoint ports and havens, wharfs and quays, public markets and fairs, to regulate weights and measures, to grant precedence, and to prevent subjects from leaving the kingdom, together with others which were obviously not taken for the American President. The only powers which could by any possibility have been copied are a few mentioned in the middle of Chapter VII., Book I, such as the veto power, the right to send and receive ambassadors, make treaties, and declare peace and war.

Let us take the first of these, the veto power,—certainly a very important one. The veto power has since then been taken away from the English king. But at the time Blackstone wrote the king was said to have an absolute veto on all the bills passed by Parliament. He could, whenever he pleased, prevent their becoming laws, and Parliament was helpless.

If the Convention of 1787 had given the President an absolute veto, it might possibly be said that they took it from the king. But they gave the President a modified veto,—a veto which he could maintain only when there were less than two-thirds of both houses of Congress against him; a sort of veto utterly unknown in England.

The history of this modified veto has been shown from time to time in the previous chapters. The colonists had been very familiar with the absolute veto power. The governors of some of the colonies had it, and in others the king had the right to annul absolutely any laws within a certain number of years after their passage. All sorts of trouble and contentions followed from this absolute veto, and the colonists were not admirers of it. Only a few of the constitutions of 1776 gave it to the governor, and it was not until the constitution of New York suggested the plan of a modified veto that it became in any degree acceptable, and New York's suggestion was adopted almost word for word in the National Constitution.

So also the right to send ambassadors was an absolute right in the British Crown, which it shared with no other department. But in the American Constitution we find that the President cannot appoint ambassadors except with the advice and consent of the Senate. The Crown had the absolute right to make treaties, but the President can make them only with the advice and consent of two-thirds of the Senate. The pardoning power was absolute in the Crown, but the President cannot pardon in cases of impeachment. The king had the power to declare peace or war, but this power is given to Congress, and not to the President; and the power to grant letters of marque, which was in the king, was given to Congress alone.

If the framers of our Constitution took the President's powers from the powers of the British Crown as described in Blackstone, they were great bunglers, and could hardly have been able to read the English language.

The only power possessed by the President which is like any of the powers of the Crown is his command of the army and navy. But the king's chief command had annexed to it, and as a part of it, the right to "raise and regulate" armies and navies; and this, in the American Constitution, was given to Congress. The President's power, which is described in the words "shall be commander-in-chief of the army and navy," was, moreover, evidently derived from the constitutions of 1776 and the colonial governors. The governors had had this power for more than a hundred years, and they were often called "Commanders-in-Chief," in the words of the National Constitution.

The President's message has been supposed to have been taken from the English king's address from the throne on opening Parliament, and perhaps there is nowadays a slight resemblance, because the President usually sends his message at the opening of Congress. But the language of the Constitution which describes the message makes it a mere report on the condition of the country to be given at any time, very much like the report of a head officer of any organization: "He shall, from time to time, give to Congress information of the state of the Union, and recommend to their consideration such measures as he shall judge necessary and expedient." This was taken, as already shown, from the New York constitution of 1777, and had appeared for the first time as far back as the New Hampshire commission of 1680.

The President was also given powers which do not even in the slightest degree resemble any of the powers of the king. He could require the opinion, in writing, of the principal officer in each of the executive departments upon any subject relating to the duties of their respective offices. His powers of appointing to public office with the consent of the Senate, of filling vacancies in the recess of the Senate, and of appointing to inferior offices without the consent of the Senate if Congress should give him the power, are also so totally unlike any similar power of the English king that it is impossible to suppose any resemblance or imitation.

The simple phrase, already noticed, which sums up the most important of the President's duties, "He shall take care that the laws be faithfully executed," had no origin in England, but first appeared, as already shown, in one of the Pennsylvania colonial constitutions, and was repeated with variations in the constitutions of 1776.

The English king had the sole power of assembling Parliament by writ. But the President can convene both houses only "on extraordinary occasions." He cannot call them except on these extraordinary occasions, and he has no power to prorogue or adjourn them when met except when they disagree as to the time of their adjournment, and then "he may adjourn them to such time as he shall think proper." This arrangement was the result of long experience in dealing with colonial governors.

In some of the colonies the royal governors had the power to adjourn the popular assemblies, and when they were displeased with an assembly, or wanted to force something from it, they would adjourn it and prevent its meeting again until it gave what was wanted. It was a most oppressive use of power, and the Pennsylvanians whose governors had not this privilege considered themselves very fortunate.

English Sources

The statement in the National Constitution which says that the President "shall commission all the officers of the United States" was not taken from any power of Blackstone's enumeration, but was the result of experience, and was a brief and sensible way of putting what had been verbosely and circuitously stated in many of the 1776 constitutions. Some of them gave in detail what officers their governors should commission. Often in each clause where the officers were created it was stated that the governor should commission them; and sometimes there were officers who were apparently not commissioned by the governor or his council. Some of the 1776 constitutions, however, had a simple clause that all their officers were to be commissioned by the governor. The framers of the National Constitution adopted this evidently clear and easy form, and it is a good illustration of the way in which the national document was developed into its rather remarkable clearness and simplicity out of the jumbled and often very careless expressions of the instruments that preceded it.

The attempt to show resemblances between the American Congress and the British Parliament is as weak as the attempt to derive the President's powers from those of the king. The opening passages of the Constitution state that the lower house is to be composed of members chosen every second year by the people, and farther on we see that both houses shall assemble at least once in every year, beginning on the first Monday in December. The President has no control whatever in dissolving Congress, or in calling them together, except to adjourn the two houses when they

Evolution of the Constitution

disagree as to the time of adjournment and to call them for a special emergency. This at the very start was totally unlike the British House of Commons, which was not elected at definite periods, but stayed in existence until dissolved by the king; and the reason for this difference was that our people had found in colonial times that great inconvenience ensued whenever the governor could in any way control the popular assembly. The fixing of a definite period for the election of Congressmen was intended to protect the popular assembly, by taking it entirely out of the control of the President, and, so far from being an imitation of the British Constitution, was intended to avoid what was supposed to be a defect in it.

Again, we find in almost the next clause that the members of the House of Representatives are to be apportioned according to population, giving one representative to every thirty thousand of the people. This was also the very reverse of the English Constitution, which allowed members of the House of Commons to be elected by pocket boroughs, by colleges, and in all sorts of ways, without any regard to an even distribution among the people. Each Congressman was also obliged to be an inhabitant of the State in which he should be chosen. But in England there was no rule as to residence, and a member of the House of Commons might reside in one county of England and be elected from any other county.

When we come to the Senate it is as unlike the House of Lords as is possible. It is not hereditary. Its members do not hold office for life, but for six years, and it is constituted expressly by localities, each State being represented by two senators who must be inhabitants of that State. In forming the Senate, the framers of the Constitution developed it, as we have already seen, out of their own experience in the constitutions of 1776 and in colonial times, where we saw the second house of legislature, or senate, gradually evolved out of the governor's council. The only provision which shows a resemblance to the House of Lords is that the Senate has the right to try impeachments, and this is also the result of experience, and not imitation; for the constitutions of 1776 made all sorts of arrangements for courts to try impeachments, and the placing of this power in the upper house was finally decided upon after many experiments.

The Senate was also intended to preserve the balance of power among the States and prevent the oppression of the small States by the larger ones. John Dickinson was in the convention as a representative from Delaware, a very small State, and he had much influence in shaping this part of the Senate's functions. Delaware had been partially annexed to Pennsylvania before the Revolution. The two provinces had the same governor, but different legislatures. At first they had been under the same governor and the same legislature, and it cost Delaware somewhat of a struggle to get an independent legislature. She knew by experience how easily a small State could be unduly controlled or ignored, and her eminent representative naturally became the champion of the weaker commonwealths. This championship resulted not only in the peculiar constitution of the

Evolution of the Constitution

Senate, but also in that clause which says, "No new State shall be formed or created within the jurisdiction of any other State, nor any State be formed by the junction of two or more States, or parts of States, without the consent of the legislatures of the States concerned, as well as of the Congress." All this was, of course, native development.

There is also a clause in the part of the Constitution devoted to the legislative department which has not often been noticed. It provides that a majority of each house shall constitute a quorum, but a smaller number may adjourn from day to day and may be authorized to compel the attendance of absent members. This was doubtless suggested by what had happened in Pennsylvania. The old Quaker assembly under Penn's constitution of 1701 had resisted the movement to make a new constitution in 1776. They had been defeated in the end by members absenting themselves so that no quorum could assemble. Less than a quorum assembled day after day, and, having no power to compel the attendance of other members, they gradually became a laughing-stock for their inefficiency, and the legislative body that had ruled the colony for nearly one hundred years became extinct. This event was fresh in the minds of the framers of the National Constitution, and they took care that nothing similar should happen to the Federal government.

Other characteristics of the American Congress might also be noted. The powers to determine their own rules of proceeding, to punish members for disorderly behavior, to expel a member, to keep a journal, not to

English Sources

adjourn for more than three days without each other's consent, privilege from arrest, and other matters, are more or less characteristic of all legislatures the world over. Some of these provisions could have been taken from England, but several of them, as we have seen, were developed out of colonial experience.

The clause which forbids a senator or a representative from holding any civil office which shall have been created or the emoluments whereof shall have been increased during the time for which he was elected was an obviously good provision which did not have to be copied from any country; and the other provision, that no person holding any office under the United States should be a member of either house during his continuance in office, had been repeated in various forms in the constitutions of 1776, and was a necessary part of the doctrine that the departments of government should be kept distinct. The clause requiring money-bills to originate in the lower house was, of course, an old English idea, but it had been worked out and contended for in the colonial governments and in the Revolutionary constitutions.

Finally, Congress is given only a limited power. Its rights and duties are enumerated, and it cannot go beyond this enumeration; but the power of the British Parliament was general and had no limits fixed to it. This attribute alone would destroy all possibility of resemblance or imitation. It was the result of the peculiar situation of the country,—a federation of States coming together in a Union, to which they intended to delegate only a portion of their sovereignty.

Evolution of the Constitution

When we come to the federalism of the Constitution, the things forbidden to the individual States,—making treaties with foreign powers, granting letters of marque, coining money, issuing bills of credit, passing bills of attainder, *ex post facto* laws, and laws impairing the obligation of contracts,—there could not of course be any possibility of imitation.

CHAPTER V.

THE EVOLUTION FROM THE COLONIAL CHARTERS SHOWN IN DETAIL.

1. ABSOLUTISM.

WE are not accustomed to associate despotism with our ideas of the origin of government in the United States. But government began with us in despotism, as it has begun with other nations. The first American charter gave Sir Walter Raleigh absolute control for six years of any colony he should establish, and this not because the persons who drew the charter were monarchists or believed in absolutism as against liberty, but because, in the absence of all experience in founding or managing colonies, this gift of absolute control was thought to be the best way of encouraging some one to take the risks of colonizing.

It was a matter of business, the most convenient way that could be devised at the time; and what was apparently very despotic power was given, as it commonly is in untried and dangerous enterprises, without any intention of establishing a theory or principle. Despotism has begun in the infancy of many nations in a similar way, as the best means of meeting present difficulties.

Twenty-two years afterwards, in the Virginia charter of 1606, the absolutism was modified in another attempt to meet the requirements of circumstances. The law-making power was given to the king, and the administration of any laws he should devise was given to councils appointed by him. This was absolutism, but not so crude and simple as in Sir Walter Raleigh's charter. It was, however, so far as practical government was concerned, the last of absolutism in America, for the next document, the Virginia charter of 1609, allowed a sort of representative government, and after that no government that could be called absolute was ever put in force.

Absolutism, however, survived in a merely formal way for a long time afterwards. The New England charter of 1620 created a close corporation which could make any laws it pleased for the government of its territory. But this corporation used this absolute power, as already shown, to establish a very free representative system of government for New England : so that, in this instance, the absolutism quickly produced republicanism. Nor was the very liberal power given to John Mason, the proprietor of New Hampshire, ever successfully enforced in practice.

The Maryland charter of 1632 also continued absolutism as an obsolete form, and, although requiring the consent of the freemen for all laws, allowed Lord Baltimore to enact laws in emergencies when there was no time for calling a meeting of the assembly. This same provision was repeated in the Carolina charters of 1663 and 1665, and in the Pennsylvania charter of 1681, which were all, like that of Maryland, proprietary charters. But the absolutism of these rather curious provisions was never enforced, and any attempt to enforce it would have brought on a popular uprising. It remained

Evolution from the Charters

as a mere survival of the past, like a part or faculty of a species of animal which has outlived its ancient usefulness.

"We for vs, our heires and successors, are likewise pleased and contented, and by these presents do giue and graunt to the said *Walter Raleigh*, his heires and assignes for ever, that hee and they, and euery or any of them, shall and may from time to time for euer hereafter, within the said mentioned remote landes and Countreis in the way by the seas thither, and from thence, haue full and meere power and authoritie to correct, punish, pardon, gouerne, and rule by their and euery or any of their good discretions and pollicies, as well in causes capital, or criminall, as ciuil, both marine and other, . . . within 6. yeeres next ensuing the date hereof, according to such statutes, lawes and ordinances, as shall bee by him the saide *Walter Raleigh*, his heires and assignes, and euery or any of them deuised, or established." (Sir Walter Raleigh's Charter of 1584.)

"And we do also ordain, establish, and agree, for Us, our Heirs, and Successors, that each of the said Colonies shall have a Council, which shall govern and order all Matters and Causes, which shall arise, grow, or happen, to or within the same several Colonies, according to such Laws, Ordinances, and Instructions, as shall be, in that behalf, given and signed with Our Hand or Sign Manual, and pass under the Privy Seal of our Realm of *England.*" (Virginia Charter of 1606.)

"Wee, by the Advice of the Lords and others of the said priuie Councill, do by these Presents ordaine, constitute, limett, and appoint, that from henceforth, there shall be for ever hereafter, in our Towne of Plymouth, in the County of Devon, one Body politicque and corporate, which shall have perpetuall Succession, which shall consist of the Number of fourtie Persons, and no more, which shall be, and shall be called and knowne by the Name the Councill established at Plymouth, in the County of Devon for the planting, ruling, ordering, and governing of New-England, in America. . . . and also to make, ordaine, and

Evolution of the Constitution

establish all Manner of Orders, Laws, Directions, Instructions, Forms, and Ceremonies of Government and Magistracy fitt and necessary for and concerning the Government of the said Collony and plantation." (Charter of New England of 1620.)

"And the said Captain John Mason doth further covenant for him, his Heirs and Assigns, that he will establish such Government in the said portion of Lands and Islands granted unto him, and the same will from time to time continue, as shall be agreeble as near as may be to the Laws and Customs of the Realm of England; and if he shall be charged at any time to have neglected his duty therein, that then he will reform the same, according to the Discretion of the President and Council, or in Default thereof, it shall be lawful for any of the aggrieved Inhabitants or Planters, being Tenants upon the said Lands, to appeal to the chief Court of Justice of the said president and Council." (Grant of New Hampshire of 1629.)

"And forasmuch, as in the government of so great a province, sudden accidents do often happen, whereunto it will be necessary to apply a remedy, before the freeholders of the said province, their delegates or deputies, can be assembled to the making of laws, . . . therefore for the better government of the said province, we will and ordain and by these presents for us, our heirs and successors do grant unto the said now Lord Baltimore and his heirs, that the said now Lord Baltimore and his heirs, by themselves or by their magistrates and officers in that behalf duly to be ordained as aforesaid may make and constitute fit and wholesome ordinances, from time to time, within the said province, to be kept and observed as well for the preservation of the peace, as for the better government of the people there inhabiting, and so as the said ordinances be not extended, in any sort to bind, charge, or take away the right or interest of any person or persons of or in their life, member, freehold, goods or chattels." (Maryland Charter of 1632.)

"With power of judicature [to John Mason] in all causes and matters whatsoever, as well criminall, capitall, and civil, ariseing or which may hereafter arise within the lymitts, bounds, and pre-

Evolution from the Charters

cincts aforesayd, to bee exercised, and executed according to the laws of England as neere as may bee, by the said capt. John Mason, his heyers and assignes, or his or their Deputys, Leeftenants, Judges, Stewards, or Officers thereunto by him or them assigned, deputed or appoynted from tyme to tyme, . . . saveing and always reserving vnto the said Counsell and their successors, power to receive, heare and determine all and singular appeale and apeales of every person and persons whatsoever, dwelling or inhabiting within the said Territorys and Yslands or any part thereof, soe granted as aforesaid, of and from all judgements, and sentences whatsoever given within the said lands and territory aforesaid." (Grant of New Hampshire of 1635.)

The provision given above from the Maryland charter of 1632 is substantially repeated in the grant of Maine of 1639.

The Carolina charter of 1663 repeats substantially the provision given above from the Maryland charter of 1632.

The grant to the Duke of York of 1664 repeats substantially the provision given above from Sir Walter Raleigh's charter of 1584.

The Carolina charter of 1665 repeats substantially the provision given above from the Maryland charter of 1632.

The grant to the Duke of York of 1674 repeats substantially the provision given above from Sir Walter Raleigh's charter of 1584.

The Pennsylvania charter of 1681 repeats the provision given above from the Maryland charter of 1632.

2. SEPARATE DEPARTMENTS.

In despotic governments the three great powers, legislative, executive, and judicial, are exercised by the same person. This is the cause of the despotism and the means by which the government remains despotic. As the three powers gradually become separated and are controlled by different persons, the government advances in freedom.

Evolution of the Constitution.

The first American government—Sir Walter Raleigh's charter of 1584—was thoroughly despotic, and Sir Walter exercised all three of the powers. In the next government—the Virginia charter of 1606—the law-making power was given to the king, and the administration of the laws to councils appointed by him. Here there was a partial separation of two of the departments; but the separation was not very distinct, for the king appointed the executive body which was to administer the laws he made, and this executive body, besides administering the laws, may have also acted as a judiciary department. But still it was a beginning of separateness.

In the Virginia charter of 1609 the laws were made by a council resident in England, which council was elected by a majority vote of the members of the corporation; and this same council appointed the governor and other officers. Here we have a legislative body elected, so to speak, by the people, and an executive department appointed by the legislature. But there is, as yet, no separate judicial department, and presumably the power of that department is to be exercised by the executive.

Apparently no attempt was made in any of the colonial governments to establish a separate judicial department until the Maryland charter of 1632, which gives Lord Baltimore express power to establish courts of justice and provide everything that relates thereto. But six years afterwards, in the fundamental orders of Connecticut of 1638, the judicial power is given to the magistrates, who were in effect a governor's council and

Evolution from the Charters

part of the executive: so that the advance of the Maryland charter is checked, and colonial government again consists of only two departments, legislative and executive, with the executive exercising the powers of a judicial department.

In 1662, however, the Connecticut charter gave express power to the general assembly to establish separate courts, both civil and criminal, and from that time, with the exception of New Hampshire, the colonial governments seem to have had the three departments, legislative, executive, and judicial.

There was still a certain amount of confusion among them. The governor's council, as we have seen, often sat with the assembly, and in this way the executive was too much mingled with the legislative. The gradual evolution of the governor's council into an upper house of the legislature was constantly remedying this defect; but in many other ways the confusion lingered. There was a tendency to give the governor's council judicial duties to perform, as in the Massachusetts charter of 1691, and, although the three powers were usually separately created, there was no express command prohibiting an individual from holding two inconsistent offices. A judge might be elected to the legislature, and there were no express words in the charter or constitution to compel him to resign his judgeship. Similarly, a member of the legislature might hold some executive office or be an officer in the militia.

The first appearance of any conscious attempt to keep the powers more distinctly separated is in the Georgia charter of 1732, which provides that no person

Evolution of the Constitution

holding an office of profit under the corporation shall be a member of the corporation. The corporation, or members of the company, under this charter, made the laws and appointed the council which carried on the company's executive business; so that the corporation was, in effect, the legislative department; and the provision for more distinct separateness meant that no member of the legislative department should hold any office in the executive department, or, presumably, in the judicial department, if there was one.

Twenty-two years afterward, in Hutchinson's plan of union of 1754, we find a similar provision, to the effect that no member of the council should be chosen to any office, civil or military. After this no more written forms of government appeared until the constitutions of 1776, and in the second one of these, the South Carolina constitution, we find a somewhat elaborate provision declaring what offices are inconsistent with each other and cannot be held by the same person.

In Virginia's constitution, which came next, the general principle is laid down for the first time that "the legislative, executive, and judiciary departments shall be separate and distinct, so that no one of them exercise the powers properly belonging to the others, nor shall any person exercise the powers of more than one of them at the same time."

It is curious, however, as showing the old condition of things still lingering, that at the close of this general principle in the Virginia constitution an exception is made allowing the justices of the county courts to be eligible to either house of assembly.

Evolution from the Charters

But the movement in favor of more distinct separateness was now well under way, and, as we pass along among the constitutions of 1776, we find nearly every one of them either laying down the broad principle first declared by Virginia or giving in detail the offices which were inconsistent and could not be held by the same person; and in some of them both the principle and the detailed description of the inconsistent offices are given.

By the time the National Constitution was framed, the doctrine of separate departments was thoroughly understood. The Constitution describes each department and assigns its duties with a clearness that leaves no doubt of their distinctness, and, to show what offices are inconsistent, contents itself with a simple phrase forbidding any person holding an office under the United States to be a member of either house during his continuance in office.

The slow growth of the principle of separate departments during two hundred years—from the confused despotism of Sir Walter Raleigh's charter of 1584 to the enlightened distinctness of the Constitution, which makes each department almost independent—is an excellent illustration of the way in which our constitutional ideas have grown naturally on our own soil, without that imitation of foreign forms upon which some writers have insisted.

At a time when the departments of our colonial governments were much confused, the departments of the British government were quite distinct, and our constitution-makers could have imitated that distinctness with a stroke of the pen. But they were not looking for anything to imitate, and they were not constructing theories or ideals. They were constructing practical governments suited to the conditions of time and place, and, among primitive conditions in a new country, a government with all the departments fused into one, or into two only slightly separated, is often the best that can be devised.

The first and original of all governments is the government of a father over the family, which, so far as a family is concerned, could not be improved by any doctrine of divided authority; and for certain simple enterprises the one-man power is still the best. The colonizers of America did not construct the single authority of Sir Walter Raleigh's charter or the very slightly separated departments of succeeding charters because they were ignorant of the principle of distinct departments; they did it because they were working out the great problem of the continent according to its needs. They were simple when their conditions were simple, and they became elaborate as the requirements became elaborate. Our present National Constitution would have been as unsuited and ridiculous to the America of 1584 as Sir Walter's charter of that year would be unsuited and ridiculous to the United States of to-day.

It is a common assertion that the doctrine of separate departments was first taught to us, as well as to the rest of the world, by Montesquieu's "Spirit of Laws," which appeared in 1748. But the colonial governments had begun to separate their departments long before that year, and separate departments were to be found

Evolution from the Charters

in the British government and in other governments on the continent of Europe. When we come to read the chapter in Montesquieu which treats of the subject (Book XI., Chap. VI.), we find that he makes no pretence of having discovered anything, but merely comments on the separated departments of the governments of Europe, and praises the British government for having advanced farther in this respect than the others. Montesquieu doubtless emphasized the importance of separated departments, and in that sense helped and encouraged their development; but he did nothing more, and professed to do nothing more.

The quotations from the charters and constitutions which show the development in this section, being too long to give in full, are summarized, a method which will be followed in other sections when the length of the quotations renders it necessary :

No person holding an office of profit under the corporation to be a member of the corporation. (Georgia Charter of 1732.)

No member of council to hold any civil or military office. (Hutchinson's Plan, 1754.)

Certain inconsistent offices not to be held by the same person. (South Carolina Constitution of 1776.)

The principle laid down that the three departments should be separate and distinct. (Virginia Constitution of 1776.)

Certain inconsistent offices not to be held by the same person. (New Jersey Constitution of 1776.)

Certain inconsistent offices not to be held by the same person. (Delaware Constitution of 1776.)

Certain inconsistent offices not to be held by the same person. (Pennsylvania Constitution of 1776.)

The principle laid down that the three departments should be separate and distinct ; and, certain inconsistent offices not to be

Evolution of the Constitution

held by the same person. (Maryland Declaration of Rights and Constitution of 1776.)

The principle laid down that the three departments should be separate and distinct. (North Carolina Declaration of Rights of 1776.)

Certain inconsistent offices not to be held by the same person. (North Carolina Constitution of 1776.)

The principle laid down that the three departments should be separate and distinct; and, certain inconsistent offices not to be held by the same person. (Georgia Constitution of 1777.)

Certain inconsistent offices not to be held by the same person. (New York Constitution of 1777.)

Certain inconsistent offices not to be held by the same person. (Rejected Constitution of Massachusetts of 1778.)

Certain inconsistent offices not to be held by the same person. (South Carolina Constitution of 1778.)

Certain inconsistent offices not to be held by the same person. (Articles of Confederation, 1778.)

Certain inconsistent offices not to be held by the same person. (Drayton's Articles of Confederation, 1778.)

Certain inconsistent offices not to be held by the same person. (Rejected Constitution of New Hampshire of 1778.)

The principle laid down that the three departments should be separate and distinct; and, certain inconsistent offices not to be held by the same person. (Massachusetts Constitution of 1780.)

The principle laid down that the three departments should be separate and distinct; and, certain inconsistent offices not to be held by the same person. (New Hampshire Constitution of 1784.)

The principle laid down that the three departments should be separate and distinct; and, certain inconsistent offices not to be held by the same person. (Vermont Constitution of 1786.)

Members of the national legislature to be ineligible to other offices under the national government, except those belonging peculiarly to the functions of the legislature. (Randolph's Plan of 1787.)

Members of the national legislature to be ineligible to other

Evolution from the Charters

offices under the national government. (Pinckney's Plan of 1787.)

The Constitution prohibits members of Congress from holding any other office under the United States. (The Constitution.)

3. THE HOUSE OF REPRESENTATIVES.

The legislative, or law-making, power is with us the foundation of government; for it is in this body that the will of the people is first shown and most completely expressed. The first article of the National Constitution, and the first words of that article, are devoted to describing the legislature, and our modern State constitutions usually begin in the same way.

This conception was reached by a process of evolution. The colonial charters were apt to begin by creating a governor and describing the executive department, and it is evident on reading them that they regarded this part of government as the foundation and the legislature as secondary and a mere check on the governor and his council, or as a privilege graciously allowed the people. But in the constitutions of 1776 we see the legislature assuming the modern position and importance which it now has without the slightest question.

Our legislative power, as now developed, consists of two bodies,—the Senate and the House of Representatives,—and of these the Senate is always spoken of as the upper house, and is regarded as the greater in dignity. But the lower house is the greater in power and importance, because it is more directly representative of the people and holds the purse-strings; that is to say, has the sole power of originating money-bills. It has sometimes been called the first house, although

Evolution of the Constitution

the Senate is called the upper house, and it is rightly called first, because it was developed first.

As the summary shows, its roots started in the Virginia charter of 1609, and it succeeded to the absolutism of the two previous charters,—the Virginia charter of 1606 and Sir Walter Raleigh's of 1584. It began in that Virginia charter of 1609 in the simple form of a council which was to be elected by the members of a corporation and make the laws for the colony. This was the real beginning of American representative government. The power of the people, on which the great fabric of our republic is now reared, was first recognized by giving power to all the members of a corporation which owned a colony. From this it was a natural step to transfer the power from the members or stockholders of the corporation to the inhabitants or people of the colony.

This step we find gradually made in the next three charters. The Virginia charter of 1611–12 gives the power to all the members of the company to make the laws in a mass-meeting. The Massachusetts charter of 1629 gives the power in the same way, but in the Maryland charter of 1632 the law-making power is given for the first time, not to the members or stockholders of a corporation, but to the inhabitants or people of the colony, and they are allowed to exercise it either in mass-meeting or, if they become too numerous for that, through delegates.

It is certainly rather strange that we should have developed our great governmental power, the power of the people and their legislature, out of the forms of a corporation. But our people have always made

Evolution from the Charters

great use of corporations, and we have now developed their use in business enterprises far beyond anything known in other countries. American corporation law has become, like our patent law, a great department of jurisprudence peculiar to the United States. Indeed, we have pushed the development of corporations so far that their enormous power for evil or good has become a political question.

The Maryland charter of 1632, as we have said, contained a suggestion that the people of the colony could, if they chose, exercise the law-making power through delegates instead of in a mass-meeting. The next document, the fundamental orders of Connecticut of 1638, carried this suggestion a step farther, and provided that the people should not exercise the law-making power in mass-meeting, but should always elect deputies, which, with the magistrates or governor's council, should constitute a body called the general court.

Thus, in the year 1638 we have a regular representative legislature established, called the general court, and consisting of the governor, the governor's council, and the delegates elected by the people. This remained the form of the legislative power all through the colonial period. We find it repeated in the Connecticut charter of 1662, the Rhode Island charter of 1663, and the Concessions of East Jersey of 1665. In 1669 Locke's curious constitution of Carolina carries out the same idea of deputies elected by the people; but instead of the governor and the governor's council he joins with the deputies several orders of the nobility, and calls the whole a parliament.

Evolution of the Constitution

In the Concessions of West Jersey of 1677 the same idea of an assembly elected by the people is continued, with no governor or governor's council added to it. The commission of New Hampshire of 1680 also has an elective assembly. The Pennsylvania frame of April 2, 1683, introduces a reaction by taking away from this now well-established assembly the right to originate laws and giving this originating right to an upper house. But in the Massachusetts charter of 1691 the form of governor, governor's council, and deputies of the people appears again; and in the frame of 1696 Pennsylvania restores to her assembly the right to originate laws. The Georgia charter of 1732 produces an apparent reaction by giving the law-making power to a corporation. But this, as already shown, was the result of very peculiar circumstances, and need not be considered.

Coming to the constitutions of 1776, we find them accepting the old colonial assembly as their principal legislative body; and in the first of these constitutions, that of New Hampshire, it is called the house of representatives, the name afterwards adopted for it in the National Constitution. As we pass on through these constitutions of 1776 we find it appearing in them all, —sometimes called the assembly, sometimes the house of delegates, but, as we near the end, more and more often called the house of representatives, until, in the simplest language of only a few lines, the old colonial assembly, over which the charters were often so wordy, becomes the House of Representatives of Congress in the National Constitution.

Evolution from the Charters

The council resident in England to be elected by a majority vote of the company, and said council to make the laws. (Virginia Charter of 1609.)

The treasurer and the whole company to meet four times a year to make the laws. (Virginia Charter of 1611–12.)

The law-making power given to the assistants and the whole body of the freemen of the company. (Massachusetts Charter of 1629.)

The law-making power given to the proprietor and the freemen or their delegates. (Maryland Charter of 1632.)

The governor, the magistrates, and the deputies elected by the towns to constitute a general court to make the laws. (Fundamental Orders of Connecticut, 1638.)

In 1643 the inhabitants of Rhode Island were given a patent which allowed them to rule themselves by such form of government as the majority of them should find most suitable to their condition.

The governor, deputy-governor, assistants, and the deputies from the towns to constitute a general assembly to make the laws. (Connecticut Charter of 1662.)

The above provision is repeated in the Rhode Island charter of 1663.

The Carolina charter of 1663 copies the provision given above from the Maryland charter of 1632.

The governor, council, and deputies of the people to constitute a general assembly to make the laws. (Concessions of East Jersey, 1665.)

The Carolina charter of 1665 copies the provision given above from the Maryland charter of 1632.

Three divisions of the nobility and the deputies of the freeholders to constitute a parliament to make the laws. (Locke's Carolina Constitution of 1669.)

One hundred deputies elected by the people to constitute the general assembly. (Concessions of West Jersey of 1677.)

The president and council to decide how many deputies elected by the people shall constitute the general assembly. (Commission for New Hampshire of 1680.)

Evolution of the Constitution

The Pennsylvania charter of 1681 copies the provision given above from the Maryland charter of 1632.

The general assembly given power only to accept or reject the bills of the upper house or make suggestions for their amendment. (Pennsylvania Frame of April 2, 1683.)

The above provision is repeated in the Pennsylvania Frame of 1683, with some changes as to the number of members of the assembly and the time of meeting.

The governor, assistants, and the deputies of the towns to constitute the general assembly. (Massachusetts Charter of 1691.)

The general assembly of Pennsylvania allowed to originate bills. (Pennsylvania Frame of 1696.)

Deputies of the people to constitute an assembly. (Pennsylvania Charter of Privileges of 1701.)

The law-making power given to the general meeting of the corporation. (Charter of Georgia of 1732.)

The lower branch of the legislature elected by the people to be called the house of representatives. (New Hampshire Constitution of 1776.)

The lower branch of the legislature to consist of representatives of the people. (South Carolina Constitution of 1776.)

The lower branch of the legislature, called the house of delegates, elected by the people. (Virginia Constitution of 1776.)

The lower house to consist of representatives of the people. (New Jersey Constitution of 1776.)

The lower house called the house of assembly. (Delaware Constitution of 1776.)

A single legislative body called the house of representatives elected by the people. (Pennsylvania Constitution of 1776.)

The lower house called the house of delegates. (Maryland Constitution of 1776.)

The lower house called the house of commons. (North Carolina Constitution of 1776.)

A single legislative body to consist of representatives of the people. (Georgia Constitution of 1777.)

The lower house called the assembly and composed of representatives of the people. (New York Constitution of 1777.)

Evolution from the Charters

The Vermont constitution of 1777 repeats the provision given above from the Pennsylvania constitution of 1776.

The lower house to be called the house of representatives, and to consist of one from each town. (Rejected Constitution of Massachusetts of 1778.)

The lower house, to be called the house of representatives, to be chosen every second year. (South Carolina Constitution of 1778.)

The house of representatives to consist of deputies from the towns. (Rejected Constitution of New Hampshire of 1778.)

The lower house to consist of representatives from the towns. (Massachusetts Constitution of 1780.)

The above provision from the Massachusetts constitution of 1780 is repeated in the New Hampshire constitution of 1784.

A single legislative body, called the house of representatives, to be chosen annually. (Vermont Constitution of 1786.)

Suggestion of a legislature, to be called the first branch of the national legislature, to be composed of representatives of the people. (Randolph's Plan, 1787.)

Suggestion of a national legislative body, chosen by the people of the several States, to be called the house of delegates. (Pinckney's Plan, 1787.)

The House of Representatives to be elected by the people every second year. (The Constitution.)

4. THE SENATE.

The line of development which led to the House of Representatives began, as was shown in the preceding section, in the Virginia charter of 1609. The Senate's line of development began apparently in the next document,—the Virginia charter of 1611–12.

This charter created what may be called an executive council, which was to sit every week and manage the casual and ordinary affairs, very much as a governor or any other executive officer might manage them. This body certainly bore a strong resemblance to the governor's council, which soon afterwards appeared; and not infrequently in the colonial period this form of an executive council, without any governor or with a governor merely subservient to the council, was made use of.

But in the next document, the Massachusetts charter of 1629, the council appears as a body of persons to advise and assist the governor, a form in which it continued, with variations and developments, for over a hundred years. In this Massachusetts charter of 1629, the assistants, as the council is called, are to sit with the whole body of the freemen to enact laws. In the next document, the Fundamental Orders of Connecticut of 1638, the freemen, instead of meeting in a body to enact laws, send delegates to a general assembly, and the council, in this instance called magistrates, is a part of this assembly.

The council as a part of the assembly, sitting and voting with it, is now well established as a regular department of colonial government, and we find it in the Connecticut charter of 1662, the Rhode Island charter of 1663, and the Concessions of East Jersey of 1665. But in Locke's Carolina constitution of 1669 we see for the first time a disposition to make the council a separate or upper house of the legislature; and Locke carried it so far that he gave to the council, as an upper house, the sole privilege of originating legislation,—an unfortunate idea, which was followed by William Penn in one of his frames of government for Pennsylvania, and not eradicated from American minds for many years.

Evolution from the Charters

In 1674, five years after Locke's constitution, an amendment to the Concessions of East Jersey provided that the council should sit apart from the assembly, but avoided Locke's excess of giving it the right to originate legislation. But a few years afterwards, in the Pennsylvania Frame of 1683, Locke's excess is followed. The notion of making the council a separate and upper house having been once acquired, it seemed impossible to prevent it from running too far; and in Pennsylvania the council was given so much control of the governor that he was a mere figure-head.

The Pennsylvania Frame of 1683 had, however, the interesting development of dividing the members of the council into classes, so that one-third should retire from office each year,—a method adopted in some of the constitutions of 1776, and afterwards followed in the Senate of the National Constitution.

In the next document, the Massachusetts charter of 1691, the council returns to its former function of sitting with the assembly, but a new and very interesting development appears for the first time. The council is to be chosen to represent certain localities or great districts,—to wit, Maine, New Plymouth, Massachusetts Bay, and the land between the Sagadahoc River and Nova Scotia,—which by their union were to form the new province of Massachusetts. Thus we have developed in the council the Senate's function of representing the States of a Union.

Soon after this, in 1696, the right to originate legislation was taken away from the council in Pennsylvania; so that we may say that in the year 1700 the

Evolution of the Constitution

American people had developed the governor's council into the two main functions of the modern senate,—namely, that it should be a separate or upper house, and that its members should represent certain large localities which by their union made up the commonwealth.

So soon as we come to the constitutions of 1776, these two ideas become more firmly established. In the first of them, the constitution of New Hampshire, the council is a separate and upper house and represents the counties. In the Virginia constitution it represents districts larger than a single county, is called for the first time a senate, and also embodies the plan which first appeared in the Pennsylvania frame of 1683, of having a certain proportion of the members retire from office each year.

In the Delaware constitution we find a slightly different plan of rotation, and in the New York constitution of 1777 the same plan as in Virginia. The other State constitutions repeated the characteristics already established for an upper house, which was thus fully developed before the close of the Revolution; and when the National Constitution was framed, in 1787, the upper house, with its name senate, its representation of large localities, and its method of rotation, was transferred easily and naturally from the governments of the States to the new government of the Union.

An executive council established to meet once a week for casual matters. (Virginia Charter of 1611–12.)

The council called assistants, and sit with the freemen to make the laws. (Massachusetts Charter of 1629.)

Evolution from the Charters

The council called magistrates, and a part of the general assembly. (Fundamental Orders of Connecticut of 1638.)

The council called assistants, and a part of the general assembly. (Connecticut Charter of 1662.)

The above provision is substantially repeated in the Rhode Island charter of 1663.

The governor's council to sit with the general assembly. (Concessions of East Jersey of 1665.)

The grand council an upper house and to originate legislation. (Locke's Carolina Constitution of 1669.)

The governor's council to sit apart from the representatives. (Amendment in 1674 to the Concessions of East Jersey of 1665; 1 N. J. Arch., 175.)

President and his council to rule the colony. (Commission for New Hampshire of 1680.)

The governor's council to be elected by the freemen, to originate legislation, and to be divided into classes so that one-third part may be elected each year. (Pennsylvania Frame of April 2, 1683.)

The above provision is repeated in the Pennsylvania Frame of 1683, except that the number of the council is reduced to eighteen.

The governor's council to be elected yearly by the general assembly and to represent certain districts (Massachusetts Bay, New Plymouth, Maine, and the territory between Sagadahoc River and Nova Scotia), and to sit in the general assembly. (Massachusetts Charter of 1691.)

Right to originate legislation taken away from the council in Pennsylvania. (Pennsylvania Frame of 1696.)

Council not to be a court, and apparently abolished, but was afterwards regularly appointed by the proprietors. (Pennsylvania Charter of Privileges of 1701.)

An executive council established for Georgia. (Georgia Charter of 1732.)

The council to be appointed by the house of representatives to represent the counties and be an upper house. (New Hampshire Constitution of 1776.)

Evolution of the Constitution

The council to be elected by the general assembly, and to be an upper house. (South Carolina Constitution of 1776.)

A senate representing districts of the State, to be elected by the districts, and to be divided into classes so that one-fourth may be elected each year. (Virginia Constitution of 1776.)

A senate representing the counties and elected by the counties. (New Jersey Constitution of 1776.)

A senate representing the counties and elected by the counties. (Delaware Constitution of 1776.)

A senate representing the counties and the towns of Baltimore and Annapolis, to be elected by electors chosen by the counties and the two towns. (Maryland Constitution of 1776.)

A senate representing the counties and elected by the counties. (North Carolina Constitution of 1776.)

An executive council representing the counties and chosen by the house of representatives to suggest amendments to the laws passed by the house of representatives. (Georgia Constitution of 1777.)

A senate chosen by certain large districts to hold office four years, and a fourth part to be elected each year. (New York Constitution of 1777.)

A senate chosen by districts. (Rejected Constitution of Massachusetts of 1778.)

A senate chosen by districts. (South Carolina Constitution of 1778.)

A council chosen by counties. (Rejected Constitution of New Hampshire of 1778.)

A senate chosen by districts. (Massachusetts Constitution of 1780.)

The above provision from the Massachusetts constitution of 1780 is repeated in the New Hampshire constitution of 1784.

A senate to be elected by the lower house from persons nominated from each State. (Randolph's Plan, 1787.)

A senate chosen by the lower house to represent each State, and to be divided into classes so that the terms of service shall not expire at the same time. (Pinckney's Plan, 1787.)

Evolution from the Charters

A senate composed of two senators from each State elected by the legislatures of the States, and divided into classes so that one-third may be chosen every second year. (The Constitution.)

5. PRESIDING OFFICER OF THE SENATE.

In colonial times, when the council was a body to assist and advise the governor, he was naturally the presiding officer of its proceedings, without any provision to that effect in the charter. But when the New Jersey constitution of 1776 was framed, in which the council was an upper house of the legislature, it was thought necessary, for the first time, to provide it in a formal way with a chairman; and the governor was made its president, with the privilege given the council to choose a vice-president, who should act in the absence of the governor.

The New York constitution of 1777 made the lieutenant-governor of the State the presiding officer of the senate, with a casting vote in case of an equal division; and this plan was followed in the National Constitution, which makes the Vice-President of the United States president of the Senate, but with no vote "unless they be equally divided."

Between the time of the New York constitution of 1777 and the National Constitution of 1787 the rejected constitution of Massachusetts of 1778 and the New Hampshire constitution of 1784 both gave the presidency of the senate to the governor.

"That the Council and Assembly jointly, at their first meeting after each annual election, shall, by a majority of votes, elect some fit person within the Colony, to be Governor for one year, who shall be constant President of the Council, and have a casting vote in their proceedings; and that the Council themselves shall choose a Vice-President who shall act as such in the absence of the Governor." (New Jersey Constitution of 1776.)

"Such lieutenant governor shall by virtue of his office be president of the Senate, and upon an equal division have a casting voice in their decisions." (New York constitution of 1777.)

"The governor shall be president of the Senate." (Rejected Constitution of Massachusetts of 1778.)

"The president of the state shall preside in the senate, shall have a vote equal with any other member; and shall also have a casting vote in case of a tie." (New Hampshire Constitution of 1784.)

"The vice president of the United States shall be president of the senate, but shall have no vote unless they be equally divided." (The Constitution.)

6. Freedom of Debate.

Freedom of speech in a legislative body seems not to have needed any safeguards in colonial times, for only one of the documents, the Concessions of West Jersey of 1669, contains any provision for it. If the right had been much interfered with by the governors or the Crown, it is probable that some of the constitutions, like those of Pennsylvania and Connecticut, which were made by the people themselves, would have had a provision for its protection. The right was secured for the British Parliament by a statute passed in the first year of the reign of William and Mary.

The Concessions of West Jersey, however, miss the important point in the right, and merely provide that every member of the assembly shall have liberty of speech, which is too general. The protection the

Evolution from the Charters

member needs is that he shall not be called to account by any power outside of the legislature for what he says at a meeting of the legislature. The legislature itself may discipline him for improper conduct or language at its meeting, but no outside power should be able to punish him. This was provided for in the Maryland constitution of 1776, as in the statute of William and Mary, and, after passing through five or six documents, the provision appeared in the Constitution. It is one of the few provisions that can be traced directly to the forms of the British government.

"That in every general free assembly every respective member hath liberty of speech." (Concessions of West Jersey, 1669.)

"That freedom of speech and debates, or proceedings in the Legislature, ought not to be impeached in any other court or judicature." (Maryland Declaration of Rights of 1776.)

"Freedom of speech and debate in Congress shall not be impeached or questioned in any court or place out of Congress." (Articles of Confederation, 1778.)

"Freedom of debate and speech shall be allowed in Congress, nor shall anything done in Congress be impeached or questioned out of it." (Drayton's Articles of Confederation, 1778.)

"The freedom of deliberation, speech, and debate, in either house of the legislature, is so essential to the rights of the people, that it cannot be the foundation of any accusation or prosecution, action or complaint, in any other court or place whatsoever." (Massachusetts Constitution of 1780.)

The above provision from the Massachusetts constitution of 1780 is repeated in the New Hampshire constitution of 1784.

The Vermont constitution of 1786 repeats the provision given above from the Massachusetts constitution of 1780.

"Freedom of speech and debate in the Legislature shall not be impeached, or questioned, in any place out of it." (Pinckney's Plan, 1787.)

Evolution of the Constitution

"For any speech or debate in either house, they [senators and representatives] shall not be questioned in any other place." (The Constitution.)

7. PRIVILEGE FROM ARREST.

The colonial charters and constitutions contained no provision protecting a member of the legislature from arrest. It seems to have been assumed that the privilege existed as a matter of course; but in at least one instance it was violated.

In 1705, Biles, a member of the Pennsylvania assembly, was arrested during the session of the assembly for speaking contemptuously of the governor. He pleaded his privilege as a member, but the court overruled the plea. The assembly passed a resolution condemning the sheriff and judges for violating the privilege of the house, and the governor thereupon called the assembly before him and, after addressing them in a most abusive speech, adjourned them. There seems to have been no definite settlement of the question on this occasion, but the general opinion was probably in favor of the existence of the privilege, for the constitutions of 1776 are usually silent about it.

"The members of Congress shall be protected in their persons from arrests and imprisonments during the time of their going to and from, and attendance on, Congress, except for treason, felony, or breach of the peace." (Articles of Confederation, 1778.)

"The delegates shall be protected in their persons from arrests and imprisonments, except for treason, felony, or breach of the peace." (Drayton's Articles of Confederation, 1778.)

"And no member of the house of representatives shall be arrested, or held to bail on mesne process, during his going unto,

Evolution from the Charters

returning from, or his attending the general assembly." (Massachusetts Constitution of 1780.)

The above provision from the Massachusetts constitution of 1780 is repeated in the New Hampshire constitution of 1784.

"The members of both houses shall, in all cases, except for treason, felony, or breach of the peace, be free from arrest during their attendance on Congress, and in going to and returning from it." (Pinckney's Plan, 1787.)

"They [senators and representatives] shall in all cases, except treason, felony, and breach of the peace, be privileged from arrest during their attendance at the session of their respective houses, and in going to and returning from the same." (The Constitution.)

8. MONEY-BILLS.

The principle that bills for raising money from the people should originate in that part of the legislature which most fully represented the people—in England the House of Commons—was familiar to the colonists, and it may be admitted that their ideas on this subject were taken directly from the forms of the British government.

None of the colonial charters or constitutions contained any clause specially securing this right, but the colonists always insisted that it belonged to them in all their legislative bodies as a matter of course because they were free-born Englishmen. In Pennsylvania, especially, they contended for it against their proprietors and deputy-governors with the greatest persistency, and insisted on the right in its fullest extent,—namely, that money-bills should not only originate in the lower house of assembly, but should also be either accepted or rejected by the council or upper house without any attempt to amend them. Some of the constitutions of 1776

Evolution of the Constitution

adopted this extreme view, which was modified in the National Constitution by allowing the Senate to propose amendments, as in the case of other bills.

"That all bills, resolves, or votes for raising, levying, and collecting money originate in the house of representatives." (New Hampshire Constitution of 1776.)

"All money-bills for the support of government shall originate in the general assembly, and shall not be altered or amended by the legislative council, but may be rejected by them." (South Carolina Constitution of 1776.)

"All laws shall originate in the house of delegates, to be approved of or rejected by the senate, or to be amended with the consent of the house of delegates; except money-bills, which in no instance shall be altered by the senate, but wholly approved or rejected." (Virginia Constitution of 1776.)

"That the council shall not prepare or alter any money-bill, which shall be the privilege of the assembly." (New Jersey Constitution of 1776.)

"All money-bills for the support of government shall originate in the house of assembly, and may be altered, amended, or rejected by the legislative council." (Delaware Constitution of 1776.)

"The house of delegates may originate all money-bills." (Maryland Constitution of 1776.)

"Excepting bills and resolves levying and granting money or other property of the State, which shall originate in the house of representatives only, and be concurred or non-concurred in whole by the senate." (Rejected Constitution of Massachusetts of 1778.)

"That all money-bills for the support of the government shall originate in the house of representatives, and shall not be altered or amended by the senate, but may be rejected by them." (South Carolina Constitution of 1778.)

"And all acts, resolves, or votes, except grants of money, lands, or other things, may originate in either house; but such

Evolution from the Charters

grants shall originate in the house of representatives only." (Rejected Constitution of New Hampshire of 1778.)

"All money-bills shall originate in the house of representatives; but the senate may propose or concur with amendments, as on other bills." (Massachusetts Constitution of 1780.)

The above provision from the Massachusetts constitution of 1780 is repeated in the New Hampshire constitution of 1784.

"All money-bills of every kind shall originate in the house of delegates, and shall not be altered by the senate." (Pinckney's Plan, 1787.)

"All bills for raising revenue shall originate in the house of representatives; but the senate may propose or concur with amendments, as on other bills." (The Constitution.)

9. ADJOURNMENT OF CONGRESS.

The adjournment of a legislative body, either of its own volition or by the action of a king or governor, is a function requiring very careful regulation, because the power to adjourn may be the bulwark of a people's liberties or the means of inflicting the greatest tyranny upon them.

If a king or a governor may keep an assembly sitting as long as he pleases, or dismiss them when he pleases, he has the means of wearing out their patience, forcing them to pass the legislation he wants, or preventing them from passing any legislation. On the other hand, a legislature may sit too long and become a public menace, or, if it consists of two branches, one may adjourn in order to defeat the intentions of the other.

It may also be very important, under certain circumstances, for a legislature to have the power of sitting indefinitely. At the time of the Revolution, a party in the Pennsylvania legislature, wishing to destroy the

Evolution of the Constitution

government of the commonwealth as it then existed, absented themselves every day, so that a quorum could not be formed. The minority attempted to hold meetings, but, as they could not pass a valid act, the legislature finally perished, and there was a revolution in the government. If the minority had had power to adjourn from day to day and to compel the attendance of absent members, they could have continued the life of the legislature until a quorum had been collected.

The colonists had much experience with all these questions, and were greatly troubled by some of them; and the clauses finally adopted in the National Constitution were as delicate a balancing of power between the President and Congress and between the two branches of Congress as could have been devised.

The summary given below from the charters and constitutions shows that in 1638 the right of the legislature to adjourn when it pleased was fully conceded in the Fundamental Orders of Connecticut of that year, which also gave the governor and his council power to call the legislature together in an emergency,—a power afterwards given to the President in the National Constitution. After that the legislature's power to adjourn was occasionally curtailed and given to the governor or the king. In 1754, in Franklin's plan of union, a sort of balancing of the power between the executive and the legislature first appears. The executive may apparently adjourn them, but not for more than six weeks without their consent or the special command of the Crown; nor can they be compelled to sit longer than six weeks except by the same consent or command.

Evolution from the Charters

This is also the first appearance of a provision to prevent an assembly from being compelled to sit too long.

In the New Hampshire constitution of 1776 a provision appears to prevent one branch of a legislature from adjourning without the consent of the other; and this is repeated in various forms until it appears in the National Constitution.

In the same year, 1776, the South Carolina constitution provides that the executive may call the legislature before the time to which they stand adjourned, when urgent necessity requires it. This is also repeated until it appears in the National Constitution, and it is a provision often made use of and considered of much value.

In the New Jersey constitution of 1776 appeared the provision that the two branches must meet at the same time. The Delaware constitution of 1776 provides that they must meet at the same time and place; and the Maryland constitution of the same year provides that, if the two branches disagree as to the time to which they shall adjourn, the governor may decide the question,—both of which provisions are to be found in the National Constitution.

> General court adjourned only by consent of majority. Governor and council may call the legislature for a special occasion. (Fundamental Orders of Connecticut, 1638.)
>
> Assembly may meet and adjourn at pleasure. (Concessions of East Jersey, 1665.) Repealed, and the right to adjourn given to the governor and council, in 1672.
>
> The palatine's court (consisting of the palatine and eight others) may dissolve the parliament at pleasure. (Locke's Carolina Constitution of 1669.)

Evolution of the Constitution

Assembly may meet and adjourn at pleasure. (Concessions of West Jersey, 1677.)

Governor and council may adjourn the assembly. (Pennsylvania Frame of April 2, 1683.)

Governor may adjourn the assembly. (Massachusetts Charter of 1691.)

Governor and council may adjourn the assembly. (Pennsylvania Frame of 1696.)

Assembly may adjourn at pleasure. (Pennsylvania Charter of Privileges, 1701.)

Assembly may adjourn for two days, but not longer without the consent of the governor. (Explanatory Charter of Massachusetts of 1726.)

Grand council not to be adjourned or continued sitting longer than six weeks without their own consent or the special command of the Crown. (Franklin's Plan of 1754.)

Council not to be adjourned or continued sitting longer than six weeks without their own consent. (Hutchinson's Plan of 1754.)

Neither branch of the legislature to adjourn longer than from Saturday to Monday without the consent of the other. (New Hampshire Constitution of 1776.)

Either branch of the legislature may adjourn at pleasure, but the president, when necessary, may call them before the time to which they stand adjourned. Sixty-nine members to be a quorum, but the speaker and any seven members may adjourn from day to day. (South Carolina Constitution of 1776.)

The above is substantially repeated in the Virginia constitution of 1776.

The assembly may adjourn at pleasure, but the council must meet at the same time as the assembly. (New Jersey Constitution of 1776.)

Either branch of the legislature may adjourn at pleasure, but the president may, with the advice of his council or on application of a majority of either house, call them before the time to which they stand adjourned, and the two houses must sit at the same time and place. (Delaware Constitution of 1776.)

Evolution from the Charters

Legislature may adjourn at pleasure, but the president, with the council, may call them before the time to which they stand adjourned. (Pennsylvania Constitution of 1776.)

Either branch of the legislature may adjourn at pleasure, but if they adjourn to different days the governor may appoint some day between, and the governor may, with the advice of his council, call them before the time to which they shall in any manner be adjourned. (Maryland Constitution of 1776.)

Either branch of the legislature may adjourn at pleasure. (North Carolina Constitution of 1776.)

Governor, with advice of council, may call assembly before the time to which they stand adjourned. (Georgia Constitution of 1777.)

Governor may convene both branches on extraordinary occasions and may prorogue them for not more than sixty days in a year, and neither branch may adjourn for more than two days without the consent of the other. (New York Constitution of 1777.)

The Vermont constitution of 1777 repeats the provision from the Pennsylvania constitution of 1776.

The council may at their pleasure require the governor to adjourn them, but neither branch shall adjourn itself for more than two days at one time. The governor may call the legislature together, if necessary, before the time to which they stand adjourned. (Rejected Constitution of Massachusetts of 1778.)

The legislature may adjourn at pleasure, but neither branch of it may adjourn for longer than three days without the consent of the other. The governor may, with the advice of the council, call the legislature before the time to which they stand adjourned. (South Carolina Constitution of 1778.)

Neither branch of the legislature may adjourn for more than two days without the consent of the other, and the president, with the advice of three or more of the council, may call the legislature before the time to which they stand adjourned. (Rejected Constitution of New Hampshire of 1778.)

The legislature may at their pleasure require the governor to adjourn them. The House of Representatives may adjourn for not more than two days at a time, and, in case of disagreement between the two branches with regard to adjournment, the governor may, with the advice of the council, adjourn them not exceeding ninety days, and he may in cases of necessity call them before the time to which they stand adjourned. (Massachusetts Constitution of 1780.)

The Congress may adjourn to any time within the year so that no period of adjournment be longer than six months. (Articles of Confederation, 1778.)

The above is substantially repeated in Drayton's Articles of Confederation, 1778.

The provision of the Massachusetts constitution of 1780 is substantially repeated in the New Hampshire constitution of 1784.

Neither house, without the consent of the other, shall adjourn for more than   days nor to any place but where they are sitting. (Pinckney's Plan, 1787.)

"The Congress shall assemble at least once in every year. . . . A majority of each [house] shall constitute a quorum to do business; but a smaller number may adjourn from day to day, and may be authorized to compel the attendance of absent members. . . . Neither house during the session of congress shall, without the consent of the other, adjourn for more than three days nor to any other place than that in which the two houses shall be sitting. . . . He [the President] may, on extraordinary occasions, convene both houses or either of them, and, in case of disagreement between them with respect to the time of adjournment, he may adjourn them to such time as he shall think proper." (The Constitution.)

10. WAR POWER.

The power to declare war and make peace is a most important function of government; for on it may depend the existence or honor of the nation. Where the power should be lodged, whether with the executive or with the legislature, or with both, has been a much debated question in our history.

Evolution from the Charters

In the early colonial governments it was often given to everybody. In several of the charters, as the summary shows, the whole company in general, and the governor and every other officer in particular, seem to have been endowed with authority to make war at any moment. This was natural enough, because in primitive governments in wild countries the war power is often the all-important function which overshadows all others.

As time went on, however, there seems to have been considerable doubt in the minds of constitution-framers as to who should be responsible for war and peace. The tendency to give the legislature a share in the responsibility is first shown in the Rhode Island charter of 1663. In the Concessions of East Jersey of 1665 the legislature alone has the power, and this method was adopted in the National Constitution, where the war power is given to Congress alone. But between the Concessions of East Jersey and the Constitution it vacillated, sometimes being given to the governor alone, and sometimes to the governor and the legislature.

The fundamental principle underlying the grant of the power seems to be that it should be given to whatever body is, in the fullest sense of the word, the nation. In England it was given to the king because he was the nation; and in the United States, where the people are the nation, it is given to Congress, which represents the people.

But, as the President controls the army and navy and the action of diplomatic agents, he can easily, by an overt act, commit the country to a war which Congress

Evolution of the Constitution

would be bound to accept; as was done in the case of our war with Mexico. In theory Congress has the power, but the real power is with one man as fully as it was in Sir Walter Raleigh's charter of 1584.

War power given to Sir Walter Raleigh. (Sir Walter Raleigh's Charter, 1584.)

Given generally to the two colonies of Virginia. (Virginia Charter of 1606.)

Given generally to the company, governor, and other officers. (Virginia Charter of 1609.)

Given generally to council, governor, and other officers. (Charter of New England of 1620.)

Given generally. (Massachusetts Charter of 1629.)

Given to the proprietor. (Maryland Charter of 1632.)

To the proprietor. (Grant of Maine of 1639.)

To the governor and officers. (Connecticut Charter of 1662.)

To the governor, assistants, and general assembly; and, when the general assembly is not sitting, to the governor and assistants. (Rhode Island Charter of 1663.)

To the proprietor. (Carolina Charter of 1663.)

To the general assembly. (Concessions of East Jersey, 1665.)

To the proprietor. (Carolina Charter of 1665.)

To the grand council. (Locke's Constitution of 1669.)

To the council. (Commission for New Hampshire of 1680.)

To the proprietor. (Pennsylvania Charter of 1681.)

To the governor. (Massachusetts Charter of 1691.)

To the corporation. (Georgia Charter of 1732.)

To the president-general and grand council. (Franklin's Plan of Union of 1754.)

To the president and council. (Hutchinson's Plan of 1754.)

To Congress. (Franklin's Articles of Confederation, 1775.)

To the president and the legislature. (South Carolina Constitution of 1776.)

To the governor. (South Carolina Constitution of 1778.)

Evolution from the Charters

To Congress; but a State may engage in war when actually invaded. (Articles of Confederation, 1778.)
To Congress. (Drayton's Articles of Confederation, 1778.)
To the governor. (Massachusetts Constitution of 1780.)
To the governor. (New Hampshire Constitution, 1784.)
To the Senate. (Pinckney's Plan, 1787.)
To Congress. (The Constitution.)

11. SPEAKERSHIP AND PROCEDURE OF CONGRESS.

A legislative body would seem to have a natural and inherent right to judge of the qualifications and elections of its own members, appoint its own speaker and other officers, and regulate its own methods of procedure, after the manner of the British House of Commons. The charters granted by the Crown made no regulation of these matters, and in some of the Colonies the governor claimed that his approval was necessary before the speaker elected by the assembly could assume his office. There were several contests in Massachusetts on this question, and in the end the Explanatory Charter of 1726 confirmed the necessity of the governor's consent in the election of a speaker. (Follett's Speaker of the House of Representatives, 12.) But whenever in colonial times the people prepared a constitution for themselves free from interference by the Crown, they usually thought it necessary to provide for the exercise of this right by the legislature, and the constitutions of 1776 carried on the development to the National Constitution.

"It is ordered and decreed, that the deputyes thus chosen shall haue power and liberty to appoynt a tyme and a place of meeting

Evolution of the Constitution

togather before any Generall Courte to aduise and consult of all such things as may concerne the good of the publike, as also to examine their owne Elections, whether according to the order, and if they or the gretest p^{r}te of them find any election to be illegall they may seclud such for p^{r}sent frō their meeting, and returne the same and their resons to the Courte; and if y^t proue true, the Courte may fyne the p^{r}ty or p^{r}tyes so intruding and the Towne, if they see cause, and giue out a warrant to goe to a newe election in a legall way, either in p^{r}te or in whole. . . . It is Ordered, sentenced and decreed, that euery Generall Courte, except such as through neglecte of the Gou^{r}nor and the greatest p^{r}te of Magestrats the Freemen themselues doe call, shall consist of the Gouernor, or some one chosen to moderate the Court, and 4 other Magestrats at lest, wth the mayor p^{r}te of the deputyes of the seuerall Townes legally chosen; and in case the Freemen or mayor p^{r}te of thē, through neglect or refusall of the Gouernor and mayor p^{r}te of the magestrats, shall call a Courte, y^t shall consist of the mayor p^{r}te of Freemen that are p^{r}sent or their deputyes, wth a Moderator chosen by thē." (Fundamental Orders of Connecticut, 1638.)

"All questions to be determined by both or either of them [council or assembly] that relate to . . . choice of officers . . . shall be resolved and determined by the ballot." (Pennsylvania Frame, April 2, 1683.)

"And the representatives so chosen either for council or assembly shall yield their attendance accordingly and be the sole judges of the regularity or irregularity of the elections of their respective members." (Pennsylvania Frame of 1696.)

"Which assembly shall have power to chuse a speaker and other their officers, and shall be judges of the qualifications and elections of their own members." (Pennsylvania Charter of Privileges of 1701.)

"Each house shall choose its own speaker, appoint its own officers, settle its own rules of proceeding." (Virginia Constitution of 1776.)

"That the assembly, when met, shall have power to choose a speaker and other their officers; to be judges of the qualifica-

Evolution from the Charters

tions and elections of their own members." (New Jersey Constitution of 1776.)

"Each house shall choose its own speaker, appoint its own officers, judge of the qualifications and elections of its own members, settle its own rules of proceedings. They may also severally expel any of their own members for misbehavior, but not a second time in the same sessions for the same offence if reelected." (Delaware Constitution of 1776.)

"The house of representatives shall have power to choose their speaker, the treasurer of the state and their other officers, judge of the elections and qualifications of their own members. They may expel a member, but not a second time for the same cause." (Pennsylvania Constitution of 1776.)

"That the house of delegates shall judge of the elections and qualifications of delegates. They may expel any member for a great misdemeanor, but not a second time for the same cause. Each house shall appoint its own officers and settle its own rules of proceeding." (Maryland Constitution of 1776.)

"That the senate and house of commons, when met, shall each have power to choose a speaker and other their officers; be judges of the qualifications and elections of their members." (North Carolina Constitution of 1776.)

"The house shall choose its own speaker, appoint its own officers and settle its own rules of proceeding." (Georgia Constitution of 1777.)

"That the assembly thus constituted shall choose their own speaker, be judges of their own members." (New York Constitution of 1777.)

The Vermont constitution of 1777 repeats the provision given above from the Pennsylvania constitution of 1776.

"The congress shall have power to make rules for regulating their proceedings." (Drayton's Articles of Confederation, 1778.)

"The senate and house of representatives shall be two separate and distinct bodies, each to appoint its own officers and settle its own rules of proceedings." (Rejected Constitution of Massachusetts of 1778.)

Evolution of the Constitution

"The council shall choose their president and the house of representatives shall choose their speaker. The council and house of representatives, respectively, shall determine all disputed elections of their own members and regulate their own proceedings." (Rejected Constitution of New Hampshire of 1778.)

"The house of representatives shall be the judge of the returns, elections, and qualifications of its own members, as pointed out in the constitution; shall choose their own speaker, appoint their own officers, and settle the rules and order of proceeding in their own house." (Massachusetts Constitution of 1780.)

The above provision from the Massachusetts constitution of 1780 is repeated in the New Hampshire constitution of 1784.

"They [the general assembly] shall have power to choose their speaker and other necessary officers, judge of the elections and qualifications of their own members; they may expel members, but not for causes known to their constituents antecedent to their election." (Vermont Constitution of 1786.)

"The house of delegates shall choose its own officers. The senate shall choose its own officers. The house of delegates shall be the judges of the election, returns, and qualifications of their members. In each house a majority shall constitute a quorum to do business. Both houses shall keep journals of their proceedings and publish them, except on secret occasions, and the yeas and nays may be entered thereon at the desire of one of the members present." (Pinckney's Plan, 1787.)

"The house of representatives shall choose their speaker and other officers. . . . Each house shall be the judge of the elections, returns, and qualifications of its own members. . . . Each house may determine the rules of its proceedings, punish its members for disorderly behavior, and, with the concurrence of two-thirds, expel a member. Each house shall keep a journal of its proceedings and from time to time publish the same, excepting such parts as may in their judgment require secrecy; and the yeas and nays of the members of either house on any question shall, at the desire of one-fifth of those present, be entered on the journal." (The Constitution.)

Evolution from the Charters

12. IMPEACHMENT.

The first appearance of the power to remove and punish an officer of government for misconduct is in the Fundamental Orders of Connecticut of 1638, but it is not until we reach the Rhode Island charter of 1663 that this power is called by its proper name,—impeachment.

The methods of trying the impeachment vary, but a strong tendency soon appears to have the assembly bring the impeachment and the council or senate try it. In the Virginia constitution of 1776 the person convicted is to be disabled from holding office, and may also be punished as the law shall direct, a description of the method of punishment which had not appeared before. This was repeated in the Delaware constitution of 1776. In the New York constitution of 1777 the manner of punishment was still more precisely detailed. Judgment in impeachment was to extend no farther than removal from office and disqualification from holding office under the State, but the guilty person might, in addition, be subject to indictment and punishment in the ordinary courts according to the laws of the land. In the Massachusetts constitution of 1780 the senators are to be sworn to try the impeachment according to the evidence. All these provisions, including the requirement of a two-thirds vote to convict, were embodied in the National Constitution, and in almost the same language in which they had appeared in the earlier documents.

The assembly is given power to deal with any magistrate or

Evolution of the Constitution

other person for any misdemeanor. (Fundamental Orders of Connecticut, 1638.)

The assembly may remove any officers of the company for misdemeanors. (Connecticut Charter of 1662.)

The above is repeated in the Rhode Island charter of 1663.

The general assembly may impeach, and the provincial council give judgment upon the impeachment. (Pennsylvania Frame of April 2, 1683.)

The above is repeated in the Pennsylvania Frame of 1683.

The assembly may impeach. (Pennsylvania Charter of Privileges, 1701.)

The house of delegates may impeach the governor when out of office, and all others guilty of maladministration; the impeachment to be tried in the general court according to law. When judges of the general court are impeached, the impeachment to be tried in the court of appeals. The guilty to be disabled from holding any office under government, and to be punished as the law shall direct. (Virginia Constitution of 1776.)

The assembly may impeach and the council try the impeachment. (New Jersey Constitution of 1776.)

The assembly may impeach the president when out of office, and all others guilty of maladministration, and the council try the impeachment. The guilty to be disabled from holding any office under government, and to be punished as the law shall direct. (Delaware Constitution of 1776.)

The general assembly may impeach and the president and council try the impeachment. (Pennsylvania Constitution of 1776.)

The general assembly or grand jury may impeach. (North Carolina Constitution of 1776.)

The assembly may impeach. (Georgia Constitution of 1777.)

The assembly may impeach by a two-thirds vote; and the impeachment be tried in a court, to consist of the president of the senate, the senators, the chancellor and judges of the supreme court; no judgment, however, of the said court to be valid unless assented to by two-thirds of the members of the court. Judgment to extend no farther than removal from office

Evolution from the Charters

and disqualification to hold office under the state. But the guilty may, nevertheless, be subject to indictment and punishment according to the laws of the land. (New York Constitution of 1777.)

The Vermont constitution of 1777 repeats the provision of the Pennsylvania constitution of 1776.

The house of representatives may impeach, and the impeachment be tried by a court composed of the governor and senate; but no judgment to be valid unless assented to by two-thirds of the court. Judgment to extend no farther than removal from office and disqualification to hold office under the state. But the guilty may, nevertheless, be subject to indictment and punishment according to the laws of the land. (Rejected Constitution of Massachusetts of 1778.)

The house of representatives may impeach by a two-thirds vote, and the impeachment be tried by a court composed of the senators and such judges as are not members of the house of representatives; no judgment, however, to be valid unless assented to by two-thirds of the members of the court. (South Carolina Constitution of 1778.)

The house of representatives may impeach, and the impeachment be tried by the senate. The senators to be sworn to try according to the evidence. Judgment to extend no farther than removal from office and disqualification to hold office under the state. But the guilty may, nevertheless, be subject to indictment and punishment according to the laws of the land. (Massachusetts Constitution of 1780.)

The above provision is repeated in the New Hampshire constitution of 1784.

The Vermont constitution of 1786 repeats the provision of the Pennsylvania constitution of 1776.

Impeachments to be tried by the inferior tribunals with an appeal to the supreme tribunal. (Randolph's Plan, 1787.)

The house of delegates may impeach, and the supreme court try the impeachment. (Pinckney's Plan, 1787.)

"The house of representatives shall have the sole power of impeachment. . . . The senate shall have the sole power to try all impeachments. When sitting for that purpose they shall be on oath or affirmation. When the president of the United States is tried, the chief-justice shall preside, and no person shall be convicted without the concurrence of two-thirds of the members present. Judgment in cases of impeachment shall not extend further than to removal from office, and disqualification to hold and enjoy any office of honor, trust, or profit, under the United States ; but the party convicted shall nevertheless be liable and subject to indictment, trial, judgment, and punishment, according to law.'' (The Constitution.)

13. THE EXECUTIVE.

The first mention of an executive in any of the documents is in the Virginia charter of 1609, where the council resident in England is to appoint governors and other officers for the colony. A governor or executive head of some sort would, of course, be necessary; but in colonial times it was not infrequently supposed that the executive could be composed of several persons. Sometimes an executive committee or council was appointed, and sometimes the governor's council was given such control over his actions that he was a mere cipher.

This tendency reached its extreme in the Articles of Confederation of 1778, where, in the recess of Congress, an executive committee ruled the country. But many-headed executives of this sort were not a success, and, in spite of their suspicions of one-man power, the people, after long experience, discovered that for certain purposes the one-man power was the only effective method, and they soon learned to place upon it the limitations that were necessary for its proper restraint.

In the summary under this section the points to be

Evolution from the Charters

noticed are the gradual appearance of a deputy- or lieutenant-governor, leading up to the Vice-President of the Constitution; the gradual appearance of the name President to describe the executive; the appointment of the executive, usually by the legislature or the Crown, until the time of the New York constitution of 1777, which gave the election of the governor to the people; and the short terms for which governors or presidents were elected. There was also not infrequently a provision to prevent their too frequent re-election. These provisions about terms and re-election suggest at once the four years' term given to the President under the Constitution, and the custom, that has become as fixed as if it were a part of the Constitution, of allowing no man to serve more than two terms.

The council resident in England to appoint a governor for Virginia. (Virginia Charter of 1609.)

An executive council to meet once a week and to deal with casual matters. (Virginia Charter of 1611-12.)

A governor and a deputy-governor to be elected by the freemen. (Massachusetts Charter of 1629.)

A governor to be chosen by the general assembly every year. (Fundamental Orders of Connecticut, 1638.)

A governor and a deputy-governor to be chosen by the general assembly every year. (Connecticut Charter of 1662.)

The above provision is repeated in the Rhode Island charter of 1663.

The governor to be appointed by the proprietors. (Concessions of East Jersey, 1665.)

The eldest lord proprietor to be palatine. (Locke's Carolina Constitution of 1669.)

The executive to consist of ten commissioners chosen by the assembly. (Concessions of West Jersey, 1677.)

Evolution of the Constitution

The governor to be appointed by the proprietor. (Pennsylvania Frame of April 2, 1683.)

The governor and lieutenant-governor to be appointed by the Crown. (Massachusetts Charter of 1691.)

A president-general appointed by the Crown. (Franklin's Plan of 1754.)

A president appointed by the Crown. (Hutchinson's Plan, 1754.)

A president-general appointed by the Crown. (Galloway's Plan, 1774.)

A president and vice-president chosen by the assembly and council. (South Carolina Constitution of 1776.)

A governor to be chosen by joint ballot of both houses every year. (Virginia Constitution of 1776.)

The governor to be chosen by the council and assembly and the vice-president by the council every year. (New Jersey Constitution of 1776.)

A president to be chosen by joint ballot of both houses for three years. (Delaware Constitution of 1776.)

The executive power to consist of a council of twelve and a president and vice-president chosen out of the council by the joint ballot of the assembly and council every year. (Pennsylvania Constitution of 1776.)

The governor to be chosen by the joint ballot of both houses every year. (Maryland Constitution of 1776.)

The governor to be chosen by joint ballot of both houses every year. (North Carolina Constitution of 1776.)

The governor to be chosen by the representatives every year. (Georgia Constitution of 1777.)

The governor to be elected by the freeholders every three years. (New York Constitution of 1777.)

The executive council, governor, and lieutenant-governor to be elected by the freemen. (Vermont Constitution of 1777.)

The governor and lieutenant-governor to be elected by the people every year. (Rejected Constitution of Massachusetts of 1778.)

The governor and lieutenant-governor to be elected by joint

Evolution from the Charters

ballot of both houses every two years. (South Carolina Constitution of 1778.)

An executive committee to be appointed by the congress of the confederation. (Articles of Confederation of 1778.)

The governor to be chosen by the people every year. (Massachusetts Constitution of 1780.)

The above provision from the Massachusetts Constitution of 1780 is repeated in the New Hampshire Constitution of 1784, except that the executive is called president.

The executive council, the governor, and the lieutenant-governor to be chosen by the freemen every year. (Vermont Constitution of 1786.)

A national executive to be chosen by the national legislature. (Randolph's Plan, 1787.)

A president suggested as an executive. (Pinckney's Plan, 1787.)

The president and vice-president to be chosen by electors elected by the people of each State every four years. (The Constitution.)

14. ELECTORS OF THE PRESIDENT.

The following quotations are given to show how the method of electing the President was taken from the method of electing Senators in Maryland:

"That the senate be chosen in the following manner: All persons, qualified as aforesaid to vote for county delegates, shall, on the first day of September, 1781, and on the same day in every fifth year forever thereafter, elect, *viva voce*, by a majority of votes, two persons for their respective counties (qualified as aforesaid to be elected county delegates) to be electors of the senate; and the sheriff of each county, or, in case of sickness, his deputy (summoning two justices of the county, who are required to attend, for the preservation of the peace), shall hold and be judge of the said election, and make return thereof, as aforesaid. And all persons, qualified as aforesaid, to vote for delegates for the city of Annapolis and Baltimore town, shall, on the same first Monday of September, 1781, and on the same day in every fifth year forever thereafter, elect, *viva voce*, by a majority of votes, one person for the said city and town respectively, qualified as aforesaid to be elected a delegate for the said city and town respectively ; the said election to be held in the same manner as the election of delegates for the said city and town ; the right to elect the said elector, with respect to Baltimore town, to continue as long as the right to elect delegates for the said town.

"That the said electors of the senate meet at the city of Annapolis, or such other place as shall be appointed for convening the legislature, on the third Monday in September, 1781, and on the same day in every fifth year forever thereafter, and they, or any twenty-four of them so met, shall proceed to elect, by ballot, either out of their own body or the people at large, fifteen senators (nine of whom to be residents on the western and six to be residents on the eastern shore), men of the most wisdom, experience, and virtue, above twenty-five years of age, residents of the State above three whole years next preceding the election, and having real and personal property above the value of one thousand pounds current money.

"That the senators shall be balloted for, at one and the same time, and out of the gentlemen residents of the western shore, who shall be proposed as senators, the nine who shall, on striking the ballots, appear to have the greatest numbers in their favour, shall be accordingly declared and returned duly elected ; and out of the gentlemen residents of the eastern shore, who shall be proposed as senators, the six who shall, on striking the ballots, appear to have the greatest number in their favour, shall be accordingly declared and returned duly elected : and if two or more on the same shore shall have an equal number of ballots in their favour, by which the choice shall not be determined on the first ballot, then the electors shall again ballot, before they separate ; in which they shall be confined to the persons who on the first ballot shall have an equal number : and they who shall have the greatest number in their favour on the second ballot, shall be accordingly declared and returned duly elected : and if the whole number should not thus be made up, because of an equal number,

Evolution from the Charters

on the second ballot, still being in favour of two or more persons, then the election shall be determined by lot, between those who have equal numbers; which proceedings of the electors shall be certified under their hands, and returned to the chancellor for the time being." (Maryland Constitution of 1776.)

"Each state shall appoint, in such manner as the legislature thereof may direct, a number of electors equal to the whole number of senators and representatives to which the state may be entitled in the congress; but no senator or representative, or person holding an office of trust or profit under the United States, shall be appointed an elector.

"The electors shall meet in their respective states, and vote by ballot for two persons, of whom one at least shall not be an inhabitant of the same state with themselves. And they shall make a list of all the persons voted for, and of the number of votes for each, which list they shall sign and certify, and transmit sealed to the seat of the government of the United States, directed to the president of the senate. The president of the senate shall, in the presence of the senate and house of representatives, open all the certificates, and the votes shall then be counted. The person having the greatest number of votes shall be the president, if such number be a majority of the whole number of electors appointed; and if there be more than one who have such a majority, and have an equal number of votes, then the house of representatives shall immediately choose by ballot one of them for president; and if no person have a majority, then from the five highest on the list the said house shall in like manner choose the president. But in choosing the president, the votes shall be taken by states, the representation from each state having one vote. A quorum for this purpose shall consist of a member or members from two-thirds of the states, and a majority of all the states shall be necessary to a choice. In every case, after the choice of the president, the person having the greatest number of votes of the electors shall be the vice-president. But if there should remain two or more who have equal votes, the senate shall choose from them by ballot the vice-president."

[The above quotation, which was Clause 3 of Section 1,

Article II., of the Constitution, has been somewhat altered by the Twelfth Amendment.]

15. DUTY TO EXECUTE THE LAWS.

The National Constitution contains the phrase "He [the President] shall take care that the laws be faithfully executed,"—a short statement, but a very important summary of a large part of the duty of the President, and one of the clauses which give him authority to put down a rebellion.

When we trace its origin in our documents we find the earliest reference to such a principle in the Massachusetts charter of 1629, which merely says that the laws must be observed and put in execution, without assigning the duty to any one in particular. But in the Maryland charter of 1632 the proprietor is assigned the duty and given the means of performing it in a very summary manner. After that the duty is usually given to the governor, and the language used becomes more and more like the simple, brief expression which finally appears in the Constitution.

"WILLING, comaunding, and requiring, and by theis Presents for Vs, our Heires, and Successors, ordeyning and appointing, that all such Orders, Lawes, Statuts and Ordinñces, Instruccõns and Direccõns, as shalbe soe made by the Governor, or Deputie Governor of the said Company, and such of the Assistants and Freemen as aforesaide, and published in Writing, vnder their comon Seale, shalbe carefullie and dulie observed, kept, performed, and putt in Execucõn, according to the true intent and meaning of the same." (Massachusetts Charter of 1629.)

"Do grant free, full, and absolute power, by virtue of these presents to him [Lord Baltimore] and his heirs for the good and

Evolution from the Charters

happy government of the said province, the same laws duly to execute upon all the people within the said province by imposition of penalties, imprisonment, or any other punishment; yea, if it shall be needful, and that the quality of the offence require it, by taking away member or life, either by him, the said now Lord Baltimore and his heirs, or by his or their deputies, lieutenants, judges, justices, magistrates, officers, and ministers, to be ordained or appointed according to the tenor and true intention of these presents." (Maryland Charter of 1632.)

"I R. W. being now chosen to be Gou'nor wthin this Jurisdiction, for the yeare ensueing, and vntil a new be chosen, doe sweare by the greate and dreadfull name of the everliueing God, to p'mote the publicke good and peace of the same, according to the best of my skill; as also will mayntayne all lawfull priuiledges of this Comonwealth; as also that all wholsome lawes that are or shall be made by lawfull authority here established, be duly executed." (Fundamental Orders of Connecticut, 1638.)

The Carolina charter of 1663 copies the provision given above from the Maryland charter of 1632.

"The governor, with his council before expressed, is to see that all courts established by the laws of the general assembly, and all ministers and officers, civil and military, do and execute their several duties and offices respectively according to the laws in force, and to punish them for swerving from the laws or acting contrary to their trust, as the nature of their offence shall require." (Concessions of East Jersey, 1665.)

The Carolina charter of 1665 copies the provision given above from the Maryland charter of 1632.

"And the same laws duly to execute unto and upon all people within the said country and the limits thereof." (Pennsylvania Charter of 1681.)

"That the governor and provincial council shall take care that all laws, statutes, and ordinances, which shall at any time be made within the said province, be duly and diligently executed." (Pennsylvania Frame of April 2, 1683.)

The above provision is repeated in the Pennsylvania Frame of 1683 and also in the Pennsylvania Frame of 1696.

"That it be his office and duty to cause them to be carried into execution." (Franklin's Plan of 1754.)

"It shall be his office and duty to cause them to be carried into execution." (Galloway's Plan, 1774.)

"The president, and, in his absence, the vice-president, with the council, are also to take care that the laws be faithfully executed." (Pennsylvania Constitution of 1776.)

"I, A. B., elected governor of the state of Georgia, do solemnly promise and swear that I will use my utmost endeavors that the laws and ordinances of the state be duly observed." (Georgia Constitution of 1777.)

"That it shall be the duty of the governor to take care that the laws are faithfully executed to the best of his ability." (New York Constitution of 1777.)

The Vermont constitution of 1777 and the Vermont constitution of 1786 repeat the provision given above from the Pennsylvania constitution of 1776.

"He [the President] shall take care that the laws of the United States be duly executed." (Pinckney's Plan, 1787.)

"He [the President] shall take care that the laws be faithfully executed." (The Constitution.)

16. THE PRESIDENT AS COMMANDER-IN-CHIEF.

The Constitution describes the President as commander-in-chief, and gives him control over the army and navy and over the militia of the several States when called into the actual service of the United States. The origin of this power and of the name commander-in-chief is perhaps as good an illustration as could be given of the growth which preceded the formation of the Constitution.

The first quotation, which is from the Concessions of East Jersey of 1665, shows the power given without the name. The proprietors of East Jersey provided that

Evolution from the Charters

the governor whom they appointed should control any militia that might be raised in their wilderness province.

Thirty-one years afterwards, when William Penn was preparing his plan for a union of all the colonies, he also thought that the person who was to be the executive to carry out the plan should have control of the militia of the colonies, and he almost gave him the name that was finally adopted, for he called him a "chief commander." Thirty-six years later the Georgia charter of 1732 called him the commander-in-chief, and from that time on this name alternates with captain-general, until the Constitution adopts it in a clause which briefly summarizes the forms that had been previously given.

"The said governor, who is commissionated by us over the several framed [train] bands and companies." (Concessions of East Jersey, 1665.)

"That in times of war the king's high commissioner shall be general or chief commander of the several quotas upon service against the common enemy, as he shall be advised, for the good and benefit of the whole." (Penn's Plan of Union, 1696.)

"And our will and pleasure is, and we do hereby, for us, our heirs and successors, declare and grant that the governor and commander-in-chief of the province of South Carolina, of us, our heirs and successors, for the time being, shall at all times hereafter have the chief command of the militia of our said province, hereby erected and established." (Georgia Charter of 1732.)

"That the supreme command of all the military force employed by the president and council be in the president." (Hutchinson's Plan, 1754.)

"That the general assembly and the said legislative council shall jointly choose by ballot from among themselves, or from the people at large, a president and commander-in-chief and a vice-president of the colony." (South Carolina Constitution of 1776.)

Evolution of the Constitution

"That the governor, or, in his absence, the vice-president of the council, shall act as captain-general and commander-in-chief of all the militia and other military force in this colony." (New Jersey Constitution of 1776.)

"The president, with the advice and consent of the privy council, may act as captain-general and commander-in-chief" [of the militia]. (Delaware Constitution of 1776.)

"The president shall be commander-in-chief of the forces of the State, but shall not command in person, except advised thereto by the council, and then only so long as they shall approve thereof." (Pennsylvania Constitution of 1776.)

"The governor, for the time being, shall be captain-general and commander-in-chief of the militia." (North Carolina Constitution of 1776.)

"The governor, for the time being, shall be captain-general and commander-in-chief over all the militia and other military and naval forces belonging to this State." (Georgia Constitution of 1777.)

"That the governor shall, by virtue of his office, be general and commander-in-chief of all the militia and admiral of the navy of this State." (New York Constitution of 1777.)

The Vermont constitution of 1777 repeats the provision given above from the Pennsylvania constitution of 1776.

"The congress shall have the sole power of appointing a generalissimo and commander-in-chief of the land forces." (Drayton's Articles of Confederation, 1778.)

"He [the governor] shall be general and commander-in-chief of the militia and admiral of the navy of this State." (Rejected Constitution of Massachusetts of 1778.)

"The governor of this commonwealth, for the time being, shall be the commander-in-chief of the army and navy and of all the military forces of the State by sea and land." (Massachusetts Constitution of 1780.)

The above provision from the Massachusetts constitution of 1780 is repeated in the New Hampshire constitution of 1784.

The Vermont constitution of 1786 repeats the provision given above from the Pennsylvania constitution of 1776.

Evolution from the Charters

"He [the President] shall be commander-in-chief of the army and navy of the United States, and of the militia of the several States." (Pinckney's Plan, 1787.)

"The President shall be commander-in-chief of the army and navy of the United States, and of the militia of the several States when called into the actual service of the United States." (The Constitution.)

17. VETO POWER.

The quotations in this section show the absolute veto power of governor or king as it existed in various forms in colonial times up to the New York constitution of 1777, when the modified veto appeared, afterwards adopted in the Constitution.

The first appearance of anything like a veto power was in the Maryland charter of 1632, which gave Lord Baltimore the power to make laws with the assent of the freemen or their delegates. The effect of this in practice was, of course, that the assembly of the freemen made the laws and submitted them to Lord Baltimore or his deputy for approval.

"Know ye therefore, moreover, that we, reposing especial trust and confidence in the fidelity, wisdom, justice, and provident circumspection of the said now Lord Baltimore, for us, our heirs and successors, do grant free, full, and absolute power, by virtue of these presents, to him and his heirs, for the good and happy government of the said province, to ordain, make, enact, and, under his and their seals, to publish any laws whatsoever appertaining either unto the public state of the said province or unto the private utility of particular persons according unto their best discretions, of and with the advice, assent, and approbation of the freemen of the said province, or the greater part of them, or of their delegates or deputies." (Maryland Charter of 1632.)

Evolution of the Constitution

The above provision is repeated in the Carolina charter of 1663.

"Which laws, etc., so made shall receive publication from the governor and council (but as the laws of us and our general assembly) and be in force for the space of one year and no more unless contradicted by the lords proprietors, within which time they are to be presented to us, our heirs, etc., for our ratification, and, being confirmed by us, they shall be in continual force till expired by their own limitation or by act of repeal in like manner to be passed as aforesaid and confirmed." (Concessions of East Jersey, 1665.)

The Carolina Charter of 1665 copies the provision given above from the Maryland Charter of 1632.

"The palatine's court shall consist of the palatine and seven proprietors. This court shall have a negative upon all acts, orders, votes, and judgments of the grand council and the parliament" [except in the appointment of landgraves, caziques, and proprietors]. "No act or order of parliament shall be of any force unless it be ratified in open parliament during the same session by the palatine or his deputy and three more of the lords proprietors or their deputies, and then not to continue longer in force but until the next biennial parliament, unless in the mean time it be ratified under the hands and seals of the palatine himself and three more of the lords proprietors themselves, and by their order published at the next biennial parliament." (Locke's Carolina Constitution of 1669.)

"And our will and pleasure is, and we do hereby declare, ordain, and grant, that all and every such Acts, Laws, and ordinances, as shall from time to time be made in and by such general Assembly or Assemblies, shall be first approved and allowed by the Pres. and Councell for the time being, and, thereupon shall stand and be in force until yᵉ pleasure of us, our heirs and successors, shall be known, whether yᵉ same Laws and ordinances shall receive any change or confirmation, or be totally disallowed and discharged." (Commission for New Hampshire of 1680.)

Evolution from the Charters

The Pennsylvania Charter of 1681 copies the provision given above from the Maryland Charter of 1632.

"Our further will and pleasure is that a transcript or Duplicate of all Lawes, which shall bee soe as aforesaid made and published within the said Province, shall within five yeares after the makeing thereof, be transmitted and delivered to the Privy Councell, for the time being, of us, our heires and successors: And if any of the said Lawes, within the space of six moneths after that they shall be soe transmitted and delivered, bee declared by us, Our heires and Successors, in Our or their Privy Councell, inconsistent with the Sovereigntey or lawful Prerogative of us, our heires or Successors, or contrary to the Faith and Allegiance due by the legall government of this Realme, from the said *William Penn*, or his heires, or of the Planters and Inhabitants of the said Province, and that thereupon any of the said Lawes shall bee adjudged and declared to bee void by us, our heires or Successors, under our or their Privy Seale, that then and from thenceforth, such Lawes, concerning which such Judgement and declaration shall bee made, shall become voyd: Otherwise the said Lawes soe transmitted, shall remaine, and stand in full force, according to the true intent and meaneing thereof." (Pennsylvania Charter of 1681.)

"*Provided* alwaies and Wee doe by these presents for vs Our Heires and Successors Establish and Ordaine that in the frameing and passing of all such Orders Laws Statutes and Ordinances and in all Elections and Acts of Government whatsoever to be passed made or done by the said Generall Court or Assembly or in Councill the Governor of our said Province or Territory of the Massachusetts Bay in New England for the time being shall have the Negative voice and that without his consent or Approbation signified and declared in Writing no such Orders Laws Statutes Ordinances Elections or other Acts of Government whatsoever soe to be made passed or done by the said Generall Assembly or in Councill shall be of any Force effect or validity anything herein contained to the contrary in anywise notwithstanding *And* wee doe for vs Our Heires and Successors Establish and Ordaine that the said Orders Laws Statutes and Ordinances be by the first opportunity after the makeing thereof sent or Transmitted vnto vs Our Heires and Successors vnder the Publique Seale to be appointed by vs for Our or their approbation or Disallowance And that in case all or any of them shall at any time within the space of three yeares next after the same shall have been presented to vs our Heires and Successors in Our or their Privy Councill be disallowed and reiected and soe signified by vs Our Heires and Successors vnder our or their Signe Manuall and Signett or by or in our or their Privy Councill vnto the Governor for the time being then such and soe many of them as shall be soe disallowed and riected shall thenceforth cease and determine and become vtterly void and of none effect *Provided* alwais that incase Wee our Heires or Successors shall not within the Terme of Three Yeares after the presenting of such Orders Lawes Statutes or Ordinances as aforesaid signifie our or their Disallowance of the same Then the said orders Lawes Statutes or Ordinances shall be and continue in full force and effect according to the true Intent and meaneing of the same vntill the Expiracon thereof or that the same shall be Repealed by the Generall Assembly of our said province for the time being." (Massachusetts Charter, 1691.)

"All which proposed and prepared bills, or such of them as the governor, with the advice of the council, shall in open assembly declare his assent unto shall be the laws of this province and territories thereof." (Pennsylvania Frame of 1696.)

"In all which cases the governor-general or lieutenant is to have a negative." (Daniel Coxe's Plan, 1722.)

"And the same [laws] shall and may present under their common seal to us, our heirs and successors, in our or their privy council for our or their approbation or disallowance: and the said laws, statutes and ordinances, being approved of by us, our heirs and successors, in our or their privy council, shall from thence forth be in full force and virtue within our said province of Georgia." (Georgia Charter of 1732.)

"That the assent of the president-general be requisite to all acts of the grand council." (Franklin's Plan of 1754.)

"That the assent of the president be made necessary to all

Evolution from the Charters

acts of the council, saving the choice of the speaker." (Hutchinson's Plan, 1754.)

"The president-general's assent shall be requisite to all acts of the grand council." (Galloway's Plan, 1774.)

"Bills having passed the general assembly and legislative council may be assented to or rejected by the president and commander-in-chief." (South Carolina Constitution of 1776.)

"And whereas laws inconsistent with the spirit of this constitution, or with the public good, may be hastily and unadvisedly passed: Be it ordained, that the governor for the time being, the chancellor, and the judges of the supreme court, or any two of them, together with the governor, shall be, and hereby are, constituted a council to revise all bills about to be passed into laws by the legislature; and for that purpose shall assemble themselves from time to time, when the legislature shall be convened; for which, nevertheless, they shall not receive any salary or consideration, under any pretence whatever. And that all bills which have passed the senate and assembly shall, before they become laws, be presented to the said council for their revisal and consideration; and if, upon such revision and consideration, it should appear improper to the said council, or a majority of them, that the said bill should become a law of this state, that they return the same, together with their objections thereto in writing, to the senate or house of assembly (in whichsoever the same shall have originated), who shall enter the objections sent down by the council at large in their minutes, and proceed to reconsider the said bill. But if, after such reconsideration, two-thirds of the said senate or house of assembly shall, notwithstanding the said objections, agree to pass the same, it shall, together with the objections, be sent to the other branch of the legislature, where it shall also be reconsidered, and, if approved by two-thirds of the members present, shall be a law. And in order to prevent any unnecessary delays, be it further ordained, that if any bill shall not be returned by the council within ten days after it shall have been presented, the same shall be a law, unless the legislature shall, by their adjournment, render a return of the said bill within ten days impracticable; in which case the bill shall be returned on the first day of the meeting of the legislature after the expiration of the said ten days." (New York Constitution of 1777.)

"No bill or resolve of the senate or house of representatives shall become a law, and have force as such, until it shall have been laid before the governor for his revisal; and if he, upon such revision, approve thereof, he shall signify his approbation by signing the same. But if he have any objection to the passing of such bill or resolve, he shall return the same, together with his objections thereto, in writing, to the senate or house of representatives, in whichsoever the same shall have originated, who shall enter the objections sent down by the governor, at large, on their records, and proceed to reconsider the said bill or resolve; but if, after such reconsideration, two-thirds of the said senate or house of representatives shall, notwithstanding the said objections, agree to pass the same, it shall, together with the objections, be sent to the other branch of the legislature, where it shall also be reconsidered, and, if approved by two-thirds of the members present, shall have the force of law; but in all such cases the vote of both houses shall be determined by yeas and nays, and the names of the persons voting for or against the said bill or resolve shall be entered upon the public records of the commonwealth. And in order to prevent unnecessary delays, if any bill or resolve shall not be returned by the governor within five days after it shall have been presented, the same shall have the force of law." (Massachusetts Constitution of 1780.)

"Every bill which shall have passed the legislature shall be presented to the President of the United States for his revision. If he approves it he shall sign it, but if he does not approve it he shall return it, with his objections, to the house it originated in, which house, if two-thirds of the members present, notwithstanding the President's objections, agree to pass it, shall send it to the other house, with the President's objections; where, if two-thirds of the members present also agree to pass it, the same shall become a law; and all bills sent to the President and not returned by him within   days shall be laws unless the legislature, by their adjournment, prevent their return, in which case they shall not be laws." (Pinckney's Plan, 1787.)

Evolution from the Charters

"Every bill which shall have passed the house of representatives and the senate shall, before it become a law, be presented to the President of the United States. If he approve he shall sign it, but if not he shall return it, with his objections, to that house in which it shall have originated, who shall enter the objections at large in their journal and proceed to reconsider it. If, after such reconsideration, two-thirds of that house shall agree to pass the bill, it shall be sent, together with the objections, to the other house, by which it shall likewise be reconsidered, and, if approved by two-thirds of that house, it shall become a law. But in all such cases the votes of both houses shall be determined by yeas and nays, and the names of the persons voting for and against the bill shall be entered on the journal of each house respectively. If any bill shall not be returned by the President within ten days (Sundays excepted) after it shall have been presented to him, the same shall be a law in like manner as if he had signed it, unless the congress, by their adjournment, prevent its return, in which case it shall not be a law. Every order, resolution, or vote, to which the concurrence of the senate and house of representatives may be necessary (except on a question of adjournment) shall be presented to the President of the United States, and before the same shall take effect shall be approved by him, or, being disapproved by him, shall be repassed by two-thirds of the senate and house of representatives, according to the rules and limitations prescribed in the case of a bill." (The Constitution.)

18. THE PARDONING POWER.

Many experiments were made with the pardoning power before it was given its present characteristics in the National Constitution. Beginning with the Virginia charter of 1609, which gave the power generally to the company and its officers, the power shifted about for over a hundred and seventy years from the governor to the legislature, and from the legislature to the governor and his council, or to a board composed of the governor, the lieutenant-governor, and the speaker of the house of representatives, until in the Constitution it rested with the President alone, except in cases of impeachment, which had been an exception in some previous documents.

In the Maryland charter of 1632 Lord Baltimore was given the right to pardon before judgment,—a right which no governor of any of our States is now believed to possess. But it seems to have been thought at one time in Massachusetts that the bare right to pardon would carry with it the right to pardon either before or after judgment, for in the constitution of that State of 1780 the right to pardon before judgment is expressly prohibited.

Of late years some of our States have returned to the old method of a board of pardons composed of the governor and other officers.

Officers of the company to punish and pardon according to such laws as should be made. In defect of law, in cases of necessity at their discretion. (Virginia Charter of 1609.)

Officers of the company to punish and pardon according to such laws as should be made. (Massachusetts Charter of 1629.)

The pardoning power given to the proprietor. (Maryland Charter of 1632.)

The above provision is repeated in the Grant of Maine of 1639.

The pardoning power given to the legislature. (Connecticut Charter of 1662.)

The above provision is repeated in the Rhode Island Charter of 1663.

The Carolina Charter of 1663 copies the provision above given from the Maryland charter of 1632.

The pardoning power given to the proprietor. (Concessions of East Jersey, 1665.)

Evolution from the Charters

The Carolina charter of 1665 copies the provision above given from the Maryland charter of 1632.

The pardoning power given to the palatine and his court. (Locke's Carolina Constitution of 1669.)

The pardoning power given to the proprietor. (Pennsylvania Charter of 1681.)

The pardoning power given to the governor and his council. (Virginia Constitution of 1776.)

The pardoning power given to the governor and his council. (New Jersey Constitution of 1776.)

The pardoning power given to the governor. (Delaware Constitution of 1776.)

The pardoning power given to the governor and his council. (Pennsylvania Constitution of 1776.)

The pardoning power given to the governor. (Maryland Constitution of 1776.)

The pardoning power given to the governor. (North Carolina Constitution of 1776.)

The pardoning power given to the legislature. (Georgia Constitution of 1777.)

The pardoning power in treason and murder given to the legislature and in other crimes to the governor. (New York Constitution of 1777.)

The Vermont constitution of 1777 repeats the provision given above from the Pennsylvania constitution of 1776.

The governor and council may reprieve for not more than six months; the pardoning power given to the governor, lieutenant-governor, and speaker of the house of representatives. (Rejected Constitution of Massachusetts of 1778.)

The governor and council may reprieve for not more than six months; the pardoning power given to the legislature. (Rejected Constitution of New Hampshire of 1778.)

The pardoning power, except in cases of impeachment, given to the governor and council, but no pardon given before conviction shall avail. (Massachusetts Constitution of 1780.)

The above provision is repeated in the New Hampshire constitution of 1784.

Evolution of the Constitution

The Vermont constitution of 1786 repeats the provision given above from the Pennsylvania constitution of 1776.

The pardoning power, except in impeachment, given to the President. (Pinckney's Plan, 1787.)

The pardoning power, except in impeachment, given to the President. (The Constitution.)

19. PRESIDENT'S MESSAGE.

"That he [the President] recommend them ye making of such Acts, Laws, and Ordinances, as may most tend to ye establishing them in obedience to our authority; their own p^{r}servation in peace and good Governm^t, and defend against their enemies, and that they do consider of the fittest ways for raising of taxes, and in such proportion as may be fit for ye support of ye s^d Governm^t." (Commission for New Hampshire of 1680.)

"That it shall be the duty of the governor to inform the legislature, at every session, of the condition of the State, so far as may respect his department; to recommend such matters to their consideration as shall appear to him to concern its good government, welfare, and prosperity." (New York Constitution of 1777.)

"It shall be the duty of the governor to inform the legislature, at every season of the general court, of the condition of the State, and from time to time to recommend such matters to their consideration as shall appear to him to concern its good government, welfare, and prosperity." (Rejected Constitution of Massachusetts of 1778.)

"He shall from time to time give information to the legislature of the state of the Union, and recommend to their consideration the measures he may think necessary." (Pinckney's Plan, 1787.)

"He [the President] shall from time to time give to the Congress information of the state of the Union, and recommend to their consideration such measures as he shall judge necessary and expedient." (The Constitution.)

Evolution from the Charters

20. Appointing Power.

The power to fill the offices of government is given in the National Constitution, in a rather curious way, to the President and Senate, with a discretion left to Congress to provide by law for appointment to inferior offices, and the summary shows that this method of dividing the power between the executive and the legislature was the result of a long development from the earliest colonial times.

In the governments of Europe it was not common for the legislature to appoint to office, and in England the appointing power was in the Crown; but in the early colonial charters and constitutions the power was frequently given solely to the legislature. As time went on, the executive was given a share in it, and it was divided up among the governor, the council, and the legislature in varying proportions until the plan adopted in the Constitution was reached.

Appointing power given to the council. (Virginia Charter of 1609.)

Appointing power given to the general courts, which were composed of the treasurer and company. (Virginia Charter of 1611–12.)

Appointing power given to the council. (Charter of New England of 1620.)

Appointing power given to the general court, which was composed of the governor, assistants, and freemen. (Massachusetts Charter of 1629.)

Appointing power given to the proprietor. (Maryland Charter of 1632.)

Appointing power given to the general assembly. (Fundamental Orders of Connecticut, 1638.)

Evolution of the Constitution

Appointing power given to the general assembly. (Connecticut Charter of 1662.)

The above provision is repeated in the Rhode Island Charter of 1663.

Appointing power given to the proprietor. (Carolina Charter of 1663.)

Appointing power given to the governor and his council. (Concessions of East Jersey of 1665.)

Appointing power given to the proprietor. (Pennsylvania Charter of 1681.)

The provincial council to nominate and the governor to appoint. (Pennsylvania Frame of April 2, 1683.)

The provincial council and assembly to nominate and the governor to appoint. (Pennsylvania Frame of 1683.)

Appointing power given to the governor, with the consent of the council, as to certain officers, such as judges, sheriffs, etc., and the other officers to be appointed by the assembly. (Massachusetts Charter of 1691.)

The freemen and justices to nominate and the governor to appoint sheriffs, coroners, and clerks of the peace. (Pennsylvania Charter of Privileges of 1701.)

Appointing power given to the common council. (Georgia Charter of 1732.)

Appointing power given to the president-general and grand council. (Franklin's Plan of 1754.)

Appointing power given to the president and council. (Hutchinson's Plan of 1754.)

Appointing power given to the Congress. (Franklin's Articles of Confederation of 1775.)

Appointing power given to the two houses of the legislature. (New Hampshire Constitution of 1776.)

Appointing power given to the legislature, except in a few instances, where the president and council could appoint. (South Carolina Constitution of 1776.)

Appointing power divided between the two houses of assembly and the governor and council. (Virginia Constitution of 1776.)

Evolution from the Charters

Appointing power given to the council and assembly. (New Jersey Constitution of 1776.)

Appointing power divided among the president, council, and assembly. (Delaware Constitution of 1776.)

Appointing power divided among the president, council, and the assembly. (Pennsylvania Constitution of 1776.)

Appointing power given to the governor and council, except in a few officers. (Maryland Constitution of 1776.)

Appointing power given to the legislature. (North Carolina Constitution of 1776.)

The governor, with the consent of a council of the senate, to appoint. (New York Constitution of 1777.)

Appointing power divided among the governor, council, and the assembly. (Vermont Constitution of 1777.)

Civil officers annually chosen to be appointed by the legislature; others by the governor and senate. (Rejected Constitution of Massachusetts of 1778.)

The appointing power divided between the governor and the legislature. (South Carolina Constitution of 1778.)

Appointing power given to the general court. (Rejected Constitution of New Hampshire of 1778.)

Appointing power given to Congress. (Articles of Confederation, 1778.)

Appointing power given to Congress. (Drayton's Articles of Confederation, 1778.)

Appointing power divided among the governor, council, and the legislature. (Massachusetts Constitution of 1780.)

Appointing power given to the president and council. (New Hampshire Constitution of 1784.)

Appointing power divided between the President and the Senate. (Pinckney's Plan, 1787.)

Appointing power given to the President and Senate, with discretion to Congress to vest the appointment of inferior officers in the President alone, in the courts of law, or in the heads of departments. (The Constitution.)

Evolution of the Constitution

21. THE JUDICIARY.

The summary in this section is not given because it shows a line of development leading to a clause in the Constitution, but merely to show the gradual growth of a judiciary department in the colonial governments. The growth of the legislative and executive departments in colonial times having been shown, it seems necessary to show the growth of the judiciary in order to complete the three great departments, even if the line of the judiciary's development is not carried down to the Constitution.

The reason for not carrying the line down to the Constitution is that the judiciary department in the Constitution seems to have a separate line of development connected with the development of federalism, and it will be treated under that head. When federalism, or the idea of having a national government controlling the people of all the States, was first developing, it was not considered necessary to have in it any judiciary department at all. The judiciary gained an entrance into federalism very slowly, and at first had jurisdiction only in cases of captures in war and piracies and felonies on the high seas, and this was, of course, not necessarily connected with the gradual rise of a judiciary department in the colonial or State governments.

The summary in this section has, accordingly, been carried only far enough to show the growth and firm establishment of a judiciary department as a part of colonial government, and it stops at the Georgia charter of 1732. The constitutions of 1776 did not usually provide for a judiciary department, because those which

Evolution from the Charters

they had had through the colonial period were already in existence and were satisfactory. Nothing was to be gained for the cause of the Revolution by creating new ones, and these constitutions of 1776 were intended to conform existing institutions to the new conditions of independence rather than to create out-and-out new forms of government. It will be observed that in the earliest documents only criminal jurisdiction is given.

Council in Virginia given authority to bind over and punish offenders or send them to England for trial. (Virginia Charter, 1611-12.)

Council given authority to correct and punish. (Charter of New England of 1620.)

Power given to the freemen to pass laws inflicting fines and imprisonment. (Massachusetts Charter of 1629.)

Power given to the proprietor to establish both civil and criminal courts. (Maryland Charter of 1632.)

Judicial power given to the magistrates, who were, in effect, the governor's council. (Fundamental Orders of Connecticut of 1638.)

The provision from the Maryland charter of 1632 is substantially repeated in the grant of Maine of 1639.

The general assembly given power to establish courts, both civil and criminal. (Connecticut Charter of 1662.)

The above provision is substantially repeated in the Rhode Island charter of 1663.

The provision from the Maryland charter of 1632 is repeated in the Carolina charter of 1663.

The general assembly given power to establish courts, and the governor and his council given power to establish criminal courts. (Concessions of East Jersey, 1665.)

The provision from the Maryland charter of 1632 is repeated in the Carolina charter of 1665.

An elaborate system of courts established by Locke's Carolina constitution. (Locke's Carolina Constitution of 1669.)

Evolution of the Constitution

The legislature given power to establish courts. (Concessions of West Jersey, 1677.)

The president and council made a court of both civil and criminal cases, with right of appeal to England. (Commission for New Hampshire of 1680.)

The proprietor may establish courts of all kinds, but appeals may be taken to England. (Pennsylvania Charter of 1681.)

The power of establishing courts given to the governor and council. (Pennsylvania Frame of April 2, 1683.)

The general assembly given power to establish courts, and the governor and council to be a court of probate and administration. (Massachusetts Charter of 1691.)

The corporation given power to establish courts. (Georgia Charter of 1732.)

22. Method of Amending.

At the time of the first settlement of America every country's form of government was supposed by its creators and upholders to last forever. As a matter of fact, however, it was well known that governments were changed by violence and revolution or by a slow, almost imperceptible process of change of custom. The governments of the colonies were often changed by new charters signed by the king, and it was understood that the power that created these governments could at any time alter or abolish them.

But still the fiction was kept up of having each charter declare that its particular form of government for the colony should be perpetual, and it was not until William Penn and his colonists were making their frame of 1683 that the idea seems to have occurred of providing, in the instrument of government itself, a regular and orderly method of changing it as time should show the necessity

Evolution from the Charters

for change. It was a natural thought, and there is no evidence that either Penn or his people believed that they were suggesting anything wonderful. But their method, as the summary shows, was repeated and repeated until, after running through many of. the constitutions of 1776, the Articles of Confederation, and other American documents, it found its place in the National Constitution.

It is generally believed to be a very important part of the Constitution, giving the elasticity which secures permanence and prevents revolution. It has already been used to make most far-reaching changes, and will probably be used for the same purpose again. As it stands in the Constitution, it is generally regarded as peculiarly American: so that it is interesting to trace its American growth for over a hundred years.

There is a curious resemblance between the clause in the Constitution and the similar clause in the Pennsylvania Charter of Privileges of 1701. The Pennsylvania document provides that it may be amended by the consent of the governor and six parts of seven of the assembly, but that the article relating to liberty of conscience shall never be altered. The National Constitution provides for amendment by consent of three-fourths of the States, but, like the Pennsylvania Charter of Privileges, adds the exceptions that no State without its consent shall be deprived of its equal suffrage in the Senate, and that prior to 1808 no amendment shall affect the right to import slaves or affect direct taxation.

"That no act, law, or ordinance whatsoever, shall at any time hereafter, be made or done by the Governor of this province, his heirs or assigns, or by the freemen in the provincial Council, or the General Assembly, to alter, change, or diminish the form, or effect, of this charter, or any part, or clause thereof, or contrary to the true intent and meaning thereof, without the consent of the Governor, his heirs, or assigns, and six parts of seven of the said freemen in provincial Council and General Assembly." (Pennsylvania Frame of April 2, 1683.)

The above provision is repeated in the Pennsylvania Frame of 1683 and in the Pennsylvania Frame of 1696.

"AND no Act, Law or Ordinance whatsoever, shall at any Time hereafter, be made or done, to alter, change or diminish the Form or Effect of this Charter, or of any Part or Clause therein, contrary to the true Intent and Meaning thereof, without the Consent of the Governor for the Time being, and *Six* Parts of *Seven* of the Assembly met.

"BUT because the Happiness of Mankind depends so much upon the Enjoying of Liberty of their Consciences as aforesaid, I do hereby solemnly declare, promise and grant, for me, my Heirs and Assigns, That the *First* Article of this Charter relating to Liberty of Conscience, and every Part and Clause therein, according to the true Intent and Meaning thereof, shall be kept and remain, without any Alteration, inviolably for ever." '(Pennsylvania Charter of Privileges of 1701.)

"As all new institutions may have imperfections which only time and experience can discover, it is agreed that the general congress, from time to time, shall propose such amendments of this constitution as may be found necessary, which, being approved by a majority of the colony assemblies, shall be equally binding with the rest of the articles of this confederation." (Franklin's Articles of Confederation, 1775.)

"No article of the declaration of rights and fundamental rules of this State, agreed to by this convention, nor the first, second, fifth (except that part thereof that relates to the right of suffrage), twenty-sixth, and twenty-ninth articles of this constitution ought ever to be violated on any pretence whatever.

"No other part of this constitution shall be altered, changed, or diminished without the consent of five parts in seven of the

Evolution from the Charters

assembly and seven members of the legislative council." (Delaware Constitution of 1776.)

"The said council of censors shall also have power to call a convention, to meet within two years after their sitting, if there appear to them an absolute necessity of amending any article of the constitution which may be defective, explaining such as may be thought not clearly expressed, and of adding such as are necessary for the preservation of the rights and happiness of the people: But the articles to be amended, and the amendments proposed, and such articles as are proposed to be added or abolished, shall be promulgated at least six months before the day appointed for the election of such convention, for the previous consideration of the people, that they may have an opportunity of instructing their delegates on the subject." (Pennsylvania Constitution of 1776.)

"That this Form of Government, and the Declaration of Rights, and no part thereof, shall be altered, changed, or abolished, unless a bill so to alter, change or abolish the same shall pass the General Assembly, and be published at least three months before a new election, and shall be confirmed by the General Assembly, after a new election of Delegates, in the first session after such new election; provided that nothing in this form of government, which relates to the eastern shore particularly, shall at any time hereafter be altered, unless for the alteration and confirmation thereof at least two-thirds of all the members of each branch of the General Assembly shall concur." (Maryland Constitution of 1776.)

"No alteration shall be made in this constitution without petitions from a majority of the counties, and the petitions from each county to be signed by a majority of voters in each county within this State; at which time the assembly shall order a convention to be called for that purpose, specifying the alterations to be made, according to the petitions preferred to the assembly by the majority of the counties as aforesaid." (Georgia Constitution of 1777.)

The Vermont constitution of 1777 repeats the provision given above from the Pennsylvania constitution of 1776.

"That no part of this constitution shall be altered without

notice being previously given of ninety days, nor shall any part of the same be changed without the consent of a majority of the members of the senate and house of representatives." (South Carolina Constitution of 1778.)

"The general court shall have no power to alter any part of this constitution, and, in case they should concur in any proposed alteration, amendment, or addition, the same being agreed to by a majority of the people, shall become valid." (Rejected Constitution of Massachusetts of 1778.)

"Nor shall any alteration at any time hereafter be made in any of them unless such alteration be agreed to in a congress of the United States and be afterwards confirmed by the legislatures of every State." (Articles of Confederation, 1778.)

"The articles of this confederation shall be strictly binding upon, and inviolably observed by, the parties interested therein; nor shall any alteration be made in them, or any of them, unless such alteration shall be agreed to in the congress and allowed by the legislature of every State in the confederacy." (Drayton's Articles of Confederation, 1778.)

"In order the more effectually to adhere to the principles of the constitution and to correct those violations which by any means may be made therein, as well as to form such alterations as from experience shall be found necessary, the general court which shall be in the year of our Lord one thousand seven hundred and ninety-five shall issue precepts to the selectmen of the several towns, and to the assessors of the unincorporated plantations, directing them to convene the qualified voters of their respective towns and plantations for the purpose of collecting their sentiments on the necessity or expediency of revising the constitution in order to amendments.

"And if it shall appear, by the returns made, that two-thirds of the qualified voters throughout the State, who shall assemble and vote in consequence of the said precepts, are in favor of such revision or amendment, the general court shall issue precepts, or direct them to be issued from the secretary's office, to the several towns to elect delegates to meet in convention for the purpose aforesaid.

Evolution from the Charters

"And said delegates to be chosen in the same manner and proportion as their representatives in the second branch of the legislature are by this constitution to be chosen." (Massachusetts Constitution of 1780.)

"To preserve an effectual adherence to the principles of the constitution and to correct any violations thereof, as well as to make such alterations therein as from experience may be found necessary, the general court shall, at the expiration of seven years from the time this constitution shall take effect, issue precepts, or direct them to be issued from the secretary's office, to the several towns and incorporated places, to elect delegates to meet in convention for the purposes aforesaid : the said delegates to be chosen in the same manner and proportioned as the representatives to the general assembly ; provided that no alteration shall be made in this constitution before the same shall be laid before the towns and unincorporated places and approved by two-thirds of the qualified voters present and voting upon the question." (New Hampshire Constitution of 1784.)

"That provision ought to be made for the amendment of the articles of union whenever it shall seem necessary, and that the assent of the national legislature ought not to be required thereto." (Randolph's Plan of 1787.)

"If two-thirds of the legislatures of the States apply for the same, the legislature of the United States shall call a convention for the purpose of amending the Constitution ; or, should Congress, with the consent of two-thirds of each house, propose to the States amendments to the same, the agreement of two-thirds of the legislatures of the States shall be sufficient to make the said amendments parts of the Constitution." (Pinckney's Plan, 1787.)

"The congress, whenever two-thirds of both houses shall deem it necessary, shall propose amendments to this constitution, or, on the application of the legislatures of two-thirds of the several states, shall call a convention for proposing amendments, which in either case shall be valid to all intents and purposes as part of this constitution when ratified by the legislatures of three-fourths of the several states, or by conventions in three-fourths thereof, as the one or the other mode of ratification may be proposed by the

Evolution of the Constitution

congress; provided that no amendment which may be made prior to the year one thousand eight hundred and eight shall in any manner affect the first and fourth clauses in the ninth section of the first article, and that no state, without its consent, shall be deprived of its equal suffrage in the senate." (The Constitution.)

23. PREVENTION OF UNCONSTITUTIONAL LAWS.

How to prevent violations of a written constitution must have been among the first questions that occurred to the early draughtsmen of those instruments. In the case of the colonial charters violations could be punished by forfeiture of the charter, and in many of the colonies the laws had to be submitted to the king for his approval. But when written constitutions were made by the people other safeguards were necessary, and the history of the experiments and struggles to invent something that would be self-acting is instructive.

The first written constitution made by the people of this country was the Fundamental Orders of Connecticut of 1638, but no attempt was made in it to provide a remedy for infringement. The subject may have been discussed,—it is difficult to suppose that it was not discussed,—but, as the problem was not even partially solved until one hundred and fifty years afterwards, the silence of our first constitution-makers can be readily excused.

Five years afterwards, in 1643, when the New England Union was formed, its framers not only considered the question, but attempted a slight and cautious solution of it. If any one of the confederated colonies should break the articles of union, "such breach of agreement, or injury," they said, "shall be duly considered and ordered by the commissioners."

Evolution from the Charters

In other words, they gave the commissioners power to devise a remedy or punishment when a case of infringement should arise, which was hardly a solution of the question, but rather a shifting of the solution to the shoulders of the commissioners. It was a beginning, nevertheless, for it at least gave the commissioners power to decide when an infringement had occurred, and the rest depended on their own skill and sagacity. It is, indeed, very interesting to see this first extremely careful step of our people in the solution of one of their most difficult problems, and I do not suppose that the most fanatical advocate of foreign sources would undertake to say that they were consciously imitating anything in the government of either England or Holland.

The proprietors of East Jersey were the next people who were bold enough to face the difficulty, by providing in their Concessions of 1665 that the laws of the assembly should not be contrary to the Concessions, and "especially that they be not repugnant to the article for liberty of conscience." This seems very inadequate, but it was a move in the right direction, because it laid down the fundamental principle that the laws must conform to the constitution.

Four years later, Locke, in his Carolina constitution of 1669, went farther, and provided that a law, when suspected of unconstitutionality on its passage, could be protested and must then be reconsidered; and, as an additional safeguard, he arranged to have all laws cease operation at the end of a hundred years from their passage. But he was outdone by the proprietors of West Jersey, who in their Concessions of 1677 declared that any member of the legislature who should move or incite any to move an infringement of the constitution should be proceeded against as a traitor.

Neither Locke nor the proprietors of West Jersey succeeded in contriving anything that was of much avail, and the summary of the subsequent documents shows for the most part mere variations of previous attempts. The violent method of the proprietors of West Jersey was, however, moderate compared to Drayton's suggestions in his articles of confederation. If Congress violated the Constitution he would allow the States to secede, and if a State violated the Constitution it might be fined or placed under ban, and, if still contumacious, punished by "the utmost vigor of arms," —a method which certainly had the merit of thoroughness.

Among all these attempts there was only one which pointed towards the final goal, and this was in the Pennsylvania Frame of 1683, where William Penn announced that if anything was procured contrary to the constitution it should be held of no force or effect. In other words, an unconstitutional law was to be void; and if he had taken the next step and said that the judges should have power to declare it void when a case involving the law came before them, he would have solved the problem as we have solved it under the National Constitution.

The framers of the Constitution took that step, but, although it was only one step, a hundred years' experience was required after Penn's Frame of 1683 before it could be taken. The way in which the power to declare laws unconstitutional and void was gradually

Evolution from the Charters

given to the judiciary in the national government as well as in the governments of the States has been very fully discussed, of recent years, in Mr. Brinton Coxe's "Judicial Power and Unconstitutional Legislation" and in Professor Thayer's "Origin and Scope of the American Doctrine of Constitutional Law."

What appears to be the first instance of such power in the judiciary is found in Virginia in the case of Josiah Philips, in the year 1778, but the case is so obscurely reported that we can only infer that the court believed themselves possessed of the power. In the next case, however,—Commonwealth *vs.* Caton, in 1782, also a Virginia case,—the court openly announce that they have "power to declare any resolution or act of the legislature, or either branch of it, to be unconstitutional and void." From this point the doctrine grew, and the cases, as originally collected by Mr. William M. Meigs, are very fully treated in Part II., Chapter XXIII., of Mr. Coxe's "Judicial Power and Unconstitutional Legislation."

The doctrine was denied in some States, and it was not firmly established until long after the Constitution had gone into operation. But in the year 1787, when the Constitution was framed, it was sufficiently well known to be accepted as a suggestion, and Gerry, one of the members of the convention, said that "in some of the States the judges had actually set aside laws as being against the Constitution."

The framers of the Constitution, of course, relied largely for its preservation on the good sense of the people, short terms of office, the mutual checking of the two houses of Congress, and the President's veto. But they inserted a clause declaring that the judicial power should extend to all cases arising under the Constitution, laws, and treaties, and another clause declaring that the Constitution and such laws as were made in pursuance of it should be the supreme law of the land. These clauses, coupled with the evident and implied necessity, have been held sufficient warrant for the courts to declare laws unconstitutional. (Marbury *vs.* Madison, 1 Cranch, 137; Coxe's "Judicial Power and Unconstitutional Legislation," prefatory note, 5.)

All we know of the origin of this doctrine of the power of the judiciary is that it first appeared in Virginia in an obscure form and gradually grew and spread. It seems to have originated, like our other forms of government, in circumstances and necessities, and was adopted for the reason that it was obviously convenient. It was not a common doctrine in Europe. On the contrary, most of the European governments expressly denied it. But, in order to show that it might possibly have a European source, Mr. Coxe has given at length and most learnedly all the instances of something similar in the ancient laws of England, France, Germany, and other countries. He gives not a particle of proof to show that the originators of the doctrine in this country were guided by, or even knew of, any of these foreign forms, and, as they are all very recondite and ancient, it is not likely that they knew of them.

In fact, in the Virginia case of Commonwealth *vs.* Caton (4 Call, 5), one of the judges expressly says that they could receive no light from foreign sources:

Evolution from the Charters

"The constitutions of other governments in Europe or elsewhere seem to throw little light upon this question, since we have a written record of that which the citizens of this State have adopted as their social compact, and beyond which we need not extend our researches." (4 Call, 17.)

When Gerry mentioned the subject in the convention which framed the Constitution, he referred not to foreign sources, but to the instances in our own country. In the Virginia case of Commonwealth *vs.* Caton the judges work out the problem by the natural process that any law violating the Constitution must necessarily be void, which was the same principle that William Penn had announced in his Frame of 1683. The Virginia judges merely take the further step of announcing that the judiciary must necessarily have the power of declaring such a law void in any case which brings it before them.

Any violation of the union to be considered by the commissioners. (New England Union of 1643.)

A proviso that the laws be not against the interest of the proprietors or contrary to the constitution. (Concessions of East Jersey, 1665.)

Laws suspected of unconstitutionality may be protested and reconsidered, and all laws shall cease their operation at the end of a hundred years. (Locke's Carolina Constitution of 1669.)

The legislature not to make laws which contradict the constitution, and those members of the legislature who take part in making such laws to be punished as traitors. (Concessions of West Jersey of 1677.)

Anything procured contrary to the constitution shall be void. (Pennsylvania Frame of April 2, 1683.)

The above provision is repeated in the Pennsylvania Frame of 1683 and in the Pennsylvania charter of privileges of 1701.

No part of the constitution, with certain exceptions, ought ever to be violated. (Delaware Constitution of 1776.)

Evolution of the Constitution

The legislature cannot alter or infringe any part of the constitution, and a council of censors is provided to protect the constitution from violation. (Pennsylvania Constitution of 1776.)

A proviso that the laws be not repugnant to the constitution. (Georgia Constitution of 1777.)

The Vermont constitution of 1777 repeats substantially the provisions from the Pennsylvania constitution of 1776.

The legislature shall not have power to alter or infringe any part of the constitution. (Rejected Constitution of Massachusetts of 1778.)

If constitution violated by Congress, the States may secede. If a State violates the constitution, it may be fined and obedience compelled by force of arms. (Drayton's Articles of Confederation, 1778.)

A proviso that the laws be not unconstitutional. (Massachusetts Constitution of 1780.)

The above provision from the Massachusetts constitution of 1780 is repeated in the New Hampshire constitution of 1784.

The Vermont constitution of 1786 repeats the provision given above from the Pennsylvania constitution of 1776, with a change as to the number and manner of electing the censors.

The national legislature to negative unconstitutional laws passed by the States, and the executive and some of the judges to be a council, with a modified veto on unconstitutional acts of Congress. (Randolph's Plan, 1787.)

Laws pursuant to the Constitution to be the supreme law of the land. (Pinckney's Plan, 1787.)

The judicial power to extend to all cases arising under the constitution and laws, and the constitution and laws made in pursuance of it to be the supreme law of the land. (The Constitution.)

24. Patents and Inventions.

"That the governor and provincial council shall . . . . encourage and reward the authors of useful sciences and laudable inventions in the said province." (Pennsylvania Frame of April 2, 1683.)

Evolution from the Charters

The above provision is repeated in the Pennsylvania Frame of 1683 and in the Pennsylvania Frame of 1696.

"The congress shall have power to promote the progress of science and useful arts by securing for limited times to authors and inventors the exclusive right to their respective writings and discoveries." (The Constitution.)

25. NATURALIZATION.

"And We do, for Us, our Heirs and Successors, further give and grant to the said Treasurer and Company, or their Successors forever, that the said Treasurer and Company, or the greater Part of them for the Time being, so in a full and general Court assembled as aforesaid, shall and may from Time to Time, and at all times forever hereafter, elect, choose and admit into their Company, and Society, any Person or Persons, as well Strangers and Aliens born in any Part beyond the Seas wheresoever, being in Amity with us, as our natural Liege Subjects born in any our Realms and Dominions: And that all such Persons so elected, chosen, and admitted to be of the said Company as aforesaid, shall thereupon be taken, reputed, and held, and shall be free Members of the said Company, and shall have, hold, and enjoy all and singular Freedoms, Liberties, Franchises, Privileges, Immunities, Benefits, Profits, and Commodities whatsoever, to the said Company in any Sort belonging or appertaining, as fully, freely and amply as any other Adventurers now being, or which hereafter at any Time shall be of the said Company, hath, have, shall, may, might, or ought to have and enjoy the same to all Intents and Purposes whatsoever." (Virginia Charter of 1611-12.)

"By act as aforesaid to give unto all strangers as to them shall seem meet a naturalization, and all such freedoms and privileges within the said province as to his Majesty's subjects do of right belong, they swearing or subscribing as aforesaid, which said strangers so naturalized and privileged shall be in all respects accounted in the said province as the king's natural subjects." (Concessions of East Jersey, 1665.)

"Whatsoever alien shall, in this form, before any precinct

Evolution of the Constitution

register, subscribe these fundamental constitutions, shall be thereby naturalized." (Locke's Carolina Constitution of 1669.)

"The legislature of the United States shall have the power to establish uniform rules of naturalization." (Pinckney's Plan, 1787.)

"The congress shall have power to establish a uniform rule of naturalization." (The Constitution.)

26. RELIGIOUS LIBERTY.

The quotations under this section show the beginning of religious liberty and the ideas that have at different times prevailed as to exactly what religious liberty was.

In colonial times and for some time after the Revolution a large part of our people were convinced that the Roman Church was unalterably opposed to both civil and religious liberty, and that it would destroy them both if opportunity offered. Accordingly we find that liberty of conscience did not always include papists, as they were called, and not infrequently in the constitutions of 1776 the members of the Roman obedience are excluded from holding public office. The most sweeping and carefully worded provision of this sort was in the North Carolina constitution of 1776, which declared that no person could hold office who denied the being of God or the truth of the Protestant religion, or who held "religious principles incompatible with the freedom and safety of the State."

Religious liberty did not always include what some have called "irreligious liberty," and we find that in several instances atheists and infidels are left without protection. Perhaps the most curious provision is in

Evolution from the Charters

the New Hampshire commission of 1680, which allows liberty of conscience to all Protestants, and commands that the Church of England be "particularly countenanced and encouraged."

"That our royall will and pleasure is, that noe person within the sayd colonye, at any tyme hereafter, shall bee any wise molested, punished, disquieted, or called in question, for any differences in opinione in matters of religion, and doe not actually disturb the civill peace of our sayd colony; but that all and everye person and persons may, from tyme to tyme, and at all tymes hereafter, freelye and fullye have and enjoye his and theire owne judgments and consciences, in matters of religious concernments, throughout the tract of lande hereafter mentioned; they behaving themselves peaceablie and quietlie, and not useing this libertie to lycentiousnesse and profanenesse, nor to the civill injurye or outward disturbeance of others; any lawe, statute, or clause, therein contayned, or to bee contayned, usage or custome of this realme, to the contrary hereof, in any wise, notwithstanding." (Rhode Island Charter of 1663.)

"That no person qualified as aforesaid within the said province at any time shall be anyways molested, punished, disquieted or called in question for any difference in opinion or practice in matters of religious concernments, who do not actually disturb the civil peace of the said province, but that all and every such person and persons may from time to time and at all times truly and fully have and enjoy his and their judgments and consciences in matters of religion throughout all the said province; they behaving themselves peaceably and quietly and not using this liberty to licentiousness, nor to the civil injury or outward disturbance of others; any law, statute, or clause contained or to be contained, usage or custom of this realm of England to the contrary thereof in any wise notwithstanding." (Concessions of East Jersey, 1665.)

"No person whatsoever shall disturb, molest, or persecute another for his speculative opinions in religion, or his way of worship." (Locke's Carolina Constitution of 1669.)

Evolution of the Constitution

"That no men, nor number of men upon earth, hath power or authority to rule over men's consciences in religious matters; therefore it is consented, agreed and ordained, that no person or persons whatsoever within the said province, at any time or times hereafter, shall be any ways upon any pretence whatsoever, called in question, or in the least punished or hurt, either in person, estate, or privilege, for the sake of his opinion, judgment, faith or worship towards God in matters of religion. But that all and every such person and persons may from time to time, and at all times, freely and fully have and enjoy his and their judgments and the exercise of their consciences in matters of religious worship throughout all the said province." (Concessions of West Jersey, 1677.)

"We do hereby require and comand that liberty of conscience shall be allowed unto all protestants; that such especially as shall be conformable to ye rites of ye Church of Eng^d shall be particularly countenanced and encouraged." (Commission for New Hampshire of 1680.)

"We do by these presents for us, our heirs and successors, grant, establish and ordain that forever hereafter there shall be liberty of conscience allowed in the worship of God to all Christians (except papists) inhabiting, or which shall inhabit, or be resident within our said province or territory." (Massachusetts Charter of 1691.)

"That no Person or Persons, inhabiting in this Province or Territories, who shall confess and acknowledge *One* almighty God, the Creator, Upholder and Ruler of the World; and profess him or themselves obliged to live quietly under the Civil Government, shall be in any Case molested or prejudiced, in his or their Person or Estate, because of his or their conscientious Persuasion or Practice, nor be compelled to frequent or maintain any religious Worship, Place or Ministry, contrary to his or their Mind, or to do or suffer any other Act or Thing, contrary to their religious Persuasion.

"AND that all Persons who also profess to believe in *Jesus Christ*, the Saviour of the World, shall be capable (notwithstanding their other Persuasions and Practices in Point of Conscience

Evolution from the Charters

and Religion) to serve this Government in any Capacity, both legislatively and executively, he or they solemnly promising, when lawfully required, Allegiance to the King as Sovereign, and Fidelity to the Proprietary and Governor, and taking the Attests as now established by the Law made at *New-Castle*, in the Year *One Thousand and Seven Hundred*, entitled, *An Act directing the Attests of several Officers and Ministers*, as now amended and confirmed this present Assembly." (Pennsylvania Charter of Privileges of 1701.)

"And for the greater ease and encouragement of our loving subjects and such others as shall come to inhabit in our said colony, we do by these presents, for us, our heirs and successors, grant, establish and ordain, that forever hereafter there shall be a liberty of conscience allowed in the worship of God to all persons inhabiting, or which shall inhabit or be resident within our said province, and that all such persons, except papists, shall have a free exercise of religion, so they be contented with the quiet and peaceable enjoyment of the same, not giving offence or scandal to the government." (Georgia Charter of 1732.)

"That religion, or the duty which we owe to our Creator, and the manner of discharging it, can be directed only by reason and conviction, not by force or violence ; and therefore all men are equally entitled to the free exercise of religion, according to the dictates of conscience ; and that it is the mutual duty of all to practice Christian forbearance, love, and charity towards each other." (Virginia Bill of Rights of 1776.)

"That no person shall ever, within this Colony, be deprived of the inestimable privilege of worshipping Almighty God in a manner agreeable to the dictates of his own conscience ; nor, under any pretence whatever, be compelled to attend any place of worship, contrary to his own faith and judgment ; nor shall any person within this Colony ever be obliged to pay tithes, taxes, or any other rates for the purpose of building or repairing any other church or churches, place or places of worship, or for the maintenance of any minister or ministry, contrary to what he believes to be right or has deliberately or voluntarily engaged himself to perform.

Evolution of the Constitution

"That there shall be no establishment of any one religious sect in this Province in preference to another; and that no Protestant inhabitant of this Colony shall be denied the enjoyment of any civil right, merely on account of his religious principles; but that all persons, professing a belief in the faith of any Protestant sect, who shall demean themselves peaceably under the government, as hereby established, shall be capable of being elected into any office of profit or trust, or being a member of either branch of the Legislature, and shall fully and freely enjoy every privilege and immunity enjoyed by others their fellow-subjects." (New Jersey Constitution of 1776.)

"There shall be no establishment of any one religious sect in this State in preference to another; and no clergyman or preacher of the gospel, of any denomination, shall be capable of holding any civil office in this State, or of being a member of either of the branches of the legislature, while they continue in the exercise of the pastoral function." (Delaware Constitution of 1776.)

"That all men have a natural and unalienable right to worship Almighty God according to the dictates of their own consciences and understanding: And that no man ought or of right can be compelled to attend any religious worship, or erect or support any place of worship, or maintain any ministry, contrary to, or against, his own free will and consent: Nor can any man, who acknowledges the being of a God, be justly deprived or abridged of any civil right as a citizen, on account of his religious sentiments or peculiar mode of religious worship: And that no authority can or ought to be vested in, or assumed by any power whatever, that shall in any case interfere with, or in any manner controul, the right of conscience in the free exercise of religious worship." (Pennsylvania Constitution of 1776.)

"That, as it is the duty of every man to worship God in such manner as he thinks most acceptable to him, all persons professing the Christian religion are equally entitled to protection in their religious liberty; wherefore no person ought by any law to be molested in his person or estate on account of his religious persuasion or profession, or for his religious practice; unless, under colour of religion, any man shall disturb the good order, peace, or

Evolution from the Charters

safety of the State, or shall infringe the laws of morality, or injure others, in their natural, civil, or religious rights; nor ought any person to be compelled to frequent or maintain, or contribute, unless on contract, to maintain any particular place of worship, or any particular ministry; yet the Legislature may, in their discretion, lay a general and equal tax for the support of the Christian religion; leaving to each individual the power of appointing the payment over of the money, collected from him, to the support of any particular place of worship or minister, or for the benefit of the poor of his own denomination, or the poor in general of any particular county: but the churches, chapels, glebes, and all other property now belonging to the church of England, ought to remain to the church of England forever. And all acts of Assembly, lately passed, for collecting monies for building or repairing particular churches or chapels of ease, shall continue in force and be executed, unless the Legislature shall, by act, supersede or repeal the same: but no county court shall assess any quantity of tobacco, or sum of money, hereafter, on the application of any vestry-men or church-wardens; and every encumbent of the church of England, who hath remained in his parish, and performed his duty, shall be entitled to receive the provision and support established by the act entitled 'An act for the support of the clergy of the church of England, in this Province,' till the November court of this present year, to be held for the county in which his parish shall lie, or partly lie, or for such time as he hath remained in his parish, and performed his duty." (Maryland Declaration of Rights of 1776.)

"That all men have a natural and unalienable right to worship Almighty God according to the dictates of their own consciences. . . . .

"That no person, who shall deny the being of God or the truth of the Protestant religion, or the divine authority either of the Old or New Testaments, or who shall hold religious principles incompatible with the freedom and safety of the State, shall be capable of holding any office or place of trust or profit in the civil department within this State. . . . .

"That there shall be no establishment of any one religious

church or denomination in this State, in preference to any other; neither shall any person, on any pretence whatsoever, be compelled to attend any place of worship contrary to his own faith or judgment, nor be obliged to pay for the purchase of any glebe, or the building of any house of worship, or for the maintenance of any minister or ministry, contrary to what he believes right, or has voluntarily and personally engaged to perform; but all persons shall be at liberty to exercise their own mode of worship:—*Provided*, That nothing herein contained shall be construed to exempt preachers of treasonable or seditious discourses from legal trial and punishment." (North Carolina Constitution of 1776.)

"All persons whatever shall have the free exercise of their religion, provided it be not repugnant to the peace and safety of the State, and shall not, unless by consent, support any teacher or teachers except those of their own profession." (Georgia Constitution of 1777.)

"And whereas we are required, by the benevolent principles of rational liberty, not only to expel civil tyranny, but also to guard against that spiritual oppression and intolerance wherewith the bigotry and ambition of weak and wicked priests and princes have scourged mankind, this convention doth further, in the name and by the authority of the good people of this State, ordain, determine, and declare, that the free exercise and enjoyment of religious profession and worship, without discrimination or preference, shall forever hereafter be allowed, within this State, to all mankind: *Provided*, That the liberty of conscience, hereby granted, shall not be so construed as to excuse acts of licentiousness, or justify practices inconsistent with the peace or safety of this State." (New York Constitution of 1777.)

"That all men have a natural and unalienable right to worship ALMIGHTY GOD, according to the dictates of their own consciences and understanding, regulated by the word of GOD; and that no man ought, or of right can be compelled to attend any religious worship, or erect or support any place of worship, or maintain any minister, contrary to the dictates of his conscience; nor can any man who professes the Protestant religion be justly

Evolution from the Charters

deprived or abridged of any civil right, as a citizen, on account of his religious sentiment, or peculiar mode of religious worship, and that no authority can, or ought to be vested in, or assumed by, any power whatsoever, that shall, in any case, interfere with, or in any manner controul, the rights of conscience, in the free exercise of religious worship: nevertheless, every sect or denomination of people ought to observe the Sabbath, or the Lord's day, and keep up, and support, some sort of religious worship, which to them shall seem most agreeable to the revealed will of GOD." (Vermont Constitution of 1777.)

"No person, unless of the Protestant religion, shall be governor, lieutenant-governor, a member of the senate or of the house of representatives, or hold any judiciary employment within this State. . . . .

"The free exercise and enjoyment of religious profession and worship shall forever be allowed to every denomination of Protestants within this State." (Rejected Constitution of Massachusetts of 1778.)

"That all persons and religious societies who acknowledge that there is one God, and a future state of rewards and punishments, and that God is publicly to be worshipped, shall be freely tolerated. The Christian Protestant religion shall be deemed, and is hereby constituted and declared to be, the established religion of this State. That all denominations of Christian Protestants in this State, demeaning themselves peaceably and faithfully, shall enjoy equally religious and civil privileges.

"No person shall be eligible to a seat in the said senate unless he be of the Protestant religion. No person shall be eligible to sit in the house of representatives unless he be of the Protestant religion." (South Carolina Constitution of 1778.)

"The future legislature of this State shall make no laws to infringe the rights of conscience or any other of the natural, unalienable rights of men, or contrary to the laws of God or against the Protestant religion. . . . .

"All the male inhabitants of the State of lawful age, paying taxes and professing the Protestant religion, shall be deemed legal voters in choosing councillors and representatives." [A property qualification was also added.] (Rejected Constitution of New Hampshire of 1778.)

"It is the right as well as the duty of all men in society, publicly and at stated seasons, to worship the Supreme Being, the great Creator and Preserver of the universe. And no subject shall be hurt, molested, or restrained, in his person, liberty, or estate, for worshipping God in the manner and season most agreeable to the dictates of his own conscience, or for his religious profession or sentiments, provided he doth not disturb the public peace or obstruct others in their religious worship. . . .

"Therefore, to promote their happiness and to secure the good order and preservation of their government, the people of this commonwealth have a right to invest their legislature with power to authorize and require, and the legislature shall, from time to time, authorize and require the several towns, parishes, precincts, and other bodies-politic or religious societies to make suitable provision, at their own expense, for the institution of the public worship of God and for the support and maintenance of public Protestant teachers of piety, religion, and morality in all cases where such provision shall not be made voluntarily. . . .

"And the people of this commonwealth have also a right to, and do, invest their legislature with authority to enjoin upon all the subjects an attendance upon the instructions of the public teachers aforesaid, at stated times and seasons, if there be any on whose instructions they can conscientiously and conveniently attend." (Massachusetts Constitution of 1780.)

"Every individual has a natural and unalienable right to worship GOD according to the dictates of his own conscience and reason; and no subject shall be hurt, molested, or restrained in his person, liberty or estate for worshipping GOD, in the manner and season most agreeable to the dictates of his own conscience, or for his religious profession, sentiments or persuasion; provided he doth not disturb the public peace, or disturb others, in their religious worship.

"As morality and piety, rightly grounded on evangelical principles, will give the best and greatest security to government, and will lay in the hearts of men the strongest obligations to due sub-

Evolution from the Charters

jection; and as the knowledge of these is most likely to be propagated through a society by the institution of the public worship of the DEITY, and of public instruction in morality and religion; therefore, to promote those important purposes, the people of this state have a right to impower, and do hereby fully impower the legislature to authorize from time to time, the several towns, parishes, bodies-corporate, or religious societies within this state, to make adequate provision at their own expence, for the support and maintenance of public Protestant teachers of piety, religion and morality. . . . .

"That no person shall be capable of being elected a senator who is not of the Protestant religion." (New Hampshire Constitution of 1784.)

The Vermont constitution of 1786 repeats the provision given above from the Pennsylvania constitution of 1776.

"The legislature of the United States shall pass no law on the subject of religion." (Pinckney's Plan, 1787.)

"No religious test shall ever be required as a qualification to any office or public trust under the United States." (The Constitution.)

"Congress shall make no law respecting an establishment of religion or prohibiting the free exercise thereof." (First Amendment to the Constitution.)

27. SEIZURES AND SEARCHES.

"That general warrants, whereby an officer or messenger may be commanded to search suspected places without evidence of a fact committed, or to seize any person or persons not named, or whose offence is not particularly described and supported by evidence, are grievous and oppressive, and ought not to be granted." (Virginia Bill of Rights of 1776.)

"That the people have a right to hold themselves, their houses, papers, and possessions free from search or seizure, and therefore warrants without oaths or affirmations first made, affording a sufficient foundation for them, and whereby any officer or messenger may be commanded or required to search suspected places, or to

Evolution of the Constitution

seize any person or persons, his or their property, not particularly described, are contrary to that right, and ought not to be granted." (Pennsylvania Constitution of 1776.)

"That all warrants, without oath or affirmation, to search suspected places, or to seize any person or property, are grievous and oppressive; and all general warrants—to search suspected places, or to apprehend suspected persons, without naming or describing the place, or the person in special—are illegal, and ought not to be granted." (Maryland Declaration of Rights of 1776.)

"That general warrants—whereby an officer or messenger may be commanded to search suspected places, without evidence of the fact committed, or to seize any person or persons, not named, whose offences are not particularly described, and supported by evidence—are dangerous to liberty, and ought not to be granted." (North Carolina Declaration of Rights of 1776.)

The Vermont constitution of 1777 repeats the provision given above from the Pennsylvania constitution of 1776.

"Every subject has a right to be secure from all unreasonable searches and seizures of his person, his houses, his papers, and all his possessions. All warrants, therefore, are contrary to this right, if the cause or foundation of them be not previously supported by oath or affirmation, and if the order in the warrant to a civil officer, to make search in suspected places, or to arrest one or more suspected persons, or to seize their property, be not accompanied with a special designation of the persons or objects of search, arrest, or seizure; and no warrant ought to be issued but in cases, and with the formalities, prescribed by the laws." (Massachusetts Constitution of 1780.)

The above provision from the Massachusetts constitution of 1780 is repeated in the New Hampshire constitution of 1784.

The Vermont constitution of 1786 repeats the provision given above from the Pennsylvania constitution of 1776.

"The right of the people to be secure in their persons, houses, papers, and effects against unreasonable searches and seizures shall not be violated, and no warrants shall issue but upon probable cause, supported by oath or affirmation and particularly

Evolution from the Charters

describing the place to be searched and the persons or things to be seized." (Fourth Amendment to the Constitution.)

28. Trial by Jury.

"That no proprietor, freeholder, or inhabitant of the said province of West New Jersey shall be deprived or condemned of life, limb, liberty, estate, property, or any ways hurt in his or their privileges, freedoms, or franchises, upon any account whatsoever, without a due trial and judgment passed by twelve good and lawful men of his neighborhood first had; and that in all causes to be tried and in all trials the person or persons arraigned may except against any of the said neighborhood, without any reason rendered (not exceeding thirty-five), and, in case of any valid reason alleged, against every person nominated for that service. . . .

"That the trials of all causes, civil and criminal, shall be heard and decided by the verdict or judgment of twelve honest men of the neighborhood, only to be summoned and presented by the sheriff of that division or propriety where the fact or trespass is committed." (Concessions of West Jersey of 1677.)

"That all trials shall be by twelve men, and, as near as may be, peers or equals, and of the neighborhood, and men without just exception; in cases of life, there shall be first twenty-four returned by the sheriffs, for a grand inquest, of whom twelve, at least, shall find the complaint to be true; and then the twelve men, or peers, to be likewise returned by the sheriff, shall have the final judgment. But reasonable challenges shall be always admitted against the said twelve men, or any of them." (Pennsylvania Laws Agreed upon in England, 1682.)

"That in all capital or criminal prosecutions a man hath a right to a speedy trial by an impartial jury of twelve men of his vicinage, without whose unanimous consent he cannot be found guilty. . . .

"That in controversies respecting property, and in suits between man and man, the ancient trial by jury is preferable to any other, and ought to be held sacred." (Virginia Bill of Rights of 1776.)

"That the inestimable right of trial by jury shall remain con-

Evolution of the Constitution

firmed as a part of the law of this colony without repeal forever." (New Jersey Constitution of 1776.)

"That in all prosecutions for criminal offences a man hath a right to a speedy public trial by an impartial jury of the country, without the unanimous consent of which jury he cannot be found guilty." (Pennsylvania Constitution of 1776.)

"That in all criminal prosecutions every man hath a right to a speedy trial by an impartial jury, without whose unanimous consent he ought not to be found guilty." (Maryland Declaration of Rights of 1776.)

"That no freeman shall be convicted of any crime, but by the unanimous verdict of a jury of good and lawful men, in open court, as heretofore used. . . . .

"That in all controversies at law, respecting property, the ancient mode of trial, by jury, is one of the best securities of the rights of the people, and ought to remain sacred and inviolable." (North Carolina Declaration of Rights of 1776.)

"Trial by jury to remain inviolate forever." (Georgia Constitution of 1777.)

"Trial by jury in all cases in which it hath heretofore been used in the colony of New York shall be established and remain inviolate forever." (New York Constitution of 1777.)

The Vermont constitution of 1777 repeats the provision given above from the Pennsylvania constitution of 1776.

"And the inestimable right of trial by jury shall remain confirmed as part of this constitution forever." (Rejected Constitution of Massachusetts of 1778.)

"The right of trial by jury in all cases as heretofore used in this State shall be preserved inviolate forever." (Rejected Constitution of New Hampshire of 1778.)

"In all controversies concerning property, and in all suits between two or more persons, except in cases in which it has heretofore been otherways used and practised, the parties have a right to a trial by jury; and this method of procedure shall be held sacred, unless, in causes arising on the high seas, and such as relate to mariners' wages, the legislature shall hereafter find it necessary to alter it." (Massachusetts Constitution of 1780.)

Evolution from the Charters

The above provision from the Massachusetts constitution of 1780 is repeated in the New Hampshire constitution of 1784.

"In all criminal prosecutions the accused shall enjoy the right to a speedy and public trial by an impartial jury of the State and district wherein the crime shall have been committed, which district shall have been previously ascertained by law, and to be informed of the nature and cause of the accusation; to be confronted with the witnesses against him; to have compulsory process for obtaining witnesses in his favor, and to have the assistance of counsel for his defence." (Sixth Amendment to the Constitution.)

"In suits at common law, where the value in controversy shall exceed twenty dollars, the right of trial by jury shall be preserved, and no fact tried by a jury shall be otherwise re-examined in any court of the United States than according to the rules of the common law." (Seventh Amendment to the Constitution.)

29. Prisoners to have Counsel and Witnesses.

"That all criminals shall have the same privileges of witnesses and council as their prosecutors." (Pennsylvania Charter of Privileges of 1701.)

"That in all capital or criminal prosecutions a man hath a right to demand the cause and nature of his accusation, to be confronted with the accusers and witnesses, to call for evidence in his favor; nor can he be compelled to give evidence against himself." (Virginia Bill of Rights of 1776.)

"That in all prosecutions for criminal offences, a man hath a right to be heard by himself and his council, to demand the cause and nature of his accusation, to be confronted with the witnesses, to call for evidence in his favor; nor can he be compelled to give evidence against himself." (Pennsylvania Constitution of 1776.)

"That, in all criminal prosecutions, every man hath a right to be informed of the accusation against him; to have a copy of the indictment or charge in due time (if required) to prepare for his defence; to be allowed counsel; to be confronted with the witnesses against him; to have process for his witnesses; to ex-

Evolution of the Constitution

amine the witnesses, for and against him, on oath." (Maryland Declaration of Rights of 1776.)

"That, in all criminal prosecutions, every man has a right to be informed of the accusation against him, and to confront the accusers and witnesses with other testimony, and shall not be compelled to give evidence against himself." (North Carolina Declaration of Rights of 1776.)

"*And it is further ordained*, That in every trial on impeachment, or indictment for crimes or misdemeanors, the party impeached or indicted shall be allowed counsel, as in civil actions." (New York Constitution of 1777.)

The Vermont constitution of 1777 repeats the provision given above from the Pennsylvania constitution of 1776.

"And on every trial, as well on impeachments as others, the party accused shall be allowed counsel." (South Carolina Constitution of 1778.)

"No subject shall be held to answer for any crime or offence until the same is fully and plainly, substantially and formally, described to him; or be compelled to accuse, or furnish evidence against himself; and every subject shall have a right to produce all proofs that may be favorable to him; to meet the witnesses against him face to face, and to be fully heard in his defence by himself, or his counsel at his election." (Massachusetts Constitution of 1780.)

The above provision from the Massachusetts constitution of 1780 is repeated in the New Hampshire constitution of 1784.

The Vermont constitution of 1786 repeats the provision given above from the Pennsylvania constitution of 1776.

"Nor shall [any person] be compelled in any criminal case to be a witness against himself." (Fifth Amendment to the Constitution.)

"In all criminal prosecutions the accused shall enjoy the right to be informed of the nature and cause of the accusation; to be confronted with the witnesses against him; to have compulsory process for obtaining witnesses in his favor, and to have the assistance of counsel for his defence." (Sixth Amendment to the Constitution.)

Evolution from the Charters

30. Excessive Bail and Fines and Cruel Punishments.

"That all fines shall be moderate." (Pennsylvania Laws Agreed upon in England, 1682.)

"That excessive bail ought not to be required, nor excessive fines imposed, nor cruel and unusual punishments inflicted." (Virginia Bill of Rights of 1776.)

"Excessive bail shall not be exacted for bailable offences, and all fines shall be moderate." (Pennsylvania Constitution of 1776.)

"That sanguinary laws ought to be avoided, as far as is consistent with the safety of the State: and no law, to inflict cruel and unusual pains and penalties, ought to be made in any case, or at any time hereafter. . . .

"That excessive bail ought not to be required, nor excessive fines imposed, nor cruel or unusual punishments inflicted, by the courts of law." (Maryland Declaration of Rights of 1776.)

"That excessive bail should not be required, nor excessive fines imposed, nor cruel or unusual punishments inflicted." (North Carolina Constitution of 1776.)

"Excessive fines shall not be levied, nor excessive bail demanded." (Georgia Constitution of 1777.)

The Vermont constitution of 1777 repeats the provision given above from the Pennsylvania constitution of 1776.

"No magistrate or court of law shall demand excessive bail or sureties, impose excessive fines, or inflict cruel or unusual punishments." (Massachusetts Constitution of 1780.)

The above provision from the Massachusetts constitution of 1780 is repeated in the New Hampshire constitution of 1784.

"Excessive bail shall not be required, nor excessive fines imposed, nor cruel and unusual punishments inflicted." (Eighth Amendment to the Constitution.)

31. Twice in Jeopardy.

"No subject* shall be liable to be tried after an acquittal for

---

*The use of the word subject instead of citizen three years after the battle of Yorktown and eight years after the Declaration of Independence

the same crime or offence." (New Hampshire Constitution of 1784.)

"Nor shall any person be subject for the same offence to be twice put in jeopardy of life or limb." (Fifth Amendment to the Constitution.)

32. Freedom of the Press.

"That the freedom of the press is one of the great bulwarks of liberty, and can never be restrained but by despotic governments." (Virginia Bill of Rights of 1776.)

"That the people have a right to freedom of speech, and of writing, and publishing their sentiments; therefore the freedom of the press ought not to be restrained." (Pennsylvania Constitution of 1776.)

"That the liberty of the press ought to be inviolably preserved." (Maryland Declaration of Rights of 1776.)

"That the freedom of the press is one of the great bulwarks of liberty, and therefore ought never to be restrained." (North Carolina Declaration of Rights of 1776.)

"Freedom of the press to remain inviolate forever." (Georgia Constitution of 1777.)

The Vermont constitution of 1777 repeats the provision given above from the Pennsylvania constitution of 1776.

"That the liberty of the press be inviolably preserved." (South Carolina Constitution of 1778.)

"The liberty of the press is essential to the security of freedom in a State; it ought not, therefore, to be restrained in this commonwealth." (Massachusetts Constitution of 1780.)

"The liberty of the press is essential to the security of freedom in a State; it ought, therefore, to be inviolably preserved." (New Hampshire Constitution of 1784.)

The Vermont constitution of 1786 repeats substantially the

---

seems curious nowadays. But the word was used for a long time after the Revolution to describe the people of a republic as well as those who lived under a monarchy. They were all alike considered as subject to the government and laws.

Evolution from the Charters

provision given above from the Pennsylvania constitution of 1776.

"The legislature of the United States shall pass no law touching or abridging the liberty of the press." (Pinckney's Plan of 1787.)

"Congress shall make no law abridging the freedom of speech or of the press." (First Amendment to the Constitution.)

33. RIGHT TO PETITION.

"That it shall be lawful for any person or persons during the session of any general free assembly in that province to address, remonstrate or declare any suffering, danger or grievance, or to propose, tender or request any privilege, profit or advantage to the said province, they not exceeding the number of one hundred persons." (Concessions of West Jersey of 1677.)

"That the people have a right to assemble together, to consult for their common good, to instruct their representatives, and to apply to the legislature for redress of grievances, by address, petition, or remonstrance." (Pennsylvania Constitution of 1776.)

"That every man hath a right to petition the Legislature, for the redress of grievances, in a peaceable and orderly manner." (Maryland Declaration of Rights of 1776.)

"That the people have a right to assemble together, to consult for their common good, to instruct their Representatives, and to apply to the Legislature, for redress of grievances." (North Carolina Declaration of Rights of 1776.)

The Vermont constitution of 1777 repeats the provision given above from the Pennsylvania constitution of 1776.

"The people have a right, in an orderly and peaceable manner, to assemble to consult upon the common good; give instructions to their representatives, and to request of the legislative body, by the way of addresses, petitions, or remonstrances, redress of the wrongs done them, and of the grievances they suffer." (Massachusetts Constitution of 1780.)

The above provision from the Massachusetts constitution of 1780 is repeated in the New Hampshire constitution of 1784.

Evolution of the Constitution

The Vermont constitution of 1786 repeats the provision given above from the Pennsylvania constitution of 1776.

"Congress shall make no law abridging the right of the people peaceably to assemble, and to petition the government for a redress of grievances." (First Amendment to the Constitution.)

34. Right to Bear Arms.

"That the people have a right to bear arms for the defence of themselves and the State." (Pennsylvania Constitution of 1776.)

"That the people have a right to bear arms for the defence of the State." (North Carolina Declaration of Rights of 1776.)

The Vermont constitution of 1777 repeats the provision given above from the Pennsylvania constitution of 1776.

"The people have a right to keep and bear arms for the common defence." (Massachusetts Constitution of 1780.)

The Vermont constitution of 1786 repeats the provision given above from the Pennsylvania constitution of 1776.

"A well-regulated militia being necessary to the security of a free state, the right of the people to keep and bear arms shall not be infringed." (Second Amendment to the Constitution.)

35. Militia Necessary; Military Subordinate.

"That a well-regulated militia, composed of the body of the people, trained to arms, is the proper, natural, and safe defence of a free state; that standing armies, in time of peace, should be avoided, as dangerous to liberty; and that in all cases the military should be under strict subordination to, and governed by, the civil power." (Virginia Bill of Rights of 1776.)

"As standing armies in the time of peace are dangerous to liberty, they ought not to be kept up; And that the military should be kept under strict subordination to, and governed by, the civil power." (Pennsylvania Constitution of 1776.)

"That a well-regulated militia is the proper and natural defence of a free government.

"That standing armies are dangerous to liberty, and ought not to be raised or kept up, without consent of the Legislature.

Evolution from the Charters

"That in all cases, and at all times, the military ought to be under strict subordination to and control of the civil power." (Maryland Declaration of Rights of 1776.)

"As standing armies in time of peace are dangerous to liberty, they ought not to be kept up; and that the military should be kept under strict subordination to, and governed by, the civil power." (North Carolina Declaration of Rights of 1776.)

The Vermont constitution of 1777 repeats the provision given above from the Pennsylvania constitution of 1776.

"That the military be subordinate to the civil power of the State." (South Carolina Constitution of 1778.)

"And as in time of peace armies are dangerous to liberty, they ought not to be maintained without the consent of the legislature; and the military power shall always be held in an exact subordination to the civil authority and be governed by it." (Massachusetts Constitution of 1780.)

"A well-regulated militia is the proper, natural, and sure defence of a state.

"Standing armies are dangerous to liberty, and ought not to be raised or kept up without the consent of the legislature.

"In all cases, and at all times, the military ought to be under strict subordination to, and governed by, the civil power." (New Hampshire Constitution of 1784.)

The Vermont constitution of 1786 repeats the provision given above from the Pennsylvania constitution of 1776.

"A well-regulated militia being necessary to the security of a free state, the right of the people to keep and bear arms shall not be infringed." (Second Amendment to the Constitution.)

36. Quartering Soldiers in Time of Peace.

"That no soldier ought to be quartered in any house, in time of peace, without the consent of the owner; and in time of war, in such manner only, as the Legislature shall direct." (Maryland Declaration of Rights of 1776.)

"In time of peace, no soldier ought to be quartered in any house without the consent of the owner; and in time of war, such quarters ought not to be made but by the civil magistrate, in a

Evolution of the Constitution

manner ordained by the legislature." (Massachusetts Constitution of 1780.)

The above provision from the Massachusetts constitution of 1780 is substantially repeated in the New Hampshire constitution of 1784.

"No soldier shall, in time of peace, be quartered in any house without the consent of the owner; nor in time of war but in a manner to be prescribed by law." (Third Amendment to the Constitution.)

37. Attainder of Treason.

"That no law, to attaint particular persons of treason or felony, ought to be made in any case, or at any time hereafter." (Maryland Declaration of Rights of 1776.)

"And that no acts of attainder shall be passed by the legislature of this State for crimes, other than those committed before the termination of the present war; and that such acts shall not work a corruption of blood." (New York Constitution of 1776.)

"No bill of attainder shall be passed [by Congress].

"No State shall pass any bill of attainder." (The Constitution.)

38. Ex Post Facto Laws.

"That retrospective laws, punishing facts committed before the existence of such laws, and by them only declared criminal, are oppressive, unjust, and incompatible with liberty; wherefore no *ex post facto* law ought to be made." (Maryland Declaration of Rights of 1776.)

"That retrospective laws, punishing facts committed before the existence of such laws, and by them only declared criminal, are oppressive, unjust, and incompatible with liberty; wherefore no *ex post facto* law ought to be made." (North Carolina Declaration of Rights of 1776.)

"Laws made to punish for actions done before the existence of such laws, and which have not been declared crimes by preceding laws, are unjust, oppressive, and inconsistent with the fundamental principles of a free government." (Massachusetts Constitution of 1780.)

Evolution from the Charters

"Retrospective laws are highly injurious, oppressive, and unjust. No such laws, therefore, should be made, either for the decision of civil causes or the punishment of offences." (New Hampshire Constitution of 1784.)

"No *ex post facto* law shall be passed [by Congress]."

"No state shall pass any *ex post facto* law." (The Constitution.)

39. TITLES OF NOBILITY, OFFICES OF PROFIT, AND PRESENTS.

"That no title of nobility or hereditary honors ought to be granted in this State, nor ought any person, in public trust, to receive any present from any foreign prince or state, or from the United States, or any of them, without the approbation of this State." (Maryland Declaration of Rights of 1776.)

"That no hereditary emoluments, privileges, or honors ought to be granted or conferred in this State." (North Carolina Declaration of Rights of 1776.)

"Nor shall any person holding any office of profit or trust under the United States accept of any present, emolument, office, or title of any kind whatever from any king, prince, or foreign state; nor shall the United States in Congress assembled grant any title of nobility." (Articles of Confederation of 1778.)

"Nor shall any person, holding any office under the United States, accept of any present, emolument, office, or title from any king or foreign state, without being thereby absolutely rendered forever incapable of any public trust under the United States." (Drayton's Articles of Confederation of 1778.)

"The United States shall not grant any title of nobility." (Pinckney's Plan, 1787.)

"No title of nobility shall be granted by the United States, and no person holding any office of profit or trust under them shall, without the consent of the congress, accept of any present, emolument, office, or title of any kind whatever from any king, prince, or foreign state.

"No state shall grant any title of nobility." (The Constitution.)

Evolution of the Constitution

40. MARTIAL LAW AND HABEAS CORPUS.

The exercise of martial law and the suspension of the privilege of the writ of *habeas corpus* are somewhat alike, because both interrupt the process of civil government and destroy for a time the liberty of the citizen.

Martial law is the right which a military commander assumes to suspend civil rights and the remedies founded on them when he thinks himself justified by the necessities of the situation. If he makes a mistake in judgment, and it is afterwards decided that the necessities of the time did not justify him, his acts are all unwarranted and void. This has been the law from time immemorial. But the framers of the colonial charters seem to have thought that the power to exercise martial law should be expressly given in their documents, probably for the reason that its use might often be very necessary in a wild country, and no question should be allowed to arise as to the right.

They usually confined its use to cases of actual war, invasion, or rebellion. The constitutions of 1776, however, omitted any mention of it, except the Massachusetts constitution of 1780 and the New Hampshire constitution of 1784. In fact, it is not usually found in modern constitutions at all, because there is no need of it. It is in any event a mere question of necessity in the desperate straits of an invasion or a rebellion, and the time and the occasion are the only tests by which the right to use it can be decided. The conditions which may have justified such a right as a part of the colonial charters have long since disappeared.

But the Massachusetts constitution of 1780 and the

Evolution from the Charters

New Hampshire constitution of 1784, which mentioned it for the last time, introduced a new power,—namely, the right to suspend the privilege of the writ of *habeas corpus;* and it was confined, as martial law had been confined, to the most urgent occasions.

We find a similar clause in the National Constitution, with the suspension limited to "cases of rebellion or invasion," when "the public safety may require it." But, unfortunately, the framers of the Constitution failed to say which department of the government should have the power to suspend; and it became a serious question in the civil war whether the President or Congress had the power. In the Massachusetts constitution of 1780 it had been given expressly to the legislature.

The governor allowed to exercise martial law in rebellion or mutiny. (Virginia Charter of 1609.)

Lord Baltimore allowed to exercise martial law in rebellion or mutiny. (Maryland Charter of 1632.)

The above provision from the Maryland charter of 1632 is substantially repeated in the Grant of Maine of 1639.

The governor allowed to exercise martial law only as occasion shall require. (Connecticut Charter of 1662.)

The governor allowed to exercise martial law only as occasion shall require. (Rhode Island Charter of 1663.)

The Carolina charters of 1663 and 1665 copy the provision given above from the Maryland charter of 1632.

The governor allowed to exercise martial law in time of actual war or rebellion as occasion shall necessarily require, but cannot grant commissions for exercising it except by consent of his council. (Massachusetts Charter of 1691.)

The corporation allowed to exercise martial law in time of actual war or rebellion where by law it may be used. (Georgia Charter of 1732.)

The governor to exercise martial law over the army and navy

in war and invasion, and in rebellion declared by the legislature to exist, as occasion shall necessarily require ; and the privilege of *habeas corpus* not to be suspended by the legislature except upon the most urgent occasions, and then for a time not exceeding twelve months. (Massachusetts Constitution of 1780.)

The above provisions from the Massachusetts constitution of 1780, relating to both martial law and *habeas corpus*, are repeated in the New Hampshire constitution of 1784, except that the time during which the writ of *habeas corpus* may be suspended is limited to three months.

The privilege of *habeas corpus* to be suspended only in rebellion or invasion. (Pinckney's Plan, 1787.)

The privilege of *habeas corpus* to be suspended only in rebellion or invasion, when the public safety may require it. (The Constitution.)

41. Eminent Domain.

"That private property ought to be subservient to public uses, when necessity requires it ; nevertheless, whenever any particular man's property is taken for the use of the public, the owner ought to receive an equivalent in money." (Vermont Constitution of 1777.)

"And whenever the public exigencies require that the property of an individual should be appropriated to public uses, he shall receive a reasonable compensation therefor." (Massachusetts Constitution of 1780.)

"That private property ought to be subservient to public uses, when necessity requires it ; nevertheless, whenever any particular man's property is taken for the use of the public, the owner ought to receive an equivalent in money." (Vermont Constitution of 1786.)

"Nor shall private property be taken for public use without just compensation." (Fifth Amendment to the Constitution.)

CHAPTER VI.

THE EVOLUTION OF FEDERALISM.

(1643 to 1787.)

WHEN we examine our present National Constitution, it is easy to see that it consists of two classes of provisions. One class is concerned with the forms and departments of administration,—the house of representatives, the senate, the president, the judiciary, and their relations to one another; and these provisions, as we have shown, were gradually evolved by two hundred years' experience with the local governments under the colonial charters and constitutions and under the constitutions of 1776.

The other class of provisions is concerned with the relations of the states to the general government, and limits the powers of the general government and restricts also the powers of the states. This federalism, as it is called, we have not yet touched upon, because there was nothing relating to it in the colonial charters or in the constitutions of 1776. It belongs to another line of development.

There were thus two lines of development. One started in the forms of the old charters for governing each individual colony, and grew through subsequent charters, constitutions, and the constitutions of 1776, producing, as we have shown, the administrative pro-

Evolution of the Constitution

visions of the National Constitution. The other line started in plans of union for defence against the Indians, and passed through a totally different set of documents, until it produced the Articles of Confederation and the federalism of the Constitution.

The development of federalism went through similar stages, and took almost as long in its processes as the development of the administrative parts of the Constitution. We usually think of it as starting about the time of the Revolution, or at least receiving its greatest impetus at that time. But it had been an important and a much-debated question for more than a hundred years before 1776, and more than twenty plans of union had been suggested and discussed. In fact, during the seventeenth and eighteenth centuries the union or confederation of the colonies was one of the great questions of the English-speaking world.*

If it had not been a great problem, and if it had not been so long and so much discussed, there would be no American federalism to-day. Such a remarkable and successful contrivance could not have been made in a year or in a decade ; could not have been the result of one war or revolution. Neither imitation of other countries nor sudden inspiration or ingenuity accounts for great political institutions ; but natural conditions, many minds, many ages, and great searchings of heart.

The material which shows the attention given to this question in colonial times and the experiments that were

---

* It is interesting to note that England is again discussing the confederation of her colonies.

Evolution of Federalism

made in it has been collected in an admirable manner by Mr. Frederick D. Stone, librarian of the Historical Society of Pennsylvania, and published as an appendix to the second volume of Carson's "One Hundredth Anniversary of the Constitution." But it is hardly as yet much known to constitutional lawyers and scholars, and certainly not so well known as it deserves.

Before we go farther in the analysis of this material it may be well to say that the progression of the subject is union, confederation, federalism. By union is meant a mere alliance of sovereignties to accomplish a certain purpose. This purpose accomplished, the union may cease, or may be continued, at the option of the contracting parties, to accomplish some other purpose. Confederation implies a stronger bond. The union is intended to be perpetual,—at any rate, it is avowedly to be perpetual,—and the sovereignties surrender some of their local rights to the union and create a general council or some form of general power to conduct what is for the general interest. But it is a consolidation of sovereignties, and not a government of the people. The general government deals with the individual states, and not directly with the people.

Federalism goes farther. More power is surrendered to the general government, which, instead of being the creature of the sovereignties, is the creature of the mass of the people that compose the sovereignties. The general government, instead of acting through the individual states, asking them for everything and relying on them to enforce its commands, now acts directly on the people and has the power to enforce its commands upon the people. The states retain their local rights and are supposed to be indestructible entities, and the union and the general government are supposed to be indestructible. By this is meant that the fusion has gone so far that, although the original elements can still be appreciated as distinct bodies, they could not be separated or resolved into their original independence without great violence,—that is, war and revolution.

What may be the development beyond federalism remains to be seen. But it presumably will be a more and more complete fusion, approaching homogeneity, and a stronger nationality, until it will be utterly impossible, by violence or any other known means, to restore the original elements.

The numerous plans of union in colonial times show the early phases of this development, and the first one of which we have any record is the confederation of the New England colonies in 1643 to protect themselves from the Indians or any hostile invasion.

The articles of this union are very particular to state that each colony retains its own local rights and jurisdiction unimpaired. The costs of any war are to be divided among the colonies in proportion to the population of each; but they are to be "left to their owne just course and custome of rating themselves." Thus the independence of each party to the union is amply secured, and the only step towards federalism is that the provinces surrender a small amount of their individual rights by agreeing not to make war without permission of the union unless suddenly invaded, and by agreeing that no two of them shall join in one jurisdiction without the consent of the others. But the local rights of each province are so strongly guaranteed that the union is still very far from federalism. This was natural; for the first and most essential element in federalism is a rigorous and distinct appreciation of local sovereignty. This is the foundation; for, as federalism is an indestructible union of indestructible states, the states must begin by feeling themselves indestructible.

Besides the emphasis it gives to local rights, the New England union of 1643 shows the beginnings of certain general provisions which can be traced afterwards until they appear in the National Constitution of 1787. This union of 1643 was quite early in the colonial period. The first of the colonies, Virginia, had been founded only a little more than thirty years, and Massachusetts was not yet twenty years old. But the situation of the colonies had already made the importance of their union very obvious. People naturally talked about it, and for the next hundred years and more we find most of the prominent people preparing plans.

Besides its very evident advantage for defence and war, a union might obviate certain inconveniences which were felt then as strongly as they would be now if we had no union. The colonists were of the same nation, spoke the same language, were living in the same zone of climate, soil, and products; and yet they were separated into distinct communities, governed by different laws, often with very strong religious differences, and with no boundaries between their jurisdictions but artificial lines, or natural ones which were very easily passed.

One of the first questions that arose among them was,

Evolution of the Constitution

How is a citizen of one colony to be treated when he goes to visit or trade in a neighboring colony, where the people do not like his opinions or where the laws of trade differ from those of his home? Shall there be certificates or passports? Suppose one colony treats the Indians in one manner, and another colony in another manner, and a third colony in a third manner, will not there be endless misunderstandings and wars, and will it not be impossible to stop the wars? Suppose a servant escapes from his master and takes refuge in another colony, can the master get him back? Will not persons accused of crime in one colony simply remove into another?

All these questions were very real and practical in colonial times, and in some respects more so than we might at first suppose. It was no light matter for a Massachusetts man in the year 1650 to go down into Rhode Island; and it was a very serious matter for a Rhode Island person to go up into Massachusetts. A Quaker woman who went from Rhode Island to Massachusetts was hanged for her temerity, and several Baptists were severely handled. In Pennsylvania, in Governor Keith's time, the people were aroused to great indignation because a Delaware sheriff had pursued a hue-and-cry after a thief across the boundary; and the matter had to be accommodated by allowing each province to pursue hue-and-cry for a certain distance across the line.

The differences between the people of the colonies were very marked; and even as late as the time of the Revolution the delegates to the Continental Congress are said to have looked upon one another at first as strangers and aliens. In the year 1643 it would have been almost impossible to join all the colonies in a union. In New England, Rhode Island was so much disliked by the other provinces that it was not included in the union we are now considering.

Massachusetts, New Plymouth, Connecticut, and New Haven were, however, sufficiently agreed among themselves, and in the union they formed each was to appoint two commissioners, and the eight thus chosen were to be the governing body of the union. If Dutch ideas were as prevalent in New England as Mr. Campbell supposes, these commissioners would have voted by colonies, after the manner of the States-General of the Netherlands. But there was no such arrangement. Six of the commissioners could decide all questions; and if six could not agree, the question was to be passed upon by each of the assemblies of the four colonies, and, if they all agreed, the decision was to be carried out. It was a simple, ordinary arrangement for a union, and was very much like other leagues of nations the world over. It described itself as a "league of friendship and amytie, offence and defence."

The problems of return of servants and fugitives from justice and intercourse between citizens of the different colonies were attempted to be solved in very much the same way as they are now solved in the National Constitution. Runaway servants and fugitives from justice were to be returned, and arrangements were to be made to give the citizens of each colony equal rights in the other colonies.

Evolution of the Constitution

But the colonists were not the only persons who saw and discussed the convenience of union. The Crown and the Privy Council saw it, although from a somewhat different point of view. Charles II., immediately after his restoration in 1660, created a council for foreign plantations, which was to correspond with the governors and devise means for bringing the colonies into a more uniform government.

Between twenty-five and thirty years later James II. attempted to go much further,—to vacate all the colonial charters and unite all the colonies from the Delaware to the St. Lawrence under one government composed of a legislative council appointed by the king and a captain-general as governor. He had gone so far as to appoint Sir Edmund Andros to be the captain-general, when he was dethroned by William III., who took no interest in his plan of union.

The council for foreign plantations which Charles II. had established was abolished in 1674, and ever after that the affairs of the colonies were in the hands of the Privy Council, who managed them through a committee known as The Lords of Trade and Plantations. This committee and the Privy Council governed the colonies. They informed themselves on all colonial affairs and recommended measures to the king. They did not properly constitute a union of the colonies, but they often proposed plans of union, usually from the point of view of military convenience to resist the French and obtain supplies and tribute from the colonies more easily. Their plans were seldom in the direction of liberty, and are not so interesting as those of the colonists themselves.

Evolution of Federalism

After the New England union of 1643 similar attempts appear in the next sixty years among other colonies to join in unions of some form or other, usually for treaties or war with the Indians. Some of them were more or less successful in accomplishing their object, but they furnish us with no elaborate provisions like those of the New England union. They were, in fact, temporary unions, and even the New England union, though intended to be perpetual, became obsolete within twenty-five years, and had accomplished little or nothing.

An attempt at union after the massacre at Schenectady in 1690 is noteworthy as including the New England colonies, New York, Virginia, and Maryland,—the nearest approach to a union of all the colonies that had as yet been tried,—but only delegates from Massachusetts, Plymouth, Connecticut, and New York attended. Although nothing remarkable was accomplished by any of these ventures, there is evidence of considerable discussion of the subject and desire and demand for union from all quarters,—from the colonists as well as from the Privy Council in England.

In 1696-97 we have a definite plan drawn up in writing by William Penn and submitted to the Lords of Trade and Plantations. It was brought about by one of those natural conditions and inconveniences which, as we have shown, were steadily driving the people towards union and federalism. Penn at that time was not only proprietor of Pennsylvania, but also one of the proprietors of East Jersey. Finding that New York was collecting customs on goods sent to the Jerseys, and that there was much difficulty in determining the quota of troops from East Jersey for the defence of New York, he proposed that such matters should be settled by a union or general government of some sort. In other words, he was striving for the settlement of two questions which are now settled by the National Constitution.

This plan of Penn's is the first which included all the colonies. The others had been sectional, although showing a tendency to increase the number of the sections.

Penn started with the same arrangement that had been adopted in the New England union of 1643, and provided for two deputies to be appointed by each colony. The twenty deputies thus appointed were to be called the congress, which is apparently the first use of that word for an American assembly; and it is rather remarkable that this congress of Penn's should be not only the first suggestion of a representative legislature for all the colonies, but should have the same name that was afterwards given in the Revolution and that is still retained.

The New England union had been merely a legislative body without any executive head. But Penn's congress was to be presided over by a commissioner appointed by the king, and, as New York would be the most central place for the congress to meet in, the New York governor should "be the king's high commissioner during the session, after the manner of Scotland."

This passage is worth observing for the phrase "after the manner of Scotland," because so much has been recently written about the Dutch origin of our institutions, and it has been particularly urged by Mr. Campbell that Penn's having had a Dutch mother and having travelled extensively in Holland gave a tinge of Dutch

Evolution of Federalism

ideas to the laws and constitutions which he established in America. But here we find him confessing that he is guided in one particular by a Scotch model, and it is not an unfair inference that if he admits an imitation in this instance he would probably admit it in others. In none of his laws or constitutions, however, can a single word be found implying a Dutch origin.

After providing for an executive, Penn's plan goes on to deal with those inconveniences of intercourse between the colonies which we found the New England union attempting to mitigate. The New England union was to preserve peace among the different colonies, carry on war against the Indians, arrange the quotas of men each colony was to furnish for war, arrange for the rights of citizens of one colony visiting another colony, adopt a general policy of dealing with the Indians, and provide for the return of servants and persons accused of crime escaping into another colony. Penn added to these subjects of general government the return of absconding debtors and the regulation of commerce.

The regulation of commerce is a most interesting addition and development. As commerce increased in the course of years its regulation became of more and more importance, and in the end the necessity for this regulation was one of the most important causes of federalism. In fact, the convention which framed the National Constitution in 1787 was originally called merely for the purpose of regulating the commerce between the States that bordered on Chesapeake Bay; and no more important clause was placed in the national document than that which gives Congress power to " regulate commerce with foreign nations and among the several states, and with the Indian tribes."

The last clause of Penn's plan provided that in time of war the king's high commissioner should be "General or Chief Commander" of the forces raised by the colonies. This sort of military power was, as we have seen in a previous chapter, often given to the governor in the constitutions of 1776, and he was called commander-in-chief or captain-general until, in the National Constitution, the term commander-in-chief was settled upon for the President.

Penn's plan of a congress of deputies, each colony sending an equal number, with a presiding officer, or executive head, appointed by the king, remained for a long time the model for all plans of union of the colonies. Names and details were varied, but the general outline remained.

It may also be observed at this point that the legislative body created by the New England plan of union had the sole power of declaring war and peace, and the other numerous temporary unions which were made from time to time were usually for the purpose of regulating war or treaties with the Indians. This may have gradually accustomed the colonists to the idea that the war and peace power of a government belonged to the representative and legislative department, and not to the executive, so that, when the National Constitution was framed, the war power, instead of being given to the President in imitation of the war power of the British king, was given to Congress.

For some years after Penn's plan appeared there was

Evolution of Federalism

a discussion of the subject of union, which shows that the idea was not only developing, but was arousing opposition in some quarters, or, in other words, that the people were becoming more and more trained to its various aspects. About the time of Penn's plan the Lords of Trade discussed another one, which they had received from the governor and assembly of Massachusetts, accompanied by several memorials from persons in neighboring colonies. It was suggested, apparently, that New York, New Jersey, and all the New England colonies be united together under one governor, who should be the person that was appointed governor of Massachusetts, and that he should also be the governor of New York and New Hampshire and general of the forces raised by the colonies that were to unite.

Connecticut objected to this arrangement, because such a military governor would have power to march her people beyond the boundaries of their province without that province's consent. This objection was a very common one in colonial times, and the feeling was strong that the people of a province should never, except by their own consent, be marched beyond its boundaries. New Hampshire also objected, because it would be an increased charge upon her without any compensating advantage; and New York objected, because most of the New England colonies had enough to do to defend their own frontiers and could not assist Massachusetts or New York. There seems also to have been an apprehension that the plan might give Boston too much advantage in trade.

The question was debated back and forth with considerable detail, and the Lords of Trade, being of the opinion that any union, except under such a military head, was impracticable, recommended that a captain-general be appointed as requested, and that his chief residence during the war be in New York, with liberty to remove to Boston from time to time as occasion should require. Richard, Earl of Bellomont, was appointed to this office, and for a time this union was in actual operation.

Two years afterwards Charles D'Avenant suggested a scheme of a Council of Trade, to which council each colony should regularly report its condition, and at the same time he approved of Penn's plan. Both his plan and Penn's were criticised in a pamphlet written by a Virginian, who objected to the provisions for equal representation from each colony. As the colonies differed vastly in numbers and extent, this was, he said, unfair, and he proposed that Virginia should have four representatives, Maryland three, New York two, Boston three, and so on. No one, he said, would deny Virginia's right to more representatives than the others, because she was the eldest and the most profitable of all the English plantations in America.

He also objected to the deputies meeting always at New York, and offered an arrangement by which they should meet in turn in different parts of the country, so that they might become better acquainted with the conditions and requirements of each part. New York, he said, should not have an opportunity of drawing so much money to it every year from all the other colonies. He commented somewhat on what D'Avenant

Evolution of Federalism

had said of Penn's plan being an imitation of the Greek Amphictyonic Council. He urged that the colonies which still remained proprietary or had charters be taken under the direct rule of the king by act of Parliament. This uniformity in the government of each would assist in a uniform plan for the government of all, which, he said, was becoming more and more necessary to resist the designs of the French and Spanish on the North American continent.

In 1701 Robert Livingston, of New York, suggested a plan which is of interest, because it is based on the sectional principle and gives up any hope of uniting all the colonies. He proposed three distinct governments, —one composed of Virginia, Maryland, and North and South Carolina; a second, of part of Connecticut, New York, the Jerseys, Pennsylvania, and Delaware; and a third, of Massachusetts, New Hampshire, Rhode Island, and the rest of Connecticut. He divided up the colonies, it will be observed, very nearly on the division, which has always existed, of New England, Middle, and Southern; and his plan shows clearly that sectionalism was always an important element in the growth or in checking the growth of federalism.

In 1721 the Earl of Stair prepared a very comprehensive scheme of twenty-six articles, which were to include the West Indies as well as all the English colonies on the continent. It followed the regulation form, which had been started by Penn, of a legislative body composed of two delegates from each province, presided over by a captain-general, who was to reside in the middlemost province. The right to local self-government in each colony was guaranteed, as it usually was in these plans, showing how persistent was this first and essential element of federalism. The method of investing the captain-general with his authority was left to be settled afterwards, and the plan suggested that he might be either nominated, elected, chosen, or appointed, which gave the colonists a possible chance for a voice in his selection, and was more liberal than most of the plans.

The plan was indeed not only liberal, but elaborate, and showed a decided tendency to develop the details of a general government. Salaries were provided for every one, a treasury department was outlined, and a general post-office system. There were also to be a secretary of state and a small navy of eight or ten vessels. It was a decided development towards a national government.

The Lords of Trade seem to have recommended the general features of the plan to the king, and they added that the utility of a union was so evident that it was unnecessary to argue the question. This seems to have been the general feeling of the time. The absurdities and inconveniences of intercourse among the colonies were obvious to every one.

In 1722, a plan by Daniel Coxe, of New Jersey, suggests, for the first time, that the captain-general, or head of the union, should be given the veto power, and argues for the importance of a union from the disasters which befell the ancient Britons for the want of one.

At the same time there was one important person, and probably others, long-headed enough to see that

Evolution of Federalism

from the point of view of the British Crown there might be a disadvantage in union. Sir William Keith, who had been a very successful governor of Pennsylvania, thought that the want of harmony among the colonies and their jealousies in trade should be encouraged rather than mitigated. "The wisdom," he said, "of the Crown of Great Britain therefore by keeping its colonies in such situation is very much to be applauded; for while they continue so it is morally impossible that any dangerous union can be formed among them." It was not good policy, he thought, "to accustom all the able men in the colonies to be well exercised in arms."

Our next plan is Franklin's of 1754, and a very important one. The Lords of Trade were anxious that all the colonies should, by their representatives, meet all the Indian tribes at Albany and make a general treaty with them which would break up the confusion of separate treaties and policies and be a precedent for general action in the future. Massachusetts took up the suggestion with much earnestness, and urged that at the same meeting there should be an attempt to confederate all the provinces. Several plans of union were offered, and Franklin's was adopted. It had been more maturely considered than the others; for before the meeting he had published his thoughts on the question in his newspaper in Philadelphia, and from these he elaborated the plan he presented to the meeting.

It contained most of the developments we have already noticed; self-government was guaranteed to each colony, salaries were provided, and a treasury department; and then we find some interesting advances.

Evolution of the Constitution

The president-general is distinctly assigned the duty of carrying into execution the acts of the council,—a detail of executive power which had not been formally expressed in the other plans, and which reminds us of that expression which, starting in one of the constitutions of Pennsylvania, passed through nearly all the documents until we find it in the National Constitution in the slightly altered form, "he shall take care that the laws be faithfully executed."

The president-general is to appoint military officers with the consent of the grand council, and civil officers are to be appointed by the grand council with the consent of the president-general, which was a more detailed description of the appointing power than had appeared before. The term president-general is worth observing. It is evidently an attempt to give a name which should be short and also express the general opinion that the head of the union must be at the same time both a civil and a military officer. The same idea was afterwards carried out in the National Constitution by calling the head of the government President and declaring that he should be commander-in-chief of the army and navy.

But the most striking advance in Franklin's plan is that the grand council, or representative body of all the colonies, is given the power "to lay and levy general duties, imposts, or taxes" on each colony according to its circumstances and ability. Previous plans had been very careful to leave to each colony the manner in which money was to be raised from it, and this was part of the guarantee of its local rights. The union might fix a colony's quota, but the colony was to lay the taxes that raised it, and this showed that the plans of union were as yet nothing but leagues or alliances of sovereignties. But here in Franklin's plan we find the provinces for the first time surrendering an important part of their sovereignty and allowing the general government to act directly on their people instead of through sovereignties, and this was evidently a strong move in the direction of federalism.

There was also another new provision in the plan, providing that no money should issue except " by joint orders of the president-general and grand council, except where sums had been appropriated to particular purposes and the president-general is previously empowered by an act to draw for such sums." This was a natural and necessary arrangement appearing for the first time, and afterwards in the National Constitution the same point was covered by the simple expression, " No money shall be drawn from the treasury but in consequence of appropriations made by law."

In the next sentence of his plan we find Franklin providing that " the general accounts shall be yearly settled and reported to the several assemblies," and in the National Constitution we find, " a regular statement and account of the receipts and the expenditures of all public money shall be published from time to time."

The general outline of Franklin's plan was, of course, the regulation one of a body of deputies sent by the colonies and called the grand council, and a president-general appointed by the Crown, who was not merely to preside over the grand council, but is described as administering the general government. The grand council were to choose their own speaker, and could not be dissolved nor continued sitting longer than six weeks at one time without their own consent or the special command of the Crown. The president-general is impliedly given the veto power in a passage which requires his assent to all acts of the grand council, and there is another veto power in the king, for the laws must be transmitted to him, and, if not disapproved within three years after presentation, are to remain in force.

It was, in fact, a complete form of government. It is important also to notice that the representation of the colonies in the grand council was not equal. Massachusetts was given seven representatives, Virginia seven, Pennsylvania six, and the others lesser numbers. After three years the representation from each colony was to be in proportion to the money raised from it each year, provided that the number chosen by any one province should not be more than seven nor less than two. This question of the representation of each colony in the union gave much trouble, and was settled in different ways. In the previous plans we find an equal representation, with occasional criticisms that it should be unequal, but here we find a plan adopted by representatives of all the colonies making the representation decidedly unequal. This shows conclusively that the colonies were working out the problem of representation in their own way, and that when in the Articles of Confederation of the Revolution the representation was made equal, by giving each State one vote, it was not, as Mr. Campbell supposes, an imitation of the States-General of the Netherlands.

Evolution of Federalism

Among the plans which seem to have been submitted at the same time as Franklin's was one which should be mentioned because it is based on sectionalism. It is supposed to have been prepared by Richard Peters, who was secretary of the province of Pennsylvania and a delegate to the Albany convention. It divides the colonies into four different governments,—one composed of the extreme southern colonies, Georgia and the two Carolinas; another of Virginia, Maryland, and Pennsylvania; a third of the Jerseys and New York, and the fourth of the New England colonies. It was almost exclusively a military suggestion, and contains nothing worthy of comment.

Franklin's plan adopted at Albany was referred by the Massachusetts assembly to a committee that prepared a substitute based on sectionalism. But both this and Franklin's plan were rejected by the Massachusetts assembly and a new committee appointed, which prepared a plan usually known as Hutchinson's. It was for the most part a mere paraphrase of Franklin's, except that it provides that no member of the council shall be chosen or appointed to any civil or military office, which shows that the desire to keep the departments of government more distinct was growing, and it also gave the president and council power to appoint officers for collecting from the people the duties levied by the council. This last provision was another advance towards federalism.

Considerable jealousy was felt against the power given to the general government in Franklin's union, and Hutchinson's plan provided that the power of the union should continue for only six years, unless at the end of

Evolution of the Constitution

that time there should be war between Great Britain and France, in which case the power should continue until the end of the war.

The other colonies also rejected Franklin's plan. They seemed to be jealous of it, and thought it created too strong a government. It was also rejected in England by the Lords of Trade, because it was too democratic. The Lords of Trade then offered a plan of their own, which was merely military and never carried into effect.

Some years afterwards, Dr. Samuel Johnson, president of King's College, in New York, proposed a plan which is noteworthy as coming from a learned source and also from a person who was evidently a high Tory. To his mind the colonies seemed to be becoming too republican. They should be brought more into conformity with the government of the mother-country, and to this end colonies like Rhode Island and Connecticut, which had rather liberal governments, should have their charters abolished. The proprietary governments should also be abolished and all brought under the direct rule of the king. This being done, a union might be formed on the general plan of a captain-general or head of some sort, with a council composed of two representatives from each province. This, he said, would be like the Amphictyonic Council of the ancient states of Greece. It would consider the common affairs of war and trade, and might also consider whether the laws passed in the different colonies should be confirmed or annulled. This last was certainly a peculiar suggestion.

But almost every plan of union that appeared added some development, and so we find even in this one the

Evolution of Federalism

first suggestion that the union should regulate the value of money so that it should be uniform in all the provinces,—a provision which afterwards appeared in nearly all the plans until it took its place in the Constitution.

During the agitations over the stamp act and other parliamentary measures which preceded the Revolution there were congresses and meetings of delegates from all the colonies, but no formal plan of union was prepared. The congresses and meetings, however, were in themselves acts of union, and could hardly have been assembled so easily without the previous experience and training of over a hundred years in unions for Indian wars and treaties and to resist the French. The French and Indian wars, which were just completed before the stamp-act agitation began, had shown more plainly than ever the need of union and at the same time strengthened the feeling for it by giving the people for the first time a common bond of sympathy against a common enemy. There is nothing so effective as a foreign enemy and invader for driving a people into union, and there has been an instance of it in our own time in the unification of Germany after the Franco-Prussian War.

In the case of the colonies the unifying tendency of the French enemy was followed immediately by the appearance of another enemy,—the British Parliament and king,—and under the pressure of this new invader delegates from all the colonies met together naturally and easily. They drew up no plan or rules of union, for the cause of their union had become too plain for rules. But their debates assisted the development towards federalism. They discussed for the first time the rights and privileges of the colonies as a whole, reviewed their history, and generalized their liberties.

The unity of feeling among them was strongly shown in the non-importation agreement, under which they voluntarily deprived themselves of foreign luxuries and set to work to increase their own arts and manufactures as well as their flocks and herds. They agreed upon the most rigid economy among themselves. On the death of a relation, "none of us," says the agreement, "will go into any further mourning dress than a black crape or ribbon on the arm or hat for gentlemen and a black ribbon and necklace for ladies, and we will discontinue the giving of gloves and scarfs at funerals." When sovereign states meet together and are willing to give up conveniences, privileges, or rights for the benefit of all, they have taken the first step beyond a mere league and in the direction of federalism.

The Continental Congress assembled in 1774, without any definite form of government, and went on from day to day and year to year conducting a war, organizing an army, and raising money by tacit understanding, with no written instrument, charter, or constitution to guide it. Three plans for a general government were suggested and debated by its members from time to time; but four years passed before any one of them was adopted, and in that time the Congress was supported in its authority and its important measures by nothing more than general opinion.

The three plans of government that were debated by the Congress were Galloway's Plan of 1774, Franklin's Plan of 1775, and the Articles of Confederation, which

Evolution of Federalism

were prepared in 1776, but not finally adopted and approved by Congress until 1778.

Galloway's plan was avowedly intended to prevent independence and unite the colonies among themselves and with the mother-country in a way that should preserve their liberties. The greater part of it is a mere copy of Franklin's plan of 1754. The local rights of each colony are first of all guaranteed, and there were to be a president-general appointed by the Crown, and a grand council elected by the colonies every three years, each colony to have representation in proportion to its importance. The president was to have the veto power and execute the laws, and the grand council was to have all the rights and privileges of the House of Commons of Great Britain. The legislative power given to the grand council was very broad and vague, and might have meant almost anything. The council were to "exercise all the legislative rights, powers, and authorities necessary for regulating and administering all the general police and affairs of the colonies, in which Great Britain and the colonies, or any of them, the colonies in general, or more than one colony, are in any manner concerned, as well civil and criminal as commercial."

This was certainly an enormous stride towards federalism, and would have given the grand council far more power than is now possessed by the Congress of the United States.

But besides this the grand council was to be a branch of the British legislature, and in all general colonial matters the two were to be a check on each other.

Either could originate colonial legislation, but no act was to be valid without the consent of both, except money-bills for aid to the Crown in war, which might become valid when approved by the grand council and the president without the assent of the British Parliament.

This plan seems to have at one time met with the approval of a majority of the Congress. But afterwards, when the feeling against England had increased, the plan and all debate on it were ordered to be stricken from the records.

Franklin's plan of the following year also contemplated a reconciliation with England, but only as a future contingency, and there was no suggestion of direct connection with the British Parliament. It was a plan for an independent government, which should be perpetually independent unless reconciliation with the mother-country were effected. It was not so strong in its federalism as Galloway's plan ; yet it was a considerable advance on plans previous to his, and showed how the idea was progressing.

The description of the rights of the States, the subjects over which they should retain jurisdiction, and the matters which should be under the control of the general government is in Franklin's plan very clear and somewhat like the modern way of expressing it. The plan, however, is intended to be suggestive in its form, and consists principally of general heads to be worked out afterwards in detail. Of this sort is the third article, which says that each colony shall " retain as much as it may think fit of its own present laws, customs, rights, privileges, and peculiar jurisdiction within its own limits and may amend its own constitution as shall seem best." The power and duty of Congress are clearly defined, and are to extend to war and peace, sending and receiving ambassadors, entering into alliance, settling boundary disputes and all other disputes between the colonies; and Congress is given power over all other matters which are necessary to the general welfare and cannot be well controlled by the assemblies of the individual States,—viz., regulations for general commerce, general currency, the post-office, and the army.

This was a large delegation of power. The assigning of the right of declaring war and peace to Congress shows how persistent was the tendency among our people to give this power to the legislative department instead of to the executive. The sending and receiving of ambassadors and the entering into alliances were, of course, new, because the people were now acting independently of the mother-country, and it was necessary that their government should have this attribute of sovereignty. The settlement of boundary disputes between colonies arose out of the circumstances of the time. There had been great difficulty over boundary questions between New Hampshire and Vermont, New York and Vermont, Pennsylvania and Connecticut, Pennsylvania and Maryland, and Pennsylvania and Virginia. Several of these disputes, notably those between Pennsylvania and Connecticut and Pennsylvania and Maryland, had already resulted in bloodshed and petty civil war. It had been found impossible to settle them except after long litigation before the Privy Council in England, which, in the case of the dispute between Pennsylvania and Maryland, lasted for over seventy years.

The settling of all other differences between colonies was also an item of power that had never appeared in any other plan. But the power to regulate the currency, the establishment of a post-office, and the regulation of commerce and of the army had appeared in other plans.

The power to appoint both civil and military officers was given by Franklin to Congress, and not to the executive. In fact, Congress was the principal power. The executive was very weak and inefficient, and was to consist merely of an executive committee or council composed of twelve members of Congress, who during the recess of the Congress should manage the general continental business, receive applications from foreign countries, prepare matters for the consideration of the next meeting of Congress, and fill such offices as during the recess should become vacant. An executive of this sort, composed of a number of persons, was a favorite notion of Franklin's, and was adopted in the constitution of Pennsylvania of 1776, largely, no doubt, through his influence. It was also adopted in the Articles of Confederation, principally because the people were very jealous of executive power and feared leaving it in the hands of one man.

The year after Franklin's plan was presented the Articles of Confederation were prepared. This was in the spring of 1776, when the movement towards the declaration of independence was in progress, and it seemed absolutely necessary to have some definite

Evolution of Federalism

form of government for the united colonies. It was therefore the most serious and earnest attempt that had ever been made to frame a union and general government.

The attempts at union in the previous hundred years had been no stronger than desires for greater convenience in managing general affairs. If they failed, nothing much was lost. The colonies were no worse off than before, and still had the mother-country to rely on. But now, if independence was declared, the colonies would be adrift in the world, and must take their place as a regularly organized nation or perish. It would be extremely difficult to conduct the war and afterwards stand before the world as an independent people unless they had a regular form of government, which would enable them to send and receive ambassadors, make alliances with foreign countries, and organize their own forces of men, money, and opinion in an efficient manner.

At the same time that the Declaration of Independence was being debated and shaped, the Continental Congress was considering with equal energy the Articles of Confederation, which were to form the most complete and advanced general government that had yet appeared. The subject was referred to a committee on June 12, 1776, and the committee reported July 12, soon after the Declaration of Independence was adopted. The articles of the new government were exhaustively debated and amended from time to time for the next two years, and were signed by the members of Congress July 9, 1778. After that three more years passed away while they were discussed by the different States, and changes suggested. They were ratified slowly, and the adoption of them was not complete until Maryland gave her consent, March 1, 1781.

The care which was required, the long years of debate, the balancing and compromising of objections and conflicting interests, show that after all the experience and attempts of the previous hundred years it was still a difficult matter to frame a general government that should be more than a mere league or alliance. Yet without the previous attempts it could not have been done ; for when we read over the completed Articles of Confederation we find them made up of everything that had before appeared in plans of union, with additions and careful elaborations.

The first draught of the Articles that was submitted to Congress had more resemblance to Franklin's plan of the year before, and was simpler in language, than the completed copy that was ratified by the States. The completed Articles, however, begin as many of the previous plans had begun,—by guaranteeing to each State its local rights and liberties. But this guarantee is expressed more completely and better than ever before. Each State is to retain its sovereignty, freedom, and independence, and every power, jurisdiction, and right which is not by the Articles expressly delegated to the United States in Congress assembled. At the same time, the States agree, in very much the same form that they had formerly agreed in the plans, to enter into a firm league of friendship with one another for their common defence and general welfare.

Evolution of Federalism

The problem which the New England union of 1643 and Penn's plan of 1696 had struggled with, that is to say the inconveniences in the intercourse of the States, is dealt with in greater detail than formerly. The people of each State are to have free ingress and regress in all the others, enjoy the same privileges and immunities in trade and commerce, be subject to the same duties and restrictions, and persons charged with crime and fleeing into another State are to be delivered up. Then appears a new provision, to the effect that full faith and credit shall be given in each State to the records and judicial proceedings of every other State, which was repeated in a slightly simplified form in the Constitution.

The general outline of the legislative department follows very closely the old forms. Each State is to send delegates to a general legislative body called the Congress. The question which had been so long discussed as to whether the States should be represented equally or in proportion to their population is settled by a compromise. Each State is to have delegates in proportion to its power, but no State shall be represented by less than two nor by more than seven. This was in conformity with the suggestions of Franklin and others in the past. But the other side, who believed in equal representation, were quieted by the provision that although each State had a proportional representation, yet all its delegates together could have only one vote. A large, powerful State would, therefore, have influence by mere numbers and speech-making in proportion to its power, but when it came to a vote on any question its vote would be no larger than that of the smallest community. This balancing arrangement was afterwards the basis for those provisions in the Constitution by which the representation in the House of Representatives was in proportion to population and in the Senate by equality of States.

Franklin's plan of an executive composed of a committee of members of Congress was carried out, and this committee was given the right to act in the recess of Congress in very much the way Franklin had recommended.

Freedom of speech in the Congress was secured, and the same paragraph also protected members from arrest and imprisonment during the session. This was a new provision made necessary by the greater importance of the government that was being created. For the same reason the individual States were forbidden to send any embassy to or to treat in any way with foreign countries. Persons holding any office under the United States or any of the States were forbidden to receive any present, emolument, or title from a foreign state; and the United States and the individual States were forbidden to grant any title of nobility. The States were also forbidden to enter into treaties or alliances with one another without the consent of Congress; nor could they lay imposts or duties which might interfere with stipulations and treaties made by the Congress; nor could they keep up any larger war establishment than was deemed necessary by the Congress; nor engage in war without the consent of Congress unless they were actually invaded or had certain advice of a contemplated invasion by Indians so

Evolution of Federalism

imminent as not to admit of delay; nor could they commission vessels of war or grant letters of marque except after a declaration of war by the Congress.

These provisions were necessarily new, but the one which forbids the States to make war on their own account unless actually invaded or threatened with invasion by the Indians is very like the provisions for the same purpose in the old plans of union, especially the New England union of 1643.

Officers of the army of and below the rank of colonel were to be appointed by the legislature of the State where the troops were raised, and officers above that rank by the Congress. The expenses of war and government were to be raised from the States and paid into a common fund in very much the same manner as in the previous plans, but the taxes were to be laid and levied by each State on its own people. Some of the previous plans, notably Franklin's of 1754, had, as we have seen, given the general government power to lay and levy these taxes. This had been a long step towards federalism,—in fact, rather too long. The people were not prepared for it, and were uncertain about allowing it. We find it appearing and disappearing in the various plans until it is established in the Constitution.

The powers given to the general government are, of course, interesting, but they are not so large nor so numerous as we might expect. Some of them had become absolutely necessary by the new circumstances of independence, such as the powers to send and receive ambassadors, enter into treaties and alliances, establish rules for captures on land and water, grant letters of marque, and establish courts to punish piracy and crimes committed at sea.

The powers to regulate affairs with the Indians and to establish a post-office were of course given, but were not new. The sole power of determining peace and war is given to the Congress, as it had in all previous plans been given to the legislative department. The provision in Franklin's plan giving Congress the power to settle boundary disputes between the States is repeated in a more elaborate form. There is also the new and very important right of fixing the standard of weights and measures.

There was no power given to regulate commerce, which is rather curious, as it had been given in previous plans. It might possibly have been inferred from the power to make commercial treaties. The general opinion seems to have been, however, that it was purposely omitted. The New Jersey legislature complained of its omission, and urged Congress to insert it by amendment; and as time went on the complaints on this point became numerous.

The few powers allowed Congress were restricted by a clause which prohibited the exercise of most of them except by the assent of nine of the thirteen States. Of the executive power still greater jealousy was shown, and for fear the presiding officer of the Congress might grow into a king they limited his term of service to one year, after which he was to be ineligible for re-election for two years. Even the committee of thirteen, which was to act as a sort of executive in the recess of Congress, could have no power delegated to it except by

Evolution of Federalism

the votes of nine States, and the special powers that could not be exercised by Congress except by the vote of nine States could not be delegated to the committee.

It was unquestionably a very weak government,—a mere league with so few of the attributes of federalism, and those few so restricted, that it was not a federal or a national government in any true sense of the word. The fashion has prevailed for a long time of attacking it in very severe terms, and even of questioning the patriotism of the men who framed it. But we must remember that it was simply a link in a long chain of evolution which had been progressing for over a hundred years, and continued, as we shall see, in the same steady course. It was a great advance on all the plans that had preceded it, and, for purposes of development, that was all that was required.

The criticisms on its lack of federal power began almost as soon as it appeared. When signed by the members of Congress and sent to the States for ratification in 1778, most of those States had finished their new constitutions, on which they had been engaged for several years. Constitution-making was the order of the day; everybody was prepared for discussion, and no previous plan of union received such serious and trained consideration.

Though the prevailing sentiment seems to have been that not enough power was given, there were many who saw in the Articles of Confederation a menace to the sovereignty of the States. But even this State-rights party, while they wished greater safeguards for local liberty, wanted at the same time more power and efficiency in

Evolution of the Constitution

the general government: so inevitable is the development of a thought when once fairly started on its way.

In South Carolina, William Henry Drayton, chief justice of the State, addressed the assembly when the Articles came before them for approval. He was an able, accomplished man, and in the course of his speech he laid before them a plan of union of his own, which has ever since been known by his name. It was simply a redraughting of the Articles in his own language, with additions and developments. He wished to secure the rights of the States, and especially the Southern interest; and he even went so far as to provide that each State should not only keep up such military establishment as it pleased, but should have a "naval seminary." Nevertheless he developed the federal power, and strongly urged the necessity for it.

He gave Congress the right to define treason and its punishment and the right to levy taxes independently of the States. The right to levy taxes, though omitted in the Articles, had appeared, as we have seen, in previous plans, and was now again introduced. But the right to define and punish treason was new, and a distinct mark of the increase of federal feeling; for treason is a crime against a nation, not against a league or union.

He created regular executive departments of war, navy, and treasury. He also provided for a census to be taken every seven years; but it was to be taken by each State, and not by the general government in the manner afterwards adopted. His greatest advance in federalism, however, was a provision to the effect that if a State failed to pay its quota it was to be assessed

Evolution of Federalism

double, and if it still refused it was to be subdued and brought to terms by Congress by force of arms.

This was the first method any one had formulated for compelling obedience to the commands of the confederacy. The weakness of Congress in this respect, and the mere advisory nature of all its acts, had been the chief points of criticism. The only remedy that Drayton could think of was for Congress to make war on the offending State. People's minds still clung to the idea that everything must be done through the States. They had not as yet advanced to the conception of a general government which enforced its commands on the people as individuals without regard to State lines. They had partially developed this thought by suggesting that the government levy taxes on the people at large; but it had gone no farther.

Drayton was very liberal in his grants of federal power; but, at the same time, like the framers of the Articles, he cramped and injured all he gave by requiring that all important acts of the Congress must have the assent of eleven out of the thirteen States,—an increase of two over the number required in the Articles.

For the next ten years the efforts for stronger federalism were continuous. In 1780 New York and the New England States met by delegates at Hartford and recommended that more power for coercing the States be given to Congress. This report was read in Congress, and Pennsylvania and New Jersey supported it. A committee of Congress also recommended an increase of power.

In 1782 there was a movement in New York to call

Evolution of the Constitution

a convention to revise the Articles, but nothing came of it. More nearly successful was the attempt to give Congress the power to levy duties on imports,—a suggestion for increased power, which now took definite shape. It was assented to by all the States except Rhode Island, but while efforts were being made to secure Rhode Island Virginia withdrew her approval.

The war with England was now over, and great difficulties were immediately experienced because Congress had not been given the power to regulate commerce. Each State was making its own regulations, and the British government, seeing its opportunity to break up the union, undertook to deal with each State separately, and prohibited American ships from trading with English colonies. It seemed as if the Revolution had been fought in vain. Congress attempted to gain prohibitory powers over commerce for fifteen years by the assent of nine States, but without success. Washington, Jefferson, and other leading men made most earnest exertions, and Washington, from his retirement at Mount Vernon, sent urgent letters to Congress and the governors of all the States. But the government grew weaker instead of stronger, and at the session of Congress in 1784 four States were absent, three withdrew in disgust, and the remaining delegates returned home.

It was at this time that Noah Webster's pamphlet, "Sketches of American Policy," appeared. It urged with much force that the government act directly on the people at large instead of on the States, and that the general government be modelled on the forms of the State governments.

Evolution of Federalism

These two suggestions, taken together, were the most important and far-reaching that had thus far been made by any one man. The conception of the general government at that time, as it had developed out of the old plans of union, was that it should consist of a simple representative body which should transact all the business of the union, executive as well as legislative. There was no separate executive department,—for the executive committee was merely a committee of Congress and its powers were very much restricted,—and there was no judicial department unless Congress chose to create one, and even if created by Congress its jurisdiction would be confined to cases of piracy, capture, and felonies committed on the high seas.

Webster suggested that all this primitive arrangement be abolished, and that the double-branch legislature, with the distinct executive and judicial departments that prevailed in the State governments, be adopted. It was a fertile suggestion, and seems to have settled the question, for when the convention met in 1787 the minds of its members were made up on this point. Thus the two lines of development of which we have been treating joined their forces in the convention that framed the Constitution,—the line that had been developing the administrative parts of government from Sir Walter Raleigh's charter of 1584 through the charters and constitutions of colonial times and the constitutions of 1776, and the line that had been developing federalism from the New England union of 1643.

Webster seems to have been the first person who wrote of the importance of joining these two lines of development, and he has not yet received full credit for it. His other suggestion was of equal if not greater importance, namely, that the government should act directly on individuals instead of on the States, and, although there seems to be no passage in the pamphlet which announces this doctrine in so many words, there are several which imply it. He wrote to Madison complaining that he had not received the full reward of recognition, and Madison replied that his services were well known and recognized. His pamphlet has now become very scarce and should be reprinted, for there seem to be only two copies of it in existence,—one in the Boston Athenæum and the other in a collection in Brooklyn.

But, in spite of plans, suggestions, and appeals to patriotism, the confusion was becoming greater. Each State was regulating its own commerce, duties on imports were unequal, and the States were discriminating against one another and soon began to levy duties on one another's goods as if each had been a foreign country to all the others. The currency of each State also varied from the currency of all the others, each had its own financial laws, and some of them passed stay laws and had other contrivances to prevent the collection of debts. The masses of the people, overwhelmed with debt, were clamoring for fresh issues of paper money. Some of them became anarchists and preached the abolition of all courts and law. In Massachusetts and New Hampshire these wild opinions brought on actual riot and rebellion; the courts were dispersed and the legislature intimidated by armed mobs.

Evolution of Federalism

In the midst of all this demoralization, in the year 1785, Maryland and Virginia wanted to connect the Potomac with the Ohio for the sake of their commercial interests, and Maryland, Pennsylvania, and Delaware wanted a canal to connect the Chesapeake with the Delaware. This slight bond of common commercial interest among four States led to the suggestion of a convention to regulate the commerce of the whole Union. The first meeting at Annapolis was of five States,—New York, New Jersey, Delaware, Pennsylvania, and Virginia,—and after a short session the members adjourned, with a recommendation for a meeting of all the States to devise measures for a general government adequate to the exigencies of the Union.

In the mean time a committee of Congress recommended that the Articles be amended so as to give Congress power to regulate foreign and domestic trade, collect duties, punish treason and crimes on the high seas, create a new system of revenue, and establish an appellate court of seven judges with jurisdiction over certain general questions. The suggestion that Congress regulate domestic trade was new. All previous powers over commerce referred to foreign commerce alone. But the last suggestion of all—the idea of an appellate federal court—was not only new, but striking, and marks the beginning of the federal judiciary.

The States were now gradually giving their approval to the assembling of a general convention, and it met in May, 1787, at Philadelphia. A few days after it had assembled, Randolph, of Virginia, presented some general propositions to show how the Articles of Confederation might be enlarged. This plan of Randolph's adopts partially the idea set forth by Noah Webster that the general government should act directly on the people instead of on the States.

He adopts, however, in its fulness, that other idea of Webster's, that the arrangement of a single representative body acting as legislature and executive be abandoned and that the government be framed on the model of the State governments, with separate departments of legislature, executive, and judiciary. Randolph's plan was the first attempt to carry out this idea, and we find him providing for two houses of legislature, an executive elected by the legislature, and a judiciary department consisting of an appellate court and inferior tribunals.

The jurisdiction given the judiciary is expressed vaguely, but is quite large, and contains the germs of a great deal that was afterwards given. Piracies and felonies on the seas and captures from enemies he of course included, and these had appeared before ; but he adds cases of revenue collection and cases in which foreigners and citizens of other States may be interested. Thus an important part of the present jurisdiction of the United States courts—namely, suits between citizens of different States—was distinctly suggested. He added the very vague jurisdiction of "questions which involve the national peace and harmony," and he also referred to these courts "impeachments of any national officer."

He recommended for the first time that a republican form of government and the integrity of its territory be guaranteed to each State. Representation in both houses of the legislature was to be in proportion to the quotas of contribution or to the number of free inhabitants, "as the one or the other might seem best in different cases." The lower house was to be elected by the people of the several States, and here he followed Webster's general recommendation that the government should be of the people at large, and not a mere representation of States.

The upper house was to be elected by the lower out of a proper number of persons nominated by the individual legislatures. Certainly a rather strange suggestion, yet showing a hint of the future Senate as the representative of the States.

In giving power to the legislature he said that it should have the same that was already exercised by Congress under the Articles of Confederation, and also should legislate in all cases in which the separate States were incompetent or in which the harmony of the United States might be interrupted by individual legislation. This was very general, and, when filled in with a few particular instances, would be ample.

The coercive power to enforce commands, which was so lacking in Congress under the Articles, he attempted to supply, as Drayton had attempted, by giving power " to call forth the force of the Union against any member of the Union failing to fulfil its duty."

But the most curious provision was a grant to the legislature of power to negative all laws passed by the several States contravening the articles of union. This was an attempt to prevent unconstitutional legislation, as we should now call it. The necessity of some such

Evolution of the Constitution

provision had been long felt, even in colonial times, and we have already considered the remedies proposed, from that in Locke's constitution for Carolina down to the council of censors in the Pennsylvania constitution of 1776.

Besides the power in the national legislature to negative unconstitutional laws of the States, Randolph added another security, in a council of revision composed of the executive and "a convenient number of the national judiciary," which should examine the acts not only of the State legislatures but also of the national legislature. The dissent of this council in the case of an act of the national legislature was to be a rejection unless the act were passed again. In the case of acts of State legislatures the council was apparently intended to act as a check upon the national legislature's declaring them unconstitutional. The council was to consider the act in question before the negative of the national legislature became final, and if the council dissented the act of the State was to stand valid unless again negatived by the national legislature. This arrangement seems to have been a combination of the plan of Locke and the council of censors of Pennsylvania.

Immediately after Randolph had presented his plan, Charles Pinckney, of South Carolina, presented another, still more advanced and complete, and so nearly like the Constitution as finally adopted that at first sight there seems to be scarcely any difference. It was a more definite and detailed plan than Randolph's, which professed to be nothing but general heads and suggestions.

It adopts in their entirety the two great ideas put

Evolution of Federalism

forth by Webster, that the government should act directly on the people and that it should be modelled on the State governments. Instead of beginning with the assertion that the States as separate bodies form the government, it begins with the words, "We the people of the States do ordain, declare," etc.,—the first use of this expression. Everything that had been in Randolph's plan, the Articles of Confederation, and all the previous plans seems to have been swept into this plan of Pinckney's. He amplifies and extends everything, adds new developments, and adopts more than ever the forms of the State governments.

He has, of course, two houses of legislature, and, like Randolph, he has the upper house elected by the lower house, with the same suggestion that a certain number shall be chosen from each State, and that it shall represent the States as the lower house represents the people. Money-bills must originate in the lower house, and cannot be altered by the Senate. This was taken from the State constitutions, and appears here for the first time in a federal document. The executive is called President, and is given the modified veto power taken from the constitution of New York, as shown in a previous chapter, and the duty of furnishing information to the legislature, which was a provision taken from the same source. He is to take care that the laws be duly executed, commission all officers, grant pardons and reprieves, be commander-in-chief of the army and navy,—all of which are ideas taken from the various constitutions of the States.

The powers granted to the legislature are given almost

Evolution of the Constitution

in the very words afterwards adopted in the Constitution. Everything that had been previously suggested is included. The legislative department is to lay and collect not only taxes, but also duties, imposts, and excises; to regulate commerce with foreign nations, and among the several States, borrow money, establish post-offices, raise armies, equip fleets, coin money, establish a judiciary, and punish treason.

The new powers are to subdue a rebellion in any State on the application of its legislature; to exercise exclusive jurisdiction in dock-yards, arsenals, and forts; to establish military and post roads, a university, and uniform rules of naturalization; to have exclusive jurisdiction in a tract of land ten miles square for the seat of government; to punish counterfeiting and offences against the laws of nations; to organize the militia of the several States; and, finally, a very necessary addition, —namely, the right "to make all laws necessary for carrying the foregoing powers into execution."

The power to declare war was given exclusively to the Senate, also the power to appoint ambassadors and judges of the Supreme Court and to regulate the manner of deciding boundary disputes between the States.

The power to regulate commerce was slightly restricted by the requirement of the assent of two-thirds of each house; and both houses were prohibited from granting any title of nobility or passing any law on the subject of religion or abridging the liberty of the press. The privilege of the writ of habeas corpus was not to be suspended except in case of rebellion or invasion, as in the Massachusetts constitution of 1780.

Evolution of Federalism

It was certainly a very advanced and complete constitution. The restrictions on the rights of the States, however, were very much the same that had appeared before, and not so numerous as they afterwards became in the Constitution. There was no provision for preventing the passage of unconstitutional laws by the general government, but the States were prevented from it by giving the national legislature the right to annul their laws, as Randolph had suggested.

Two other plans were afterwards offered to the convention, one by Paterson, of New Jersey, and the other by Alexander Hamilton. But neither of them was as complete as Pinckney's, and they seem to have been aside from the line of development. Pinckney's was directly in the line, and so close to the Constitution as adopted, not only in its general provisions, but also in language, that the difference can be dismissed in a few words.

Pinckney's plan began with the words, "We the people of the States of New Hampshire, Massachusetts," etc., mentioning each one. The Constitution begins, "We the people of the United States," getting still closer to the conception that it is the people, and not the States, that create the government. In the Constitution the Senate is elected by the legislatures of the different States, two from each State, instead of being elected by the lower house from citizens in each State, as in Pinckney's and Randolph's plans. In the Constitution the Senate is to try impeachments instead of the judiciary; a vice-president is added, and duties, imposts, and excises must be uniform throughout the

Evolution of the Constitution

United States. In the powers of Congress there are the new ones of regulating commerce with the Indian tribes, establishing uniform laws on the subject of bankruptcies, and granting patents and copyrights. The others are all taken from Pinckney's plan, in many instances word for word.

The President's powers in the Constitution differ somewhat from those given in Pinckney's plan. The President shares with the Senate the right to make treaties and to appoint ambassadors and judges, which Pinckney gave exclusively to the Senate; and the judicial department has a wider scope than Pinckney gave it.

The provision in the Constitution prohibiting the States from passing any law impairing the obligation of contracts was altogether new, and requires some discussion. It was unknown to any of the laws of Europe or, indeed, of the world, and seems to have been altogether the result of some very bitter experience in Pennsylvania. It was introduced into the Constitution by James Wilson, one of the delegates from that State.

During colonial times, the College of Philadelphia, founded by Franklin, had been in the hands of the Church of England people and the proprietary party of the colony. The provost of the college, Dr. Smith, had been a party man of considerable violence, and the college, Dr. Smith, and the proprietary party were greatly disliked by the masses of the people in Pennsylvania. When the Revolution came the masses got into power and proceeded to revenge themselves on their old enemies. They drove from office, and even from social influence, the class of men who had formerly ruled the commonwealth, until that class were gathered together in the college as their last stronghold.

Among this class were Robert Morris and James Wilson, signers of the Declaration of Independence, who stood high in national councils, but were in a minority in the government of their State. The majority saw an opportunity to injure them by destroying their college, and an act of the State legislature was passed in November, 1779, declaring the college charter void, dissolving the board of trustees and the faculty, and giving all the property of the institution to new trustees, who were, of course, selected by the majority party. This was a severe blow to the interests of higher education in Pennsylvania, from which they are only just recovering.

The new college created on the ruins of the old one was a failure, and in 1789 the legislature repented of its act of spoliation and returned the confiscated property to the old College of Philadelphia. The two colleges—the old, restored one and the new one—existed side by side for some years, until at last a union was effected which produced the present University of Pennsylvania.

This spoliation of the college had been done in the teeth of a provision of the State constitution which protected chartered institutions from such attacks. But there was no way of enforcing the State constitution, and the legislature did what it pleased. People began to realize that all educational institutions, as well as charitable and business enterprises, were at the mercy of the State legislature, and this feeling was intensified

Evolution of the Constitution

when the same legislature, in 1785, annulled the charter of the Bank of North America. Something, it was generally believed, must be done to give the new national government the power to prevent such deeds. Wilson, who had been a friend and supporter of both the bank and the college, solved the problem by providing in the national document that "no State shall pass any law impairing the obligation of contracts." It is a simple, short sentence; but it has stood the test of nearly a hundred years of judicial decision, and the principle is now well established that the granting of a charter is a contract between the legislature and the corporation which cannot afterwards be impaired or altered by the legislature without the corporation's consent.

Under this decision has been built up the enormous power of railroads, manufactories, and other business corporations which have played so important a part in the development of the United States. This simple sentence, backed by the power of the general government, has protected those enterprises from Granger, Populist, and other fanatical movements in different States which would otherwise have crippled or destroyed them. Sometimes a belief has seemed to be gaining ground that this clause protected the corporations too well, and gave them too much power; but the havoc that State legislatures committed before there was such protection seems to show that if the protection is excessive it is excess on the safer side. It has given a stability to investments and enterprises, commercial as well as religious, collegiate, and scientific, which could not have been had without it.

Evolution of Federalism

When the Constitution was finally adopted by the people in 1789, the desire for a firmer union and stronger government was gratified, and development almost ceased. The hundred years that have since elapsed have brought little change except a few amendments extending somewhat the federal power over the States, and some restricting the federal power. The first eleven amendments are usually considered as a part of the original Constitution, because they were adopted immediately after the Constitution went into effect, and they contain, for the most part, those bills-of-rights provisions, securing trial by jury, freedom of religion and of the press, and freedom from unreasonable search, which, as we have seen, had grown up as restrictions on the power of the individual States. The people insisted that there should be similar restrictions on the national government.

The essential features of the Constitution, however, are unchanged. The Senate and the House of Representatives and their relations to each other are the same. The President and his duties and relations to Congress have not altered. In fact, our government has been in these respects almost stationary during a century in which the most conservative European governments have suffered considerable change.

Not only have the administrative parts of the government which were evolved from the forms of the State constitutions remained unchanged, but the federalism, the nationality, and the indestructibility of the Union are unaltered. As soon as the new Constitution was submitted to the States for approval in 1788, the party that had always been jealous of any interference with State rights complained bitterly that it was a national government, and not a confederacy,—that it was a creation of the people, and not of the States. Opposition to its approval was organized on this ground, and the debates of the State conventions, especially those of Virginia, Maryland, and Pennsylvania, disclose in full the arguments of those who urged its rejection, because, as Patrick Henry put it, the opening sentence was "We the people" instead of "We the States." But the majority of the people ratified it in the form the framers gave it and intended to give it,—a national Union which could be broken only by rebellion and revolution.

CHAPTER VII.

THE EVOLUTION OF FEDERALISM SHOWN IN DETAIL.

1. UNION AND REPRESENTATION.

THIS section shows the beginnings of the various plans of union, and also the attempts to solve the question how the provinces should be represented in a union. It was thought by some that the provinces should be all equal in their representation, and by others that each should be represented according to its population, or power, or by the amount of its contribution towards the objects of the union. The small provinces, of course, favored equal representation, and the large ones representation by population or power. It seems probable, however, that there was a majority in favor of representation by population, but all were agreed that it could not be accomplished without an accurate census, which in colonial times was difficult to obtain.

Attempts were made to satisfy all parties by giving representatives to each province according to its population, but allowing each province only one vote. In the Constitution this same plan was carried out by allowing representation by population in the lower house and representation by States in the Senate, and for carrying this into effect it was provided that a census should be taken every ten years.

Some quotations from State constitutions are given because they show the development of the idea that representation should be based on an accurate enumera-

Evolution of the Constitution

tion of the people. In England the representation in Parliament was not based on any such enumeration, but was confessedly unequal, and large bodies of the people were without any representation at all.

"It is also agreed that for the managing and concluding of all affairs proper and concerning the whole confederation two commissioners shall be chosen by and out of each of these four jurisdictions,—namely, two for the Massachusetts, two for Plymouth, two for Connecticut, and two for New Haven,—being all in church fellowship with us." (New England Union of 1643.)

"That in order to it two persons well qualified for sense, sobriety, and substance be appointed by each province as their representatives or deputies, which, in the whole, make the congress to consist of twenty persons." (Penn's Plan of Union, 1696.)

"Deputies would be more equally proportioned in manner following,—viz.: Virginia, 4; Maryland, 3; New York, 2; Boston, 3; Connecticut, 2; Rhode Island, 2; Pennsylvania, 1; the two Carolinas, 1; each of the two Jerseys, 1." (A Virginian's Plan, 1701.)

"That the said captain-general . . . be attended with a general council, to be constituted of two members from the assembly of each province, and that one representative or deputy from each province be changed or re-elected every year, which would the better inform the said council of the condition of every province to the contributing towards the preservation of the whole." (Lord Stair's Plan, 1721.)

"It is further humbly proposed that two deputies shall be annually elected by the council and assembly of each province, who are to be in the nature of a great council or general convention of the estates of the colonies, and by the order, consent, or approbation of the lieutenant or governor-general, shall meet together, consult, and advise for the good of the whole." (Daniel Coxe's Plan, 1722.)

"That within   months after the passing of such act the house of representatives in the several assemblies that happened to be sitting within that time, or that shall be especially for that

Federalism in Detail

purpose convened, may and shall choose members for the grand council in the following proportions, that is to say:

"Massachusetts Bay	7
New Hampshire	2
Connecticut	5
Rhode Island	2
New York	4
New Jerseys	3
Pennsylvania	6
Maryland	4
Virginia	7
North Carolina	4
South Carolina	4
	48

"That after the first three years, when the proportion of money arising out of each colony to the general treasury can be known, the number of members to be chosen for each colony shall from time to time in all ensuing elections be regulated by that proportion (yet so as that the number to be chosen by any one province be not more than seven nor less than two)." (Franklin's Plan of 1754.)

"It is humbly proposed by act of parliament that the house of representatives of each colony be enjoined, within a limited time after the passing of such act, to choose members to represent them in a grand council in the following proportion, viz.:

"Massachusetts Bay	7
Connecticut	5
New York	4
Pennsylvania	6
Virginia	7
South Carolina	4
New Hampshire	2
Rhode Island	2
New Jersey	3
Maryland	4
North Carolina	4
In the whole	48"

(Hutchinson's Plan, 1754.)

Evolution of the Constitution

"That the several assemblies shall choose members for the grand council in the following proportions, viz." [The proportion for each colony is left blank.] (Galloway's Plan, 1774.)

"The number of delegates to be elected and sent to congress by each colony shall be regulated, from time to time, by the number of such polls returned, so as that one delegate be allowed for every five thousand polls." (Franklin's Articles of Confederation, 1775.)

"But as representation in proportion to the number of taxable inhabitants is the only principle which can at all times secure liberty, and make the voice of a majority of the people the law of the land; therefore the general assembly shall cause complete lists of the taxable inhabitants in the city and each county in the commonwealth respectively, to be taken and returned to them, on or before the last meeting of the assembly elected in the year one thousand seven hundred and seventy-eight, who shall appoint a representation to each, in proportion to the number of taxables in such returns; which representation shall continue for the next seven years afterwards, at the end of which a new return of the taxable inhabitants shall be made, and a representation agreeable thereto appointed by the said assembly, and so on septennially forever." (Pennsylvania Constitution of 1776.)

"That as soon after the expiration of seven years (subsequent to the termination of the present war) as may be a census of the electors and inhabitants in this State be taken, under the direction of the legislature. And if, on such census, it shall appear that the number of representatives in assembly from the said counties is not justly proportioned to the number of electors in the said counties respectively, that the legislature do adjust and apportion the same by that rule. And further, that once in every seven years, after the taking of the said first census, a just account of the electors resident in each county shall be taken, and if it shall thereupon appear that the number of electors in any county shall have increased or diminished one or more seventieth parts of the whole number of electors, which, on the said first census, shall be found in this State, the number of representatives for such county shall be increased or diminished accordingly, that is to say, one

Federalism in Detail

representative for every seventieth part as aforesaid." (New York Constitution of 1777.)

"For the more convenient management of the general interests of the United States, delegates shall be annually appointed in such manner as the legislature of each state shall direct, to meet in congress on the first Monday in November in every year, with a power reserved to each state to recall its delegates, or any of them, at any time within the year, and to send others in their stead for the remainder of the year.

"No state shall be represented in congress by less than two nor by more than seven members; and no person shall be capable of being a delegate for more than three years, in any term of six years; nor shall any person, being a delegate, be capable of holding any office under the United States for which he, or another for his benefit, receives any salary, fees, or emolument of any kind.

"Each state shall maintain its own delegates in any meeting of the states, and while they act as members of the committee of the states.

"In determining questions in the United States in congress assembled, each state shall have one vote." (Articles of Confederation, 1778.)

"Each state shall be represented in congress by not less than three nor more than seven delegates, and shall have one vote in congress, where all questions shall be determined by a majority of votes, except such as shall be hereafter mentioned." (Drayton's Articles of Confederation, 1778.)

"That at the expiration of seven years after the passing of this constitution, and at the end of every fourteen years thereafter, the representation of the whole state shall be proportioned in the most equal and just manner according to the particular and comparative strength and taxable property of the different parts of the same, regard being always had to the number of white inhabitants and such taxable property." (South Carolina Constitution of 1778.)

"The rights of suffrage in the national legislature ought to be proportioned to the quotas of contribution, or to the number of

Evolution of the Constitution

free inhabitants, as the one or the other rule may seem best in different cases." (Randolph's Plan, 1787.)

"Until a census of the people shall be taken, in the manner hereinafter mentioned, the house of delegates shall consist of   , to be chosen from the different states in the following proportions: For New Hampshire,   ; for Massachusetts,   ; for Rhode Island,   ; for Connecticut,   ; for New York,   ; for New Jersey,   ; for Pennsylvania,   ; for Delaware,   ; for Maryland,   ; for Virginia,   ; for North Carolina,   ; for South Carolina,   ; for Georgia,   ; and the legislature shall hereinafter regulate the number of delegates by the number of inhabitants, according to the provisions hereinafter made, at the rate of one for every   thousand." (Pinckney's Plan, 1787.)

"Representatives and direct taxes shall be apportioned among the several states which may be included within this Union, according to their respective numbers, which shall be determined by adding to the whole number of free persons, including those bound to service for a term of years, and excluding Indians not taxed, three-fifths of all other persons. The actual enumeration shall be made within three years after the first meeting of the Congress of the United States, and within every subsequent term of ten years in such manner as they shall by law direct. The number of representatives shall not exceed one for every thirty thousand, but each state shall have at least one representative; and until such enumeration shall be made the State of New Hampshire shall be entitled to choose three; Massachusetts, eight; Rhode Island and Providence Plantations, one; Connecticut, five; New York, six; New Jersey, four; Pennsylvania, eight; Delaware, one; Maryland, six; Virginia, ten; North Carolina, five; South Carolina, five; and Georgia, three.

"The senate of the United States shall be composed of two senators from each state." (The Constitution.)

"Representatives shall be apportioned among the several states according to their respective numbers, counting the whole number of persons in each state, excluding Indians not taxed. But when the right to vote at any election for the choice of electors for President and Vice-President of the United States, representa-

Federalism in Detail

tives in congress, the executive and judicial officers of a state, or the members of the legislature thereof, is denied to any of the male inhabitants of such state, being twenty-one years of age and citizens of the United States, or in any way abridged, except for participation in rebellion or other crime, the basis of representation therein shall be reduced in the proportion which the number of such male citizens shall bear to the whole number of male citizens twenty-one years of age in such state." (Fourteenth Amendment to the Constitution.)

2. CENSUS.

The clause in the Constitution providing for a census of all the inhabitants every ten years is of great importance, for on it depend the representation in Congress and the confidence of the people that they are fairly represented. Unless there always had been this feeling that they were fairly represented, it would have been impossible to preserve the Union. Equality in this, as in other matters, is one of our essentials, and from the earliest colonial times it was felt that it could be accomplished only by mathematical accuracy, or the nearest approximation to such accuracy as could be attained.

"That the commissioners for each jurisdiction from time to time, as there shall be occasion, bring a true account and number of all the males in every plantation, or any way belonging to, or under their several jurisdictions, of what quality, or condition soever they be, from sixteen years to three score, being inhabitants there." (New England Union of 1643.)

"And the delegates are to bring with them to every congress an authenticated return of the number of polls in the respective provinces, which is to be taken triennially for the purposes above mentioned" [*i.e.*, for apportioning the number of delegates to be allowed each colony]. (Franklin's Articles of Confederation, 1775.)

Evolution of the Constitution

"That as soon after the expiration of seven years (subsequent to the termination of the present war) as may be a census of the electors and inhabitants in this state be taken under the direction of the legislature. And, further, that once in every seven years after the taking of the said first census a just account of the electors resident in each county shall be taken." (New York Constitution of 1777.)

"The legislature in the several states shall, from time to time, cause all the white inhabitants therein to be numbered as nearly as may be; the persons appointed to number them shall be sworn to make the most diligent and accurate inquiry that they can, and to return to the executive power in the state the true number they shall so find; they shall be paid for their trouble and punished for their neglect, if any there shall be; the executive authority in each state, having received such a return, shall without loss of time send it, or an exact copy of it, to the congress; such a return to the congress shall be made before the first day of January next, and in every seventh year thereafter." (Drayton's Articles of Confederation, 1778.)

"The actual enumeration shall be made within three years after the first meeting of the congress of the United States and within every subsequent term of ten years, in such manner as they shall by law direct." (The Constitution.)

3. NAME.

"Wherefore it is fully agreed and concluded . . . that they all be and henceforth be called by the name of the United Colonies of New England." (New England Union of 1643.)

"The name of this confederacy shall henceforth be the United Colonies of North America." (Franklin's Articles of Confederation, 1775.)

"The style of this confederacy shall be 'The United States of America.'" (Articles of Confederation, 1778.)

"The style of the confederacy shall be the United States of America." (Drayton's Articles of Confederation, 1778.)

"The style of this government shall be 'The United States of America.'" (Pinckney's Plan, 1787.)

Federalism in Detail

"We, the people of the United States, ... do ordain and establish this constitution for the United States of America." (The Constitution.)

4. GENERAL POWERS OF CONGRESS.

"Which shall bring full power from their several general courts respectively to hear, examine, weigh, and determine all affairs of our war or peace, leagues, aids, charges, and numbers of men for war, division, and spoils, and whatsoever is gotten by conquest, receiving of more confederates for plantations into combination with any of the confederates, and all things of like nature which are the proper concomitants or consequence of such a confederation, for amity, offence, and defence, not intermeddling with the government of any of the jurisdictions, which, by the third article, is preserved entirely to themselves." (New England Union of 1643.)

"That the president-general, by and with the advice and consent of the general council, hold and exercise all the legislative rights, powers, and authorities necessary for regulating and administering all the general police and affairs of the colonies, in which Great Britain and the colonies, or any of them, the colonies in general, or more than one colony, are in any manner concerned, as well civil and criminal as commercial." (Galloway's Plan, 1774.)

"That the national legislature ought to be empowered to enjoy the legislative rights vested in congress by the confederation, and, moreover, to legislate in all cases to which the separate states are incompetent, or in which the harmony of the United States may be interrupted by the exercise of individual legislation." (Randolph's Plan, 1787.)

"The legislature of the United States shall have the power to make all laws for carrying the foregoing powers into execution." (Pinckney's Plan, 1787.)

"The congress shall have power to lay and collect taxes, duties, imposts, and excises, to pay the debts and provide for the common defence and general welfare of the United States.

Evolution of the Constitution

"To make all laws which shall be necessary and proper for carrying into execution the foregoing powers, and all other powers vested by this constitution in the government of the United States, or in any department or officer thereof." (The Constitution.)

5. Presiding Officer of Congress.

Besides the quotations given under this section from the plans of union, many more might be given from the colonial charters and constitutions and the constitutions of 1776. But, as they are all to the same effect in giving the lower house of the legislature the power to choose their presiding officer, it seems hardly necessary to print them.

"It is further agreed that at each meeting of these eight commissioners, whether ordinary or extraordinary, they, or six of them agreeing, as before, may choose their president out of themselves, whose office and work shall be to take care and direct for order and a comely carrying on of all proceedings in the present meeting. But he shall be invested with no such power or respect as by which he shall hinder the propounding or progress of any business, or any way cast the scales, otherwise than in the precedent article is agreed." (New England Union of 1643.)

"That the king's commissioners, for that purpose specially appointed, shall have the chair and preside in the said congress." (Penn's Plan of Union, 1696.)

"That the grand council have power to choose their speaker." (Franklin's Plan of 1754.)

"That the assent of the president be made necessary to all acts of the council, saving the choice of a speaker." (Hutchinson's Plan, 1754.)

"That the general council shall have power to choose their own speaker." (Galloway's Plan, 1774.)

"The United States in congress assembled shall have authority to appoint one of their number to preside: provided, that no person be allowed to serve in the office of president more than

Federalism in Detail

one year in any term of three years." (Articles of Confederation, 1778.)

"The congress shall have power to appoint one of their number to preside in it; nor shall any person officiate as president of the congress longer than one year in any term of three years." (Drayton's Articles of Confederation, 1778.)

"The House of Representatives shall choose their speaker and other officers." (The Constitution.)

6. Restrictions on Congress.

The idea of expressly limiting the legislative powers of the Union was of late growth, and began with the Articles of Confederation, which make the consent of nine States necessary to certain acts of Congress.

But even then it was taken for granted that besides these express prohibitions all powers not expressly given Congress were impliedly denied. The Constitution was framed on this principle, but the fears and caution of the people compelled the adoption of the ninth and tenth amendments as additional safeguards, which declare that the rights possessed by Congress shall not be construed to disparage others possessed by the people, and that all powers not expressly given are reserved to the States or the people.

"The United States, in congress assembled, shall never engage in a war, nor grant letters of marque and reprisal in time of peace, nor enter into any treaties or alliances, nor coin money, nor regulate the value thereof, nor ascertain the sums and expenses necessary for the defence and welfare of the United States, or any of them, nor emit bills, nor borrow money on the credit of the United States, nor appropriate money, nor agree upon the number of vessels of war to be built or purchased, or the number of land or sea forces to be raised, nor appoint a commander-in-

Evolution of the Constitution

chief of the army or navy, unless nine states assent to the same; nor shall a question on any other point, except for adjourning from day to day, be determined, unless by the votes of a majority of the United States, in congress assembled." (Articles of Confederation, 1778.)

"But the congress shall not declare what shall be treason against the United States, nor the punishment of it, but by the voice of each of the United States in congress; nor shall the congress engage in war, nor enter into or conclude any treaty or alliance, nor ascertain the military land quota of the states, nor build, furnish or equip a naval force, nor rate or cause a general tax to be levied, nor appoint a generalissimo, nor nominate an admiralissimo, nor emit or borrow money, nor grant letters of marque and reprisal in time of peace, except by the consent of eleven votes in the congress; nor shall the congress vest any of these powers in the committee of the United States; nor shall the congress exercise any power but what is hereby expressly delegated to them." (Drayton's Articles of Confederation, 1778.)

"The executive and a convenient number of the national judiciary ought to compose a council of revision, with authority to examine every act of the national legislature before it shall operate, and the dissent of the said council shall amount to a rejection unless the act of the national legislature be again passed." (Randolph's Plan of 1787.)

"All laws regulating commerce shall require the assent of two-thirds of the members present in each house." (Pinckney's Plan of 1787.)

"The migration or importation of such persons as any of the states now existing shall think proper to admit shall not be prohibited by the congress prior to the year one thousand eight hundred and eight; but a tax or duty may be imposed on such importation not exceeding ten dollars for each person.

"The privilege of the writ of *habeas corpus* shall not be suspended unless when, in cases of rebellion or invasion, the public safety may require it.

"No bill of attainder or *ex-post-facto* law shall be passed.

"No capitation or other direct tax shall be laid unless in proportion to the *census* or enumeration hereinbefore directed to be taken.

"No tax or duty shall be laid on articles exported from any state. No preference shall be given by any regulation of commerce or revenue to the ports of one state over those of another; nor shall vessels bound to or from one state be obliged to enter, clear, or pay duties in another.

"No title of nobility shall be granted by the United States." (The Constitution.)

"The enumeration in the Constitution of certain rights shall not be construed to deny or disparage others retained by the people." (Ninth Amendment to the Constitution.)

"The powers not delegated to the United States by the constitution nor prohibited by it to the states are reserved to the states, respectively, or to the people." (Tenth Amendment to the Constitution.)

7. Restrictions on the States.

Federalism is impossible unless the uniting States surrender some of their rights. To persuade them to such a surrender was a long and slow process; yet it was seen to be a necessity from the beginning, and in the earliest union—the New England union of 1643—there is a slight surrender.

"And for that the justest wars may be of dangerous consequence, especially to the smaller plantations in these united colonies, it is agreed that neither the Massachusetts, Plymouth, Connecticut, nor New Haven, nor any of the members of any of them, shall, at any time hereafter, begin, undertake, or engage themselves or this confederation, or any part thereof, in any war whatsoever (sudden exigents with the necessary consequences thereof excepted, which are also to be moderated as much as the case will permit) without the consent and agreement of the forenamed eight commissioners, or at least six of them, as in the sixth Article is provided: And that no charge be required of any of the Confederates in case of a defensive war till the said Commissioners have met and approved the justice of the war, and have agreed upon the sum of money to be levied, which sum is then to be paid by the several Confederates in proportion according to the fourth Article. Nor shall any other plantation or jurisdiction in present being, and not already in combination or under the jurisdiction of any of these Confederates, be received by any of them; nor shall any two of the Confederates join in one jurisdiction without consent of the rest, which consent to be interpreted as is expressed in the sixth Article ensuing." (New England Union of 1643.)

"But no colony shall be at liberty to declare war against any enemy, or to begin any hostilities, except they have the direction and allowance of the president and council." (Hutchinson's Plan, 1754.)

"No colony shall engage in an offensive war with any nation of Indians without the consent of the congress, or grand council above mentioned, who are first to consider the justice and necessity of such war." (Franklin's Articles of Confederation, 1775.)

"No state, without the consent of the United States, in congress assembled, shall send any embassy to, or receive any embassy from, or enter into any conference, agreement, alliance, or treaty, with any king, prince, or state; nor shall any person holding any office of profit or trust under the United States, or any of them, accept of any present, emolument, office, or title of any kind whatever, from any king, prince, or foreign state; nor shall the United States, in congress assembled, or any of them, grant any title of nobility.

"No two or more states shall enter into any treaty, confederation, or alliance whatever, between them, without the consent of the United States, in congress assembled, specifying accurately the purposes for which the same is to be entered into, and how long it shall continue.

"No state shall lay any imposts or duties which may interfere with any stipulations in treaties, entered into by the United States, in congress assembled, with any king, prince, or state, in pursu-

Federalism in Detail

ance of any treaties already proposed by congress to the courts of France and Spain.

"No vessels of war shall be kept up in time of peace, by any state, except such number only as shall be deemed necessary, by the United States, in congress assembled, for the defence of such state or its trade; nor shall any body of forces be kept up, by any state, in time of peace, except such number only as, in the judgment of the United States, in congress assembled, shall be deemed requisite to garrison the forts necessary for the defence of such state; but every state shall always keep up a well-regulated and disciplined militia, sufficiently armed and accoutred, and shall provide and constantly have ready for use, in public stores, a due number of field-pieces and tents, and a proper quantity of arms, ammunition, and camp-equipage.

"No state shall engage in any war without the consent of the United States, in congress assembled, unless such state be actually invaded by enemies, or shall have received certain advice of a resolution being formed by some nation of Indians to invade such state, and the danger is so imminent as not to admit of a delay till the United States, in congress assembled, can be consulted; nor shall any state grant commissions to any ships or vessels of war, nor letters of marque or reprisal, except it be after a declaration of war by the United States, in congress assembled, and then only against the kingdom or state, and the subjects thereof, against which war has been so declared, and under such regulations as shall be established by the United States, in congress assembled, unless such state be infested by pirates, in which case vessels of war may be fitted out for that occasion, and kept so long as the danger shall continue, or until the United States, in congress assembled, shall determine otherwise.

"Every state shall abide by the determinations of the United States, in congress assembled, on all questions which, by this confederation, are submitted to them. And the articles of this confederation shall be inviolably observed by every state, and the Union shall be perpetual." (Articles of Confederation, 1778.)

"Any state neglecting to have a representation in congress shall

Evolution of the Constitution

nevertheless be bound by the act of congress as if its representation was present.

"Provided that such restrictions [by one state on citizens of another state] shall not extend to defeat the articles of this confederation or any part thereof. Provided, also, that no duty, imposition, or restriction shall be laid by any state on the property of the United States, or of the government, in either of them, except in cases of embargo.

"No state shall lay or allow to continue any prohibition, impost, or duty which may interfere with any treaty which shall be made by the congress with any foreign power; no state shall engage in any war without the consent of the congress unless such state be actually invaded by an enemy or shall have received certain intelligence of such hostile design formed by some nation of Indians and the danger is so imminent as not to admit of a delay; no state shall grant letters of marque and reprisal but after a declaration of war by the congress, and then only against the power against whom the war has been so declared, except such state be infested by piracies, in which case vessels of war may be fitted out by that state for the occasion only; no state shall enter into any conference, agreement, treaty, or alliance with any king, prince, or foreign states; nor shall any person holding any office under the United States, or under any of them, accept of any present, emolument, office, or title from any king or foreign state without being thereby absolutely rendered forever incapable of any public trust under the United States, or any of them; nor shall any of these states grant any title of nobility.

"No state shall exercise any power hereby delegated to the congress." (Drayton's Articles of Confederation, 1778.)

"The national legislature ought to be empowered to negative all laws passed by the several states contravening, in the opinion of the national legislature, the articles of union or any treaty subsisting under the authority of the union, and to call forth the force of the union against any member of the union failing to fulfil its duty under the articles thereof.

"The executive and a convenient number of the national judiciary ought to compose a council of revision, with authority

Federalism in Detail

to examine every act of a particular legislature before a negative thereon shall be final, and the dissent of the said council shall amount to a rejection unless the act of the particular legislature be again negatived by   of the number of each branch." (Randolph's Plan, 1787.)

"No state shall grant letters of marque and reprisal, or enter into treaty, or alliance, or confederation ; nor grant any title of nobility ; nor, without the consent of the legislature of the United States, lay any impost on imports ; nor keep troops or ships of war in time of peace ; nor enter into compacts with other states or foreign powers ; nor emit bills of credit ; nor make anything but gold, silver, or copper a tender in payment of debts ; nor engage in war, except for self-defence when actually invaded or the danger of invasion be so great as not to admit of a delay until the government of the United States can be informed thereof. And, to render these prohibitions effectual, the legislature of the United States shall have the power to revise the laws of the several states that may be supposed to infringe the powers exclusively delegated by this constitution to congress, and to negative and annul such as do." (Pinckney's Plan, 1787.)

"No state shall enter into any treaty, alliance, or confederation ; grant letters of marque and reprisal, coin money, emit bills of credit, make anything but gold and silver coin a tender in payment of debts, pass any bill of attainder, *ex-post-facto* law, or law impairing the obligation of contracts, or grant any title of nobility.

"No state shall, without the consent of the congress, lay any imposts or duties on imports or exports except what may be absolutely necessary for executing its inspection laws, and the net produce of all duties and imposts laid by any state on imports or exports shall be for the use of the treasury of the United States, and all such laws shall be subject to the revision and control of the congress. No state shall, without the consent of congress, lay any duty of tonnage, keep troops or ships of war in time of peace, enter into any agreement or compact with another state or with a foreign power, or engage in war, unless actually invaded, or in such imminent danger as will not admit of delay." (The Constitution.)

8. State Sovereignty.

While it is essential to federalism that the uniting States should surrender some of their rights, it is equally essential that they should preserve their remaining rights. Only in this way can the ideal of federalism be attained,—an indestructible union of indestructible States. As we have shown in the preceding section, the first attempt at union—the New England union of 1643—contained a slight surrender of State rights. It also contained a guarantee that the remaining State rights should be inviolably preserved. These two counterpoising essentials of our system appeared at the very beginning, at the same time, and in the same document. American federalism, at its first appearance in the year 1643, contained that foundation principle without which it cannot be preserved.

"It is further agreed that the Plantations which at present are, or hereafter shall be, settled within the limits of the Massachusetts, shall be forever under the Massachusetts, and shall have peculiar jurisdiction among themselves in all cases as an entire body; and that Plymouth, Connecticut, and New Haven shall each of them have like peculiar jurisdiction and government within their limits, and in reference to the Plantations which already are settled, or shall hereafter be erected, or shall settle within their limits respectively: provided, that no other jurisdiction shall hereafter be taken in as a distinct head or member of this confederation; nor shall any other Plantation or jurisdiction in present being, and not already in combination or under the jurisdiction of any of these Confederates, be received by any of them; nor shall any two of the Confederates join in one jurisdiction without consent of the rest, which consent to be interpreted as is expressed in the sixth article ensuing." (New England Union of 1643.)

Federalism in Detail

"That this general council do not meddle with or alter the manner of government in any province, but that the said general council may send advice to the assembly of any province touching any matter which they conceive may be to the advantage of the province." (Lord Stair's Plan, 1721.)

"The quota or proportion, as above allotted and charged on each colony, may, nevertheless, be levied and raised by its own assembly in such manner as they shall judge most easy and convenient and the circumstances of their affairs will permit." (Daniel Coxe's Plan, 1722.)

"Each colony may retain its present constitution except in the particulars wherein a change may be directed by the said act as hereafter follows."

"But they shall not impress men in any colony without the consent of its legislature." (Franklin's Plan of 1754.)

"The president and council shall not have power to impress men in any colony without the consent of its legislature." (Hutchinson's Plan, 1754.)

"That a British and American legislature, for regulating the administration of the general affairs of America, be proposed and established in America, including all the said colonies, within and under which government each colony shall retain its present constitution and powers of regulating and governing its own internal police in all cases whatever." (Galloway's Plan, 1774.)

"That each colony shall enjoy and retain as much as it may think fit of its own present laws, customs, rights, privileges, and peculiar jurisdictions within its own limits; and may amend its own constitution, as shall seem best to its own assembly or convention." (Franklin's Articles of Confederation, 1775.)

"Each state retains its sovereignty, freedom, and independence, and every power, jurisdiction, and right, which is not by this confederation expressly delegated to the United States in congress assembled.

"When land forces are raised by any state for the common defence, all officers of or under the rank of colonel shall be appointed by the legislature of each state respectively by whom such forces shall be raised, or in such manner as such state shall direct, and all vacancies shall be filled up by the state which first made the appointment.

"The taxes for paying that proportion [of the common fund for the general welfare] shall be laid and levied by the authority and direction of the legislatures of the several states within the time agreed upon by the United States.

"Provided that no treaty of commerce shall be made [by the United States in congress assembled] whereby the legislative power of the respective states shall be restrained from imposing such imposts and duties on foreigners as their own people are subjected to, or from prohibiting the exportation or importation of any species of goods or commodities.

"No state shall be deprived of territory for the benefit of the United States.

"The United States, in congress assembled, shall also have the sole and exclusive right and power of regulating the trade and managing all affairs with the Indians not members of any of the states; provided that the legislative right of any state, within its own limits, be not infringed or violated." (Articles of Confederation, 1778.)

"But it is declared the several states do possess and enjoy all those natural rights and powers of sovereignty not by this act delegated. And it is also declared that whenever the congress shall cease to observe these articles of confederation the several states shall be at liberty to declare themselves absolved from all obedience to that government." (Drayton's Articles of Confederation, 1778.)

"That the territory of each state ought to be guaranteed by the United States to each state." (Randolph's Plan, 1787.)

"No tax or duty shall be laid on articles exported from any state. No preference shall be given by any regulation of commerce or revenue to the ports of one state over those of another; nor shall vessels bound to or from one state be obliged to enter, clear, or pay duties in another.

"No new state shall be formed or erected within the jurisdiction of any other state; nor any state be formed by the junction of two or more states, or parts of states, without the consent of

Federalism in Detail

the legislatures of the states concerned as well as of the congress." (The Constitution.)

"The powers not delegated to the United States by the constitution nor prohibited by it to the states are reserved to the states respectively, or to the people." (Tenth Amendment to the Constitution.)

9. Raising Money and Taxation.

"It is by these confederates agreed that the charge of all just wars, whether offensive or defensive, upon what part or member of this confederation soever they fall, shall, both in men and provisions, and all other disbursements, be borne by all the parts of this confederation, in different proportions according to their different ability, in manner following, namely, that the commissioners for each jurisdiction from time to time, as there shall be occasion, bring a true account and number of all the males in every plantation, or any way belonging to or under their several jurisdictions, of what quality or condition soever they be, from sixteen years old to threescore, being inhabitants there. And that according to the different numbers which from time to time shall be found in each jurisdiction, upon a true and just account, the service of men and all charges of the war be borne by the poll; each jurisdiction or plantation being left to their own just course and custom of rating themselves and people according to their different estates, with due respects to their qualities and exemptions among themselves, though the confederation take no notice of any such privilege; and that according to their different charge of each jurisdiction and plantation, the whole advantage of the war (if it please God to bless their endeavors), whether it be in lands, goods or persons, shall be proportionably divided among the said confederates." (New England Union of 1643.)

"That the general council, with the captain-general, have power to allot the portion of men and money (or money and men) which shall be the appointment of each province, to be fixed in gross, and the assembly of the province to direct by a law the ways of raising it." (Lord Stair's Plan of 1721.)

Evolution of the Constitution

"That for these purposes they have power to make laws and lay and levy such general duties, imposts, or taxes, as to them shall appear most equal and just, considering the ability and other circumstances of the inhabitants in the several colonies, and such as may be collected with the least inconvenience to the people, rather discouraging luxury than loading industry with unnecessary burdens." (Franklin's Plan of 1754.)

"And in order to raise moneys sufficient for these purposes:

"That the said president and council be empowered to lay general duty on wines and spirituous liquors or other luxurious consumptions as shall appear to them just and equal on the several colonies, each colony to pay in proportion to their members; and if it shall appear that the sum raised by any colony fall short of such proportion and the deficiency shall not forthwith be paid by such colony, then and as oft as it shall so happen the said president and council shall have power to lay additional duty on such colony until the deficiency be made good; and if the sum raised from any colony shall exceed its proportion, the surplus shall remain or be paid into the general treasury of such colony. And the accounts of the deposition of all moneys raised shall be annually settled, that the members of the council may make report of the same to the respective assemblies.

"That the president and council shall appoint officers for collecting all such duties as shall be agreed on, and all laws and orders for enforcing the payment thereof in any and every colony, and also all laws and orders for restraining supplies to, and communication with, his Majesty's enemies, whether by flags of truce or in any other manner, shall be as fully and effectively observed and executed as if they had been the laws of that particular colony where any offence shall be committed, and all offences against such laws and orders shall be tried and determined accordingly." (Hutchinson's Plan, 1754.)

"All charges of wars, and all other general expenses to be incurred for the common welfare, shall be defrayed out of a common treasury, which is to be supplied by each colony in proportion to its number of male polls between sixteen and sixty years

Federalism in Detail

of age. The taxes for paying that proportion are to be laid and levied by the laws of each colony." (Franklin's Articles of Confederation, 1775.)

"All charges of war, and all other expenses that shall be incurred for the common defence or general welfare and allowed by the United States, in congress assembled, shall be defrayed out of a common treasury, which shall be supplied by the several states, in proportion to the value of all land within each state, granted to, or surveyed for, any person, as such land and the buildings and improvements thereon shall be estimated, according to such mode as the United States, in congress assembled, shall from time to time direct and appoint. The taxes for paying that proportion shall be laid and levied by the authority and direction of the legislatures of the several states, within the time agreed upon by the United States, in congress assembled." (Articles of Confederation, 1778.)

"The congress shall have the sole power of rating and causing taxes to be levied throughout the United States for the service of the confederacy." (Drayton's Articles of Confederation, 1778.)

"The legislature of the United States shall have power to lay and collect taxes, duties, imposts, and excises." (Pinckney's Plan, 1787.)

"The proportion of direct taxation shall be regulated by the whole number of inhabitants of every description, which number shall, within   years after the first meeting of the legislature and within the term of every   year after, be taken in the manner to be prescribed by the legislature.

"No tax shall be laid on articles exported from the states; nor capitation tax, but in proportion to the census before directed." (Pinckney's Plan, 1787.)

"The congress shall have power to lay and collect taxes, duties, imposts, and excises, to pay the debts and provide for the common defence and general welfare of the United States; but all duties, imposts, and excises shall be uniform throughout the United States. No capitation or other direct tax shall be laid unless in proportion to the census or enumeration hereinbefore directed to be taken." (The Constitution.)

Evolution of the Constitution

10. Intercourse between the States.

"It is also agreed that the commissioners for this confederation hereafter at their meetings, whether ordinary or extraordinary, as they may have commission or opportunity, do endeavor to frame and establish agreements and orders in general cases of a civil nature wherein all the plantations are interested for preserving peace among themselves, and preventing as much as may be all occasions of war or difference with others, as about the free and speedy passage of justice in every jurisdiction to all the confederates equally as their own, receiving those that remove from one plantation to another without due certificates; how all the jurisdictions may carry it towards the Indians, that they neither grow insolent nor be injured without due satisfaction, lest war break in upon the confederates through such miscarriage. It is also agreed that if any servant run away from his master into any other of these confederated jurisdictions, that, in such case, upon the certificate of one magistrate in the jurisdiction out of which the said servant fled, or upon other due proof, the said servant shall be delivered either to his master or any other that pursues and brings such certificate or proof. And that upon the escape of any prisoner whatsoever or fugitive for any criminal cause, whether breaking prison or getting from the officer or otherwise escaping, upon the certificate of two magistrates of the jurisdiction out of which the escape is made that he was a prisoner or such an offender at the time of the escape, the magistrates, or some of them of that jurisdiction where for the present the said prisoner or fugitive abideth, shall forthwith grant such a warrant as the case will bear for the apprehending of any such person, and the delivery of him into the hands of the officer or other person that pursues him. And if there be help required for the safe returning of such offender, then it shall be granted to him that craves the same, he paying the charges thereof." (New England Union of 1643.)

"That their business shall be to hear and adjust all matters of complaint or differences between province and province,—as, 1st, where persons quit their own province and go to another that

Federalism in Detail

they may avoid their just debts, though they be able to pay them; 2d, where offenders fly justice or justice cannot well be had upon such offenders in the provinces that entertain them." (Penn's Plan of Union, 1696.)

"The better to secure and perpetuate mutual friendship and intercourse among the people of the different states in this union, the free inhabitants of each of these states, paupers, vagabonds, and fugitives from justice excepted, shall be entitled to all privileges and immunities of free citizens in the several states; and the people of each state shall have free ingress and regress to and from any other state, and shall enjoy therein all the privileges of trade and commerce, subject to the same duties, impositions, and restrictions as the inhabitants thereof respectively; provided that such restrictions shall not extend so far as to prevent the removal of property imported into any state to any other state, of which the owner is an inhabitant; provided, also, that no imposition, duties, or restriction shall be laid by any state on the property of the United States, or either of them.

"If any person guilty of, or charged with, treason, felony, or other high misdemeanor in any state shall flee from justice and be found in any of the United States, he shall, upon demand of the governor or executive power of the state from which he fled, be delivered up, and removed to the state having jurisdiction of his offence.

"Full faith and credit shall be given, in each of these states, to the records, acts, and judicial proceedings of the courts and magistrates of every other state." (Articles of Confederation, 1778.)

"There shall be a mutual friendship and intercourse among the people of the several states in this union; the free white inhabitants of each of these states (those who refuse to take up arms in defence of the confederacy, paupers, vagabonds, and fugitives from justice excepted) shall be entitled to all privileges and immunities of free citizens in the several states, according to the laws of such state respectively, for the government of their own free white inhabitants, having uninterrupted ingress and regress, together with their property, to and from any other of the

Evolution of the Constitution

United States, subject, nevertheless, to the duties, impositions, and restrictions as the inhabitants thereof respectively.

"If any person charged with, or guilty of, treason, felony, or other high misdemeanors, in any of the respective states, shall flee from justice, and be found in any of the states, upon the demand of the executive power in the state from which he fled, he shall be delivered up and removed to the state having jurisdiction of the offence, that state defraying the expense of the removal. And full faith and credit shall be given throughout the United States to the acts, records, and judicial proceedings of the courts and magistrates in each." (Drayton's Articles of Confederation, 1778.)

"The citizens of each state shall be entitled to all privileges and immunities of citizens in the several states. Any person, charged with crimes in any state, fleeing from justice to another, shall, on demand of the executive of the state from which he fled, be delivered up and removed to the state having jurisdiction of the offence.

"Full faith shall be given, in each state, to the acts of the legislature, and to the records and judicial proceedings of the courts and magistrates of every state." (Pinckney's Plan, 1787.)

"Full faith and credit shall be given in each state to the public acts, records, and judicial proceedings of every other state. And the congress may, by general laws, prescribe the manner in which such acts, records, and proceedings shall be proved, and the effect thereof.

"The citizens of each state shall be entitled to all privileges and immunities of citizens in the several states.

"A person charged in any state with treason, felony, or other crime, who shall flee from justice, and be found in another state, shall, on demand of the executive authority of the state from which he fled, be delivered up, to be removed to the state having jurisdiction of the crime.

"No person held to service or labor in one state, under the laws thereof, escaping into another, shall, in consequence of any law or regulation therein, be discharged from such service or labor, but shall be delivered up on claim of the party to whom such service or labor may be due." (The Constitution.)

Federalism in Detail

11. REGULATION OF COMMERCE.

"3rd, to prevent injuries in point of commerce." (Penn's Plan of Union, 1696.)

"That the president-general, with the advice of the grand council, make such laws as they judge necessary for regulating all Indian trade." (Franklin's Plan of 1754.)

"The president, by the advice of the council, shall have the sole power of restraining and regulating all Indian trade by laws and orders, with penalties annexed not extending to life and limb; all offences against such laws or orders to be tried and determined within the government where the offence shall be committed, according to the course of judicial proceeding in such government, in like manner as if such offence had been committed against the laws of such colony, and any offence that may be committed in any parts that shall not be within the certain bounds of any colony shall and may be tried and determined in the colony where the offender shall be taken." (Hutchinson's Plan, 1754.)

"The congress shall also make such general ordinances as may relate to our general commerce." (Franklin's Articles of Confederation, 1775.)

"The United States, in congress assembled, shall also have the sole and exclusive right and power of regulating the trade and managing all affairs with the Indians not members of any of the states; provided that the legislative right of any state, within its own limits, be not infringed or violated." (Articles of Confederation, 1778.)

"The congress shall have the sole power of regulating the affairs and trade of the Indians not members of any state." (Drayton's Articles of Confederation, 1778.)

"The legislature of the United States shall have the power to regulate commerce with all nations and among the several states." (Pinckney's Plan, 1787.)

"The congress shall have power to regulate commerce with foreign nations and among the several states and with the Indian tribes." (The Constitution.)

Evolution of the Constitution

12. Sending and Receiving Ambassadors.

"That the power and duty of congress shall extend to the sending and receiving ambassadors." (Franklin's Articles of Confederation, 1775.)

"The United States, in congress assembled, shall have the sole and exclusive right and power of sending and receiving ambassadors." (Articles of Confederation, 1778.)

"The congress shall have sole power of sending ambassadors to, and receiving therefrom, foreign princes and states." (Drayton's Articles of Confederation, 1778.)

"The senate shall have the sole and exclusive power to appoint ambassadors and other ministers to foreign nations.

"He [the President] shall receive public ministers from foreign nations, and may correspond with the executives of the different states." (Pinckney's Plan, 1787.)

"He [the President] shall nominate, and, by and with the advice of the senate, shall appoint ambassadors and other public ministers.

"He shall receive ambassadors and other public ministers." (The Constitution.)

13. Captures.

"The United States, in congress assembled, shall have the sole and exclusive right and power of establishing rules for deciding in all cases what captures on land or water shall be legal, and in what manner prizes taken by land or naval forces in the service of the United States shall be divided or appropriated." (Articles of Confederation, 1778.)

"The congress shall have the sole power of declaring what captures on land and on water shall be legal, and in what manner such captures, by the land and naval forces in the service of the United States, shall be divided and appropriated." (Drayton's Articles of Confederation, 1778.)

"The legislature of the United States shall have the power to make rules concerning captures from an enemy." (Pinckney's Plan, 1787.)

Federalism in Detail

"The congress shall have power to make rules concerning captures on land and water." (The Constitution.)

14. THE JUDICIARY.

The New England union of 1643 contemplated nothing more than a legislative department, which was to exercise all the powers of the Union. Penn's plan of 1696 added an executive, and subsequent plans down to the time of the Revolution were usually based on those two departments, which, however, were not always entirely distinct from each other. A judicial department was never mentioned, because the plans and the situation were not sufficiently complex to require the function of regularly organized government. It was not until the time of the Articles of Confederation of 1778 that the judicial power was cautiously introduced, and confined at first to piracies and felonies on the high seas and cases of capture.

"The United States, in congress assembled, shall have the sole and exclusive right and power of appointing courts for the trial of piracies and felonies committed on the high seas; [and] courts for receiving and determining finally appeals in all cases of captures." (Articles of Confederation, 1778.)

"The congress shall have the sole power of appointing courts in the several United States for trial of piracies committed on the high seas, and for deciding finally appeals in all cases of capture arising in such states respectively." (Drayton's Articles of Confederation, 1778.)

"That a national judiciary be established; to consist of one or more supreme tribunals and of inferior tribunals; to be chosen by the national legislature; to hold their offices during good behavior, and to receive punctually, at stated times, fixed compensation for their services, in which no increase or diminution shall

Evolution of the Constitution

be made so as to affect the persons actually in office at the time of such increase or diminution. That the jurisdiction of the inferior tribunals shall be to hear and determine, in the first instance, and of the supreme tribunal to hear and determine, in the *dernier ressort*, all piracies and felonies on the high seas ; captures from an enemy ; cases in which foreigners, or citizens of other states, applying to such jurisdictions, may be interested ; or which respect the collection of the national revenue, impeachments of any national officers, and questions which may involve the national peace and harmony." (Randolph's Plan, 1787.)

"The legislature of the United States shall have the power to constitute tribunals inferior to the supreme court.

"The legislature of the United States shall have the power, and it shall be their duty, to establish such courts of law, equity, and admiralty as shall be necessary.

"The judges of the courts shall hold their offices during good behavior and receive a compensation which shall not be increased or diminished during their continuance in office. One of these courts shall be termed the supreme court, whose jurisdiction shall extend to all cases arising under the laws of the United States, or affecting ambassadors, other public ministers, and consuls ; to the trial or impeachment of officers of the United States ; to all cases of admiralty and maritime jurisdiction. In cases of impeachment affecting ambassadors and other public ministers this jurisdiction shall be original and in all other cases appellate." (Pinckney's Plan, 1787.)

"The congress shall have power to constitute tribunals inferior to the supreme court.

"The judicial power of the United States shall be vested in one supreme court and in such inferior courts as the congress may from time to time ordain and establish. The judges, both of the supreme and inferior courts, shall hold their offices during good behavior, and shall, at stated times, receive for their services a compensation which shall not be diminished during their continuance in office.

"The judicial power shall extend to all cases in law and equity arising under this constitution, the laws of the United States and

Federalism in Detail

treaties made, or which shall be made, under their authority; to all cases affecting ambassadors, other public ministers, and consuls; to all cases of admiralty and maritime jurisdiction; to controversies to which the United States shall be a party; to controversies between two or more states; between a state and citizens of another state; between citizens of different states; between citizens of the same state claiming lands under grants of different states; and between a state, or the citizens thereof, and foreign states, citizens, or subjects.

"In all cases affecting ambassadors, other public ministers, and consuls, and those in which a state shall be a party, the supreme court shall have original jurisdiction. In all the other cases before mentioned the supreme court shall have appellate jurisdiction, both as to law and fact, with such exceptions and under such regulations as the congress shall make." (The Constitution.)

"The judicial power of the United States shall not be construed to extend to any suit in law or equity commenced or prosecuted against one of the United States by citizens of another state, or by citizens or subjects of any foreign state." (Eleventh Amendment to the Constitution.)

15. Power to Borrow Money.

"The United States, in congress assembled, shall have authority to borrow money or emit bills on the credit of the United States, transmitting every half year to the respective states an account of the sums of money so borrowed or emitted." (Articles of Confederation, 1778.)

"The congress shall have the sole power of emitting and borrowing money upon the credit of the United States, from time to time, not exceeding the sum ascertained as necessary to be raised for the service of the confederacy, transmitting to the several states, half yearly, an account of the sums of money so emitted and borrowed, applying the said sums of money ascertained to be raised, and allowed to be emitted and borrowed, for defraying the public expense." (Drayton's Articles of Confederation, 1778.)

"The legislature of the United States shall have the power to borrow money and emit bills of credit." (Pinckney's Plan, 1787.)

"The congress shall have power to borrow money on the credit of the United States." (The Constitution.)

16. Regulation of the Value of Money.

"And, lastly, whether considering the trouble and confusion attending the endless diversity of money, it would not be best, by an act of the legislature at home, to establish one medium to obtain in the colonies." (Dr. Johnson's Plan of 1660.)

"The congress shall also make such general ordinances as relate to our general currency." (Franklin's Articles of Confederation, 1775.)

"The United States, in congress assembled, shall also have the sole and exclusive right and power of regulating the alloy and value of coin struck by their own authority, or by that of the respective states." (Articles of Confederation, 1778.)

"The congress shall have the sole power of regulating the alloy and value of coin struck by their authority." (Drayton's Articles of Confederation, 1778.)

"The legislature of the United States shall have the power to coin money and regulate the value of all coins, [and] to declare the law and punishment of counterfeiting coin." (Pinckney's Plan of 1787.)

"The congress shall have power to coin money, regulate the value thereof and of foreign coin, [and] to provide the punishment of counterfeiting the securities and current coin of the United States." (The Constitution.)

17. Standard of Weights and Measures.

"The United States, in congress assembled, shall also have the sole and exclusive right and power of fixing the standard of weights and measures." (Articles of Confederation, 1778.)

"The legislature of the United States shall have the power to fix the standard of weights and measures." (Pinckney's Plan, 1787.)

"The congress shall have power to fix the standard of weights and measures." (The Constitution.)

18. ARMY.

An army is an essential part of a federal government if the federalism is to endure. In fact, the earliest forms of federalism had in view an army as their principal object. The New England union of 1643 was established almost for the sole purpose of raising an army to protect the provinces that were associated in the union.

At the same time there is the danger that the army may become so large as to be a menace to liberty, or that it may be used to coerce some one or more of the States for the benefit of the others. To guard against this, the early plans of union usually left much of the control to the individual provinces, each of which was to furnish its quota of men and no more, appoint the officers, and furnish arms and equipments, while ammunition, food, and general expenses were to be provided by the union. As federalism developed, and less and less was left to the individual States, the control of the army was placed in the Congress, or whatever body most fully represented the people, who have always proved to be very jealous of standing armies, and, in this respect, most careful guardians of their liberty.

"It is further agreed that if any one of these jurisdictions, or any plantations under it, or in any combination with them be invaded by any enemy whomsoever, upon notice and request of any three magistrates of that jurisdiction so invaded, the rest of

Evolution of the Constitution

the confederates, without any further meeting or expostulation, shall forthwith send aid to the confederate in danger, but in different proportions,—namely, the Massachusetts an hundred men sufficiently armed and provided for such a service and journey, and each of the rest forty-five so armed and provided, or any less number, if less be required, according to this proportion. But if such confederate in danger may be supplied by their next confederate not exceeding the number hereby agreed, they may crave help there, and seek no further for the present. The charge to be borne as in this article is expressed, and, at the return, to be victualled and supplied with powder and shot for their journey (if there be need) by that jurisdiction which employed or sent for them; but none of these jurisdictions to exceed these numbers till by a meeting of the commissioners for this confederation a greater aid appear necessary. And this proportion to continue till, upon knowledge of greater numbers in each jurisdiction which shall be brought to the next meeting, some other proportion be ordered. But in any such case of sending men for present aid, whether before or after such order or alteration, it is agreed that at the meeting of the commissioners for this confederation the cause of such war or invasion be duly considered, and, if it appear that the fault lay in the parties so invaded, that then that jurisdiction or plantation make just satisfaction, both to the invaders whom they have injured, and bear all the charges of the war themselves without requiring any allowance from the rest of the confederates towards the same. And further, that if any jurisdiction see any danger of any invasion approaching, and there be time for a meeting, that in such case three magistrates of that jurisdiction may summon a meeting at such convenient place as themselves shall think meet, to consider and provide against the threatened danger, provided when they are met they may remove to what place they please, only whilst any of these four confederates have but three magistrates in their jurisdiction, their request or summons from any two of them shall be accounted of equal force with the three mentioned in both the clauses of this article till there be an increase of magistrates there." (New England Union, 1643.)

Federalism in Detail

[The Congress] "to consider of ways and means to support the union and safety of these provinces against the public enemies." (Penn's Plan of Union, 1696.)

"That there be a reasonable sum raised and paid every year from each province for erecting forts, where proper, and repairing the old ; and for providing the said forts with arms and ammunition, etc., the better to enable the provinces to extend their territories backward.

"That the standing military forces that shall be thought needful for the defence of all the provinces be on any vacancies filled up by the said captain-general, to be confirmed by his Majesty's commission.

"That the said captain-general have power to remove any officer in the militia of any province when under his command upon service, but to fill up the vacancies with persons only of the province to which the said militia belonged.

"That the captain-general have power to order and march the militia of any province to the defence of another (this article to be settled under reasonable rules, allowances, and restrictions)." (Lord Stair's Plan, 1721.)

"That they [the grand council] raise and pay soldiers and build forts for the defence of any of the colonies." (Franklin's Plan of 1754.)

"That one company, consisting of one hundred men complete, exclusive of officers, shall be raised by every province, and a regiment formed of the thirteen companies to be called the union regiment, to be commanded by one colonel, lieutenant-colonel, and major, to be appointed by the king.

"That this little standing army shall assist in making roads, building forts, or any other necessary work." (Peters's Plan, 1754.)

"That the president and council shall have power to raise and pay soldiers and build forts for the defence of any of the colonies, and for removing all encroachments upon his Majesty's territories, and for the annoyance of his Majesty's enemies." (Hutchinson's Plan, 1754.)

"The congress shall also make such general ordinances as

Evolution of the Constitution

may relate to the establishment of posts and the regulation of our common forces." (Franklin's Articles of Confederation, 1775.)

"The United States, in congress assembled, shall also have the sole and exclusive right and power of making rules for the government and regulation of the said land and naval forces, and directing their operations.

"The United States, in congress assembled, shall have authority to agree upon the number of land forces, and to make requisitions from each state for its quota in proportion to the number of white inhabitants in such state, which requisition shall be binding; and thereupon the legislature of each state shall appoint the regimental officers, raise the men, and clothe, arm, and equip them, in a soldier-like manner, at the expense of the United States; and the officers and men so clothed, armed, and equipped shall march to the place appointed, and within the time agreed on by the United States in congress assembled. But if the United States, in congress assembled, shall, on consideration of circumstances, judge proper that any state should not raise men, or should raise a smaller number than its quota, and that any other state should raise a greater number of men than the quota thereof, such extra number shall be raised, officered, clothed, armed, and equipped in the same manner as the quota of such state, unless the legislature of such state shall judge that such extra number cannot be safely spared out of the same; in which case they shall raise, officer, clothe, arm, and equip as many of such extra number as they judge can be safely spared; and the officers and men so clothed, armed, and equipped shall march to the place appointed, and within the time agreed on by the United States in congress assembled." (Articles of Confederation, 1778.)

"The congress shall have the sole power of ascertaining the military land quota of each state in proportion to the number of white inhabitants therein respectively; making rules for the government of the said military quotas,—directing, ordering, and commanding the said military quotas, generalissimo, major-generals, principal staff officer, subordinate officers, war office, in all their operations and proceedings; collecting military stores and provisions, and issuing them for the service of the United States.

Federalism in Detail

"The military land quota of each of the United States shall be in proportion to the number of white inhabitants in each. The several states shall, in due time, embody the several military quotas required by the congress, and shall raise, clothe, arm, and maintain them at the general expense rated by the congress. The several states shall appoint all the regimental and deputy staff officers incidental to their quotas; and into as many brigades as the congress shall brigade their respective quotas, so many brigadier-generals shall such respective state nominate,—the whole to be commissioned by the congress. All vacancies in a quota shall be supplied by its state. The executive power in each state, except that in which the congress be sitting, shall, under the authority and control of the congress, direct the land forces, ships, and vessels of war, and all officers incidental thereto, in the service of the United States within such state. The proportionate pecuniary quotas of the several states shall be regulated in proportion to the number of inhabitants in each state respectively. Whenever such pecuniary quotas for the service of the United States shall be required by congress they shall state the capitation rate. Each state shall then appoint persons to number its whole inhabitants, according to the mode stated, to ascertain the number of white inhabitants in each state; such persons being also caused to specify the number of white, mustizo, mulatto, and negro inhabitants respectively. Such a numeration being duly returned, the legislature in each state shall levy the sum of money to arise therefrom in such mode as they shall deem expedient; and a true copy of the said return shall, without loss of time, be sent to congress. The several states shall duly pay their pecuniary quotas into the treasury office of America by the time mentioned by the congress for such payment, unless to the contrary directed for the good of the public service; in which case, such state so directed shall, within twelve months, duly account with the said treasury office for the pecuniary quota, or part thereof so directed to be retained." (Drayton's Articles of Confederation, 1778.)

"The legislature of the United States shall have power to raise armies; to pass laws for arming, organizing, and disciplining the militia of the United States; to provide such arsenals and erect such fortifications as may be necessary for the United States, and to exercise exclusive jurisdiction therein; to establish military roads." (Pinckney's Plan, 1787.)

"The congress shall have power to raise and support armies, but no appropriation of money to that use shall be for a longer term than two years.

"To make rules for the government and regulation of the land and naval forces.

"To provide for calling forth the militia to execute the laws of the union, suppress insurrections, and repel invasions.

"To provide for organizing, arming, and disciplining the militia, and for governing such part of them as may be employed in the service of the United States, reserving to the states respectively the appointment of the officers and the authority of training the militia according to the discipline prescribed by congress.

"And to exercise like authority [*i.e.*, exclusive authority] over all places purchased by the consent of the legislature of the state in which the same shall be for the erection of forts, magazines, arsenals, dock-yards, and other needful buildings." (The Constitution.)

19. NAVY.

"That, until the said provinces shall be enabled thereto, his Majesty would allow eight or ten small men-of-war constantly to attend this general government and to protect the trade; which ships to be under the command and direction of the said captain-general, and to be paid their wages by the joint government of the whole continent so soon as the ability of this new general government can allow of." (Lord Stair's Plan, 1721.)

"That the president-general, with the advice of the grand council, equip vessels of force to guard the coasts and protect the trade on the ocean, lakes, or great rivers." (Franklin's Plan of 1754.)

"The United States, in congress assembled, shall also have the sole and exclusive right and power of making rules for the

Federalism in Detail

government and regulation of the said land and naval forces and directing their operation.

"The United States, in congress assembled, shall have authority to build and equip a navy." (Articles of Confederation, 1778.)

"The congress shall have the sole power of building, purchasing, and equipping a naval force in the service of the United States of America; making rules for the government of the said naval force, admiralty office; directing, ordering, and commanding the said naval force, admiralissimo, subordinate officers, naval office in all their operations and proceedings. Each state shall, within five years, establish a foundation for a naval seminary, making suitable provision for the constant maintenance, education, and fitting for sea five youths for every thousand white inhabitants within such state." (Drayton's Articles of Confederation, 1778.)

"The legislature of the United States shall have the power to build and equip fleets; to provide such dock-yards as may be necessary for the United States, and to exercise exclusive jurisdiction therein." (Pinckney's Plan, 1787.)

"The congress shall have power to provide and maintain a navy.

"And to exercise like authority [*i.e.*, exclusive authority] over all places purchased by the consent of the legislature of the state in which the same shall be, for the erection of forts, magazines, arsenals, dock-yards, and other needful buildings." (The Constitution.)

20. CONTROVERSIES BETWEEN STATES.

"That the power and duty of congress shall extend to the settling all disputes and differences between colony and colony about limits or any other cause." (Franklin's Articles of Confederation, 1775.)

"The United States, in congress assembled, shall also be the last resort on appeal in all disputes and differences now subsisting, or that hereafter may arise, between two or more states concerning boundary, jurisdiction, or any other cause whatever." (Articles of Confederation, 1778.)

"The congress shall have the sole power of being the *dernier ressort* on appeal in all cases of dispute between any two or more of the United States." (Drayton's Articles of Confederation, 1778.)

"They [the senate] shall have the exclusive power to regulate the manner of deciding all disputes and controversies now existing, or which arise, between the states, respecting jurisdiction or territory." (Pinckney's Plan, 1787.)

"The judicial power shall extend to controversies between two or more states." (The Constitution.)

21. Treaty-making Power.

"That the president-general, with the advice of the grand council, hold or direct all Indian treaties in which the general interest or welfare of the colonies may be concerned." (Franklin's Plan of 1754.)

"That the president, by the advice of the council, may hold and manage all Indian treaties in which the general interest or welfare of the colonies may be concerned." (Hutchinson's Plan, 1754.)

"That the power and duty of congress shall extend to entering into alliances." (Franklin's Articles of Confederation, 1775.)

"That the president and commander-in-chief shall have no power to make war or peace, or enter into any final treaty, without the consent of the general assembly and legislative council." (South Carolina Constitution of 1776.)

"The United States, in congress assembled, shall have the sole and exclusive right and power of entering into treaties and alliances, provided that no treaty of commerce shall be made whereby the legislative power of the respective states shall be restrained from imposing such imposts and duties on foreigners as their own people are subjected to, or from prohibiting the exportation or importation of any species of goods or commodities whatsoever." (Articles of Confederation, 1778.)

"The congress shall have the sole power of entering into and concluding treaties and alliances with foreign powers." (Drayton's Articles of Confederation, 1778.)

Federalism in Detail

"The senate shall have the sole and exclusive power to make treaties." (Pinckney's Plan, 1787.)

"He [the President] shall have power, by and with the advice and consent of the senate, to make treaties, provided two-thirds of the senators present concur." (The Constitution.)

22. Money not to Issue from Treasury except by Law.

"Yet no money to issue but by joint orders of the president-general and grand council, except where sums have been appropriated to particular purposes and the president-general is previously empowered by an act to draw for such sums." (Franklin's Plan of 1754.)

"But no money shall issue out of any treasury without the special order of the president, by the advice of the council, except where sums have been appropriated to particular purposes, and the president shall be specially empowered to draw for such sums." (Hutchinson's Plan, 1754.)

"No moneys shall be issued out of the treasury of this commonwealth and disposed of (except such sums as may be appropriated for the redemption of bills of credit or treasurer's notes, or for the payment of interest arising thereon), but by warrant under the hand of the governor for the time being, with the advice and consent of the council for the necessary defence and support of the commonwealth, and for the protection and preservation of the inhabitants thereof, agreeably to the acts and resolves of the general court." (Massachusetts Constitution of 1780.)

The above provision from the Massachusetts constitution of 1780 is repeated in the New Hampshire constitution of 1784.

"No money shall be drawn from the treasury but in consequence of appropriations made by law." (The Constitution.)

23. Post-Office.

"That there be a post established to pass once a week, at least, through all the provinces from the southernmost settlement to the most northerly, that is possible, with orders to send intelligences; and that every governor may correspond with the general on all occasions." (Lord Stair's Plan, 1721.)

"The United States, in congress assembled, shall also have the sole and exclusive right and power of establishing and regulating post-offices from one state to another throughout all the United States, and exacting such postage on the papers passing through the same as may be requisite to defray the expenses of the said office." (Articles of Confederation, 1778.)

"The congress shall have the sole power of establishing and regulating post-offices throughout the United States, exacting such postage as may be necessary to defray the expense of the said offices, or any part thereof." (Drayton's Articles of Confederation, 1778.)

"The legislature of the United States shall have the power to establish post-offices; to establish post-roads." (Pinckney's Plan, 1787.)

"The congress shall have power to establish post-offices and post-roads." (The Constitution.)

24. TREASON.

"The congress shall have power to declare what shall be deemed treason against the United States of America, and in what manner such treason shall be punished." (Drayton's Articles of Confederation, 1778.)

"The legislature of the United States shall have the power to declare the punishment of treason, which shall consist only in levying war against the United States, or any of them, or in adhering to their enemies. No person shall be convicted of treason but by the testimony of two witnesses." (Pinckney's Plan, 1787.)

"Treason against the United States shall consist only in levying war against them, or in adhering to their enemies, giving them aid and comfort. No person shall be convicted of treason unless on the testimony of two witnesses to the same overt act, or on confession in open court.

"The congress shall have power to declare the punishment of treason, but no attainder of treason shall work corruption of

Federalism in Detail

blood, or forfeiture, except during the life of the person attainted." (The Constitution.)

25. LETTERS OF MARQUE.

"The United States, in congress assembled, shall have the sole and exclusive power of granting letters of marque and reprisal in times of peace." (Articles of Confederation, 1778.)

"The congress shall have the sole power of granting letters of marque and reprisal." (Drayton's Articles of Confederation, 1778.)

"The congress shall have power to grant letters of marque and reprisal." (The Constitution.)

26. NATIONALITY.

"The right of making laws for the United States should be vested in all their inhabitants.

"In all the affairs that respect the whole, congress must have the same power to enact laws and compel obedience throughout the continent as the legislatures of the respective states have in their several jurisdictions. If congress have any power, they must have the whole power of the continent.

"Let every state reserve its sovereign right of directing its own internal affairs; but give to congress the sole right of conducting the general affairs of the continent." (Noah Webster's "Sketches of American Policy," 1785.)

"We, the people of the states of New Hampshire, Massachusetts, Rhode Island and Providence Plantations, Connecticut, New York, New Jersey, Pennsylvania, Delaware, Maryland, Virginia, North Carolina, South Carolina, and Georgia, do ordain, declare, and establish the following Constitution for the government of ourselves and posterity." (Pinckney's Plan, 1787.)

"We, the people of the United States, in order to form a more perfect union, establish justice, insure domestic tranquillity, provide for the common defence, promote the general welfare, and secure the blessings of liberty to ourselves and our posterity, do ordain and establish this Constitution for the United States of America." (The Constitution.)

CHAPTER VIII.

CLAUSES OF THE CONSTITUTION WHICH WERE OF SHORT DEVELOPMENT.

IN the course of the evolution which has been traced in the preceding chapters it is noticeable that almost every document contained a few points that were new, and in this way the development progressed. Almost every colony, State, or person that was considered contributed its share, and it would be extremely difficult to decide what place or what person did the most. When the Constitution had absorbed all this development, it also, like its predecessors, added some new provisions which were suggested by circumstances, and these are the only parts of the Constitution which can be said to have been "struck off at a given time."

They were not, however, imitations of anything in Europe. Most of them were very simple and necessary provisions, which speak for themselves:

1. The debts contracted by the government under the Articles of Confederation to be valid against the government under the Constitution.

2. Congress to have exclusive jurisdiction over such district (not exceeding ten miles square) as should become the seat of government.

3. The United States to protect each state from invasion, and also from domestic violence, on application of the legislature of the state, or, if it is not in session, on application of the governor.

Clauses of Short Development

4. The ratification by the conventions of nine states to be sufficient to establish the Constitution between the states so ratifying.

5. The United States to guarantee to every state a republican form of government.

6. The times, places, and manner of holding elections for senators and representatives to be prescribed in each state by the legislature thereof; but the congress may, at any time, by law, make or alter such regulations, except as to the places of choosing senators.

7. The President may require the opinion, in writing, of the principal officer in each of the executive departments, upon any subject relating to the duties of their respective offices.

8. The congress to have power to establish uniform laws on the subject of bankruptcies.

9. No senator or representative to hold any office which shall have been created or the emoluments thereof increased during the time for which he was elected.

10. The importation of slaves not to be prohibited prior to the year 1808, but a tax on such importation not exceeding ten dollars for each person may be imposed.

11. New states to be admitted into the Union by congress.

12. The congress to have power to dispose of and make rules and regulations for the territory or other property of the United States.

13. No tax or duty to be laid on articles exported from any state. No preference to be given by any regulation of commerce or revenue to the ports of one state over those of another. Vessels bound to or from one state not to be obliged to enter, clear, or pay duties in another.

Among the amendments, the ninth, which says that the enumeration of certain rights shall not be construed to disparage others retained by the people, and the tenth, which says that the powers not delegated to the United States nor prohibited to the States are reserved to the States or to the people, were the result of the

Evolution of the Constitution

agitation of the State-rights party, and were adopted immediately after the Constitution went into effect. The eleventh amendment, which prohibits the extension of the judicial power to any suit against any one of the States by citizens of another or by citizens of a foreign state, was also the result of the same agitation.

There were also two parts of the fifth amendment which are not to be found in previous American constitutions,—the guarantee that no person shall be held to answer for a capital or infamous crime except on indictment of a grand jury, and the guarantee that no person shall be deprived of life, liberty, or property without due process of law. These were old principles well known for centuries among the English race, and they had appeared in colonial statutes. It was thought that their enforcement would be better secured by making them a part of the National Constitution.

Since the adoption of the twelfth amendment, which altered the method of electing the President, there have been no amendments except those made immediately after the civil war, and, as they were the result of that war, and their history is well known, they need not be considered.

There are three clauses in the Constitution still remaining undiscussed which were preceded by a slight development, and their history can be traced to some extent in colonial times.

The first is the provision that, when vacancies occur in the representation from any State, the executive authority of the State may issue writs of election to fill such vacancies. Some of the colonial charters, like

Clauses of Short Development

those of Massachusetts and of Rhode Island, gave the assembly authority to fill vacancies in executive offices until there should be another election; but vacancies in the assembly were not specially provided for. Some of the constitutions of 1776, particularly those of Delaware, Georgia, and North Carolina, directed that the legislature should issue writs of election for filling any vacancies that might occur in its membership. The Maryland constitution of 1776 provided that such writs should be issued by the speaker; and the Pennsylvania constitution of the same year gave general power to the president and council to fill all vacancies in office, but whether this would include vacancies in the legislature is doubtful. The provision in the Maryland constitution was like the English practice of that time, by which, when a vacancy occurred in the House of Commons, the Speaker could order another election to fill the vacancy.

The Constitution also directs that the President shall receive a salary, and that the senators and representatives shall receive a compensation for their services. The members of the British Parliament received no salaries, and it seems to have been a disputed question at the time our National Constitution was framed whether members of Congress should be paid for their services. Franklin argued very earnestly that they should not be paid. The previous documents had usually been silent on this subject; but some of the constitutions of 1776, notably that of Virginia and the Massachusetts constitution of 1780, had provided for the salaries of the governor and other officers; and the Pennsylvania Frame of 1696 gave the members of the council five shillings a day, the members of the assembly four shillings a day, and the members of both bodies twopence a mile for travelling expenses.

The provision in the Constitution requiring the publication, from time to time, of a statement and account of the receipt and expenditure of all public money had appeared before in several of the plans of union.

This completes our analysis of the Constitution, every clause of which has been traced to its origin. The analysis seems to show that the Constitution was a growth, and that it is as much the result of the natural development of progressive history as is the British Constitution. It was not, as Mr. Gladstone says, "struck off at a given time;" nor was it, as Herbert Spencer would have us think, "obtained by a happy accident, not by normal progress;" and the description of it given by Von Holst and others as "a mere experiment" is equally inaccurate.

CHAPTER IX.

DUTCH SOURCES.

THE appearance of Mr. Campbell's work, "The Puritan in Holland, England, and America," was a great surprise to both lawyers and scholars. It was an unexpected, stunning blow; a clap of thunder out of a clear sky. Two large, handsome volumes, written in an attractive, even brilliant manner, informing us in sharp, sarcastic sentences, with an immense array of facts, that our most cherished liberties and customs were neither English nor native, but Dutch, was so dazing that no one at first knew what to say, and we have scarcely yet mustered courage enough to frame a reply.

In all other books that describe or criticise our institutions,—whether written by ourselves or by foreigners,—there is not even a suggestion that our sources were Dutch. In all our political histories in which every event of our growth is given, from the settlement of Virginia in 1607 down to the present decade, there is not a sentence or a hint that would have led one to this discovery of Mr. Campbell's. More than that, if we examine the original authorities, the writings and documents of the colonists and of the framers of the constitutions of the States and of the Constitution of the nation, we find not a word to show that those men, our ancestors, were conscious that they were copying from

Holland. I certainly never saw an original document, letter, speech, or writing of any kind in which a father of the republic said that American institutions were of Dutch origin, or in which an argument was made in favor of transplanting Dutch institutions to America. Mr. Campbell quotes no writings of this sort, and it is not unfair to infer that none exist.

His method of proof is not at all documentary, although in his preface he tells us that documents are the only sure tests for the truth of history, and he has much to say of modern scientific methods of investigation. In the past, he tells us, history was written by legends, tradition, and rumor. Public documents were considered parts of the private library of the king, and it is only of recent years that official records, diplomatic correspondence, and state papers have become accessible to historians. "One can imagine," he says, "the position of a writer who sat down to compose a work upon his own or any other country when such material was everywhere kept a secret." But Mr. Campbell seems to have taken the place of those ancient kings, and fails to furnish his readers with anything in the nature of documentary proof.

A great deal of his information, as he frankly admits, has been obtained at second hand from miscellaneous reading in books like Carnegie's "Triumphant Democracy," "The Chautauquan," and magazine articles. The results of the original research among documents of which he says so much in the preface we look for in vain, and we find him generously acknowledging that he is greatly indebted to Carnegie's "Triumphant De-

Dutch Sources

mocracy" for a large number of valuable facts (vol. i. p. 22).

His method of proof may be called the speculative method,—the method of suggestion, presumption, probability. He wanders round and round his subject with telling anecdotes, witticisms, gibes at the ancient historians, and pæans to liberty. All European nations except Holland have been so cruel and wicked, and have had such ridiculous laws and governments, that, as the United States is the only other nation in the world that has not been cruel, wicked, and ridiculous, the reader may judge for himself as to the possibility, if not probability, and perhaps certainty, of the one being derived from the other.

He informs us at great length that the English are prone to exaggerate their own merits, trace everything to themselves, and ignore the services of other nations. The writers of New England have all been men of English origin, and would naturally, therefore, be silent about the Dutch sources and assign their institutions to English causes. But if New England was so thoroughly permeated with Dutch ideas, as he elsewhere maintains, how was it that the writers escaped? If the Dutch influence had been powerful enough to create institutions, would it not have been powerful enough to compel acknowledgment, or at least an admission or a complaint?

He has a very clever way of throwing out a suggestion which will leave a significant impression on the mind of an ordinary reader. Thus, in his preface, after saying that in 1563 the Dutch were famous for their

Evolution of the Constitution

ingenuity in inventing all sorts of machines for shortening labor, he says, "Here is the Yankee of Europe," and this hint, mixed with others of a similar kind, gradually builds up the feeling that of two countries so nearly alike one must be the copy of the other.

After wandering through hundreds of pages heaping up these possibilities, insinuations, and suggestions, and doing it in a manner irresistibly bright and attractive, Mr. Campbell has completely accomplished his purpose,—at least temporarily,—for an untrained mind can hardly resist the impression that America was thoroughly Dutch in origin; that our Constitution, the New England township system, our land laws, our customs, and our general principles of dealing, conduct, and government are from Holland, not England; and one begins to wonder how it is that the language still remains English.

The book is in its individual sentences very clear, but the general arrangement is most confusing to any one who wants definiteness and accuracy. It is a mere collection of points mixed in with a vast assemblage of facts and anecdotes taken from the history of nearly the whole world. There is no regular, orderly statement of propositions to be proved; no separate statement of each individual item of Dutch imitation followed by its proof, and no thorough analysis.

For example, why should not that little item of the recording of deeds and mortgages, which he says came from Holland, be in a chapter or at least a paragraph by itself, with all that can be said in favor of the imitation, and then done with it; and so on with the next item?

Dutch Sources

Why should the recording item be spread out in various parts of the book, with references to it every now and then? Why should the careful reader, seeking definite, positive knowledge, feel that he must go through the ten hundred and twenty-one pages of the two volumes with a pencil, setting down any distinct item of imitation he can find and putting under it any proof he can collect from the whole? If the work had been divided into distinct topics of positive imitations it could all have been written in one chapter with sub-headings for each imitation, and would hardly have extended much beyond the limits of a magazine article.

In reading the book one examines table of contents, text, and chapter-headings in vain in the search for a definite division of topics, with proof and argument assigned to each, and it is not until near the end of the second volume that a page (vol. ii. p. 465) is found where the author sums up, with some degree of explicitness, the American institutions which he thinks he has proved were copied from Holland. I shall give the list in his own words:

1. The Federal Constitution as a written instrument.
2. The provisions in this instrument placing checks on the power of the President in declaring war and peace and in the appointment of judges and all important executive officers.
3. The whole organization of the Senate.
4. Our State constitutions.
5. Freedom of religion.
6. Free press.
7. Wide suffrage.
8. Written ballot.

9. Free schools for boys and girls.
10. The township system (with its sequence of local self-government in county and State).
11. The independence of the judiciary.
12. The absence of primogeniture.
13. The subjection of land to execution for debt.
14. The system of recording deeds and mortgages.
15. Public prosecutors for crime in every county.
16. The constitutional guarantee that every accused person shall have subpœnas for his witnesses and counsel for his defence.
17. The reforms in our penal and prison system.
18. The emancipation of married women.
19. The whole organization of our public charitable and reformatory work.

In taking up the instances of imitation I cannot treat them either in the order in which Mr. Campbell has summed them up or in the order in which they occur throughout the book, for neither order would disclose the true bearings of the subject. Nor is it necessary to discuss every one of them. I shall begin with No. 10, "The township system (with its sequence of self-government in county and State)," because this brings us at once to fundamental principles and decides the question, which is, of course, at the bottom of all the others, How did the Dutch influence reach America?

It is obvious to any one who notices the way in which Mr. Campbell has worded this item of imitation, "The township system (with its sequence of self-government in county and State)," that it is overwhelming in its effects. If it is true that the Dutch established the New England township system and that that created self-government in the counties, and that thence came

Dutch Sources

State sovereignty, the Dutch undoubtedly created the whole United States. If Mr. Campbell could establish that one item No. 10, I for one should be willing to surrender all the others. They would not be worth contending for, and it would remain merely to call on Mr. Campbell to explain by what accident it was that our language still remained English and why our courts still continued to cite authorities from the English law reports.

Mr. Campbell's argument I understand to be this: The Pilgrim Fathers, so called, were a sect of Brownists or Independents who were terribly persecuted for their religion in England, and fled to Holland, where they lived, first at Amsterdam, afterwards at Leyden, for twelve years. During that time they probably acquired a knowledge of Dutch institutions, especially the Dutch towns, which governed themselves with more or less independence. At the end of the twelve years about one hundred of them came to America and settled on the coast of Massachusetts at a place they called New Plymouth, about fifty miles from Boston.

About ten years after their arrival a large number of English people called Puritans came upon the coast and settled in the neighborhood of Boston. These people continued to come for about ten years, and vastly outnumbered the Independents, or Pilgrim Fathers, who had settled at New Plymouth. The new-comers, or Puritans, were not Dutch, and had not, as a class, been in Holland; but two of them had,—namely, Dudley, who was afterwards governor, and had been a soldier in the Dutch army, and Hugh Peters, a minister, who had

Evolution of the Constitution

once had a congregation in Holland; and doubtless others whom we have not heard of had been in Holland. They had, however, nearly all of them come from the southern and eastern parts of England, where, half a century before, large numbers of Dutch immigrants had settled. As we find that all these people in Massachusetts established towns which governed themselves in purely local matters, and as there were similar towns in Holland, the Massachusetts town system was clearly of Dutch origin.

So much for the entering in of the influence. Mr. Campbell goes on to show how it spread. People from Massachusetts, some from the Plymouth colony, and some from the Puritans, founded Connecticut and established self-governing towns, which were also clearly of Dutch origin, because the people who established them had been under the Dutch influence in Massachusetts, and one of these Connecticut settlers, Thomas Hooker, the minister, had lived for a time in Holland. About the same time that these events occurred in New England, or soon after, the Dutch established these same self-governing towns in their colony at New York. And from these Dutch sources in Massachusetts, New York, and Connecticut, establishing the idea of local self-government in a town, that idea has spread to the whole country, creating the local self-government of our counties all over the Union and the self-government of our States, or State sovereignty, as we call it.

This Dutch influence prevailed not only in Massachusetts, Connecticut, and New York, but, according to

Dutch Sources

Mr. Campbell, in New Jersey, which was originally a part of the New York Dutch colony; and it also prevailed in Pennsylvania and Delaware, because William Penn's mother had been a Dutchwoman, and Penn himself had travelled in Holland and was familiar with its language and people. The northern and middle Atlantic States were therefore pervaded by this influence, and, as those are the States which have in effect created the Union and given forth the dominating principles of American civilization, it is ridiculous to say that our ideas and institutions are English. The only part of the country where English notions prevailed was the South, and all it gave was slavery. Virginia may have contributed the idea of the natural equality of man, but she borrowed this from the Roman law.

The Dutch influence, being thus firmly established in the dominating part of the country, and having evidently created the township system with all its consequences, was also fruitful in establishing other customs, laws, and institutions. The Connecticut people, at their first settlement, drew up a document creating a legislature and government, and this has been called the first American written constitution. This idea of reducing the principles or form of government to writing must have been taken from Holland, because the Netherland Republic had existed for about half a century under the Union of Utrecht, which was a written constitution. These written constitutions became the regulation forms for the States after the Revolution, copied, of course, from Connecticut's instrument, which was copied from Holland; and, as our Federal Constitution is written, it follows that, so far as it is a written instrument, it also is of Dutch origin.

One would suppose that, having proved that our local self-government in towns, our State governments, our State constitutions as written instruments, and our National Constitution as a written instrument were of Dutch origin, Mr. Campbell would be content. But he is not, and he goes on piling up the resemblances.

Religious liberty existed in Holland before it was established anywhere else in Europe. We also find it among the Dutch in New York and in the laws made by Penn for Pennsylvania: so that the American principle of religious freedom may be said to have come from Holland. It is true that in Massachusetts we find a church established by law and heresy punished with death; but this, Mr. Campbell assures us, was because the Puritans had not, in this particular, imbibed the full measure of the Dutch influence.

Similarly, we find free schools in Holland, New England, and New York: so that the American public-school system had its source in the Netherlands, and it has now filled the whole Union. So, also, the system of recording deeds and mortgages was unknown in England, but was common practice in the Netherlands, whence it was introduced into Massachusetts, New York, New Jersey, and Pennsylvania, and thence to the whole country.

In England the distribution of land among small holders was fettered by primogeniture, which has now given the soil of Great Britain into the hands of a few aristocrats and left the mass of the people in poverty,

Dutch Sources

with scarcely space on which to stand. The Dutch law, which gave equal inheritance to all children, prevailed in New York, and was, of course, well known to William Penn and the people who settled New England. Hence we have in the United States an absence of primogeniture and an easy and approximately equal distribution of land, which has prevented grinding poverty and encouraged the energy and enterprise of our people.

Such is, in brief, Mr. Campbell's argument. And now for something on the other side.

First of all, we must have a clear idea of the exact nature of the New England town system, which Mr. Campbell says was introduced from Holland. The New England town was a little democracy of people who elected their own officers and through them governed a district of land much smaller than a county. Each town also sent its representatives to the general assembly of the colony. It was a system of local government by means of small districts, each of which had entire charge of its own affairs. The peculiarities about it were the small size of each district, the absolute control over its own affairs, the free voice and vote of all the people in exercising that control, and their right to be represented as a town in the general assembly.

But Mr. Campbell's rather vague description of the Dutch towns would not imply that they had these characteristics at the time the English colonies in America were settled. The most important one of all—the free suffrage and democracy—was absent. "In few, if any of them," he says, "was there an approach to democracy in later times. That had passed away with the advance of wealth, the rich merchants and manufacturers who secured the charters having generally absorbed the power originally lodged in the whole body of the freemen." (Vol. i. p. 147.)

Elsewhere (vol. ii. p. 429) he says that the free suffrage had been retained in some of the most obscure provinces of the northeast, and, as the Pilgrim Fathers who came to Massachusetts were not in those provinces of the Netherlands, he has a labored argument to show how they might, nevertheless, probably have heard about it.

Apparently the only resemblance which the Dutch towns near where the Pilgrim Fathers lived bore to those established in Massachusetts was that the six important ones could send representatives to the assembly of the States. The right of the small towns to send representatives and their democratic government had been lost hundreds of years before. This makes the resemblance somewhat lame; and the argument is still further weakened by an admission in another passage (vol. i. p. 75) that the township system prevailed in Central Asia and still exists in Upper India. So the Dutch were, after all, not its inventors.

But let us pass all this for the present, for we shall see the Dutchman's idea of town government when we come to the history of New York. Let us suppose, for the sake of argument, that the towns in Holland were all self-governing and represented as towns in the legislature, just as Mr. Campbell would like to have them,— how does he prove that the Massachusetts people imitated them? He must show some connecting link; he

Dutch Sources

must give positive proof of imitation, because without this it is perfectly possible that the people of New England developed their town system out of natural conditions, as the people of Central Asia or of Upper India, or the Dutch themselves, developed towns to suit their purpose.

Mr. Campbell, however, neither quotes nor cites any document, pamphlet, letter, or writing of any kind in which any of the people who settled Massachusetts expressed a liking for the Dutch town system or urged its adoption in the colony. If they were so infected by the Dutch influence, would they not have said something about it? Would they not have argued in its favor and urged its extension? They were great writers. Many of them kept diaries and journals that have come down to us. We have also their letters, the pamphlets, and the books they wrote, all preserved with the scrupulous care with which Massachusetts guards every scrap of paper relating to her history. How was it that none of the Cottons or Mathers—men of such vast learning, the authors of so many books and essays on all sorts of subjects—never touched on Holland? How is it that in all the writings of Massachusetts, from beginning to end, there is nothing Mr. Campbell can quote to show a Dutch influence, not merely in this township question, but in other things or in general?

If there is nothing that shows Dutch influence in general, would not the introduction of some special Dutch institution like the towns have aroused comment or resistance, and would there not at least be something to quote on this point? Even Mr. Campbell does not contend that every one of the Puritans was literally an out-and-out Dutchman. If there was even a small minority of out-and-out Englishmen in the colony, would they not have protested against the introduction of a foreign method of government, and, like those minorities that followed Roger Williams or Anne Hutchinson, raised a controversy about it of which there would at least be some scrap of evidence?

As a matter of fact, we all know that there were in the colony from the very beginning Church of England people and others who objected most strenuously to the Puritan methods of government, and sent home reports finding all the fault they could think of. Other disgruntled persons went to England in person to make complaints. Many of these complaints were addressed to royalists and to the Crown with the intention of bringing down vengeance on the Puritans of Massachusetts and depriving them of their charter. They continued to be made for fifty years, and in the end were successful, and the charter was annulled in 1684.

Now, is it possible that, among all these complaints made by Tories, none can be found to the effect that the colonists had adopted a foreign system of local government? Charles II. and James II. had no love for Holland, their enemy, and, in the end, the destroyer of their dynasty and house. What appeal to their resentment against Puritan Massachusetts would have been more effective than to tell them that the colony was adopting the laws and methods of Holland?

Mr. Campbell meets none of these points. In fact, he admits, in the fullest manner, not only that there was

Dutch Sources

no general resemblance to Holland in Massachusetts, but that in most respects the colony was the very reverse of Holland in the things for which Holland was most famous. Freedom of religion, freedom of the press, separation of church and state, and humane laws were the great Dutch principles which Mr. Campbell says were copied by the United States. But Massachusetts punished heretics with death or banishment, had the severest sort of censorship of the press, a church established by law, the right to vote and hold office confined to church-members, a set of the most bloody and cruel laws, punishing more than twenty offences with death; and, as is well known, she kidnapped the Indians and sold them as slaves, killed hundreds of people for witchcraft, whipped hundreds of Quakers at the cart's tail, and hung four of them for persisting in their religious belief.

But a little difficulty like this is nothing to a man of Mr. Campbell's ingenuity, and, accordingly, we find him saying in explanation (vol. ii. p. 415), "But at this period she was in a few respects less advanced than her sister colonies, simply because she had absorbed less from the Netherland Republic."

In other words, the colony where, as Mr. Campbell contends, the Netherland influence entered—the colony where there was more direct Netherland influence than in any other part of the country except New York—was less like Holland and had fewer of the great Netherland principles than parts of the country where there was no Netherland influence at all.

But let us do some of Mr. Campbell's work for him,

Evolution of the Constitution

and examine the early writings of Massachusetts to see what they say of this Dutch influence, and also what they say about the beginning of the town system. The first and most important is Bradford's "History of Plymouth Plantation."

Bradford was the leader of the Pilgrim Fathers. He started with them in England when they fled to Holland. He lived with them during the twelve years' sojourn in Amsterdam and Leyden. He came with them to Massachusetts, assisted in founding the settlement at New Plymouth, was elected their governor over and over again, and remained with them until his death in 1657. He was a man of good education, familiar with French, Latin, Greek, and Hebrew, and a student of history and theology. His "History of Plymouth Plantation" is the history of an eye-witness, and, as it goes very much into details, it is an authority of the highest importance. If there was strong Dutch influence among his people after they came to Massachusetts, it would surely show itself in his book.

But when we read the book there is nothing Dutch about it. Indeed, when we consider that he and his people had been in the Low Countries for twelve years, it is surprisingly free from anything of the sort; and our first thought is, that, as usually happens when people of mature years sojourn in a foreign country, very little impression had been made upon their minds, and they remained the out-and-out Englishmen they had been born and bred. If the Pilgrim Fathers had gone to the Netherlands when they were children, and had grown up in the country, their ideas and conduct

Dutch Sources

might have been different. But in the whole book there is only one passage showing any liking for Dutch ways or giving a Dutch reason for anything, and that is an account of the first marriage-ceremony that was performed :

"May 12 was the first marriage in this place which according to the laudable custom of the Low Countries, in which they had lived, was thought most requisite to be performed by the magistrate, as being a civil thing, upon which many questions about inheritances do depend with other things most proper to their cognizance and most consonant to the Scriptures, Ruth 4, and nowhere found in the Gospel to be laid on the ministers as a part of their office. This decree or law about marriage was published by the States of the Low Countries A.D. 1590. That those of any religion after lawful and open publication coming before the Magistrates in the Town or State House were to be orderly (by them) married to one another. Peters Hist. Fol. 1029. And this practice hath continued amongst, not only them, but hath been followed by all the famous churches of Christ in these parts to this time. Ano. 1646." (Mass. Hist. Coll., 4th series, vol. iii. p. 101.)

I cannot tell, of course, whether Mr. Campbell knew of this passage ; but at any rate he does not quote it, and it would help him very little. He does not contend, so far as I know, that the Dutch, through the Pilgrim Fathers, or in any other way, introduced into this country the custom of being married before a magistrate instead of before a minister of religion. It would be in vain to make such a contention, for no such custom exists. Our people are almost universally married by ministers of religion, although marriages before magistrates, mayors, or competent witnesses of any kind are usually held valid, as they were in the old common law of England.

So far as it goes, this passage from Bradford would prove that the Pilgrim Fathers attempted to introduce a Dutch method which has been rejected by the American people. And the passage is the more noteworthy on this account, because it is a rebuke to all those spread-eagle writers who assume that everything that was done near Plymouth Rock spread out into the whole United States, and must be traced back to the rock as a cause.

The passage is the only one I know of in the whole range of Massachusetts literature that gives a Dutch origin for anything. I was once quite familiar with many of the original authorities of the colonial history of Massachusetts, and I can remember nothing Dutch in them. I have not gone over all of them again to write this chapter, for it would be a great labor, and is not necessary. But I have gone over those which relate to the first settlement, the time when the town system was introduced, and the twenty years that followed. These are the ones which are relevant and essential, for, if there was as much Dutch influence among the colonists as Mr. Campbell asserts, it would have shown itself at once, certainly within the first twenty years. If there are no signs of it within those twenty years, there is, in my opinion, no proof of it.

I have selected the first twenty years—that is, from 1620 to 1640—because after that immigration ceased, and there were no more important additions to the population by migration until long after the Revolution.

Dutch Sources

So far as the Plymouth Plantation is concerned, those twenty are more than covered by Bradford's history. But the Plymouth colony was very small and unsuccessful, and the large majority of the Massachusetts population was made up of the Puritans, who, ten years after the arrival of the Pilgrims, came and settled in the neighborhood of Boston. They increased very rapidly for ten or more years by immigration until there were about twenty thousand, and after that their increase was also rapid by births.

These people were direct from England, and had never sojourned in Holland. But, as Mr. Campbell says that they had come from the southern and eastern parts of England, to which many Hollanders had migrated half a century before, it is necessary to examine an authority which will include them. There is an excellent one,—"Winthrop's Journal,"—which has sometimes been published as "Winthrop's History of New England." It is much more voluminous and detailed than Bradford's history, and comes down to a later time.

Winthrop was an accomplished man of some means, who came out with the first of the Puritans, was their first governor, and was re-elected governor again and again for many years. He was a lawyer by education, and at the time of his arrival in the colony was forty-three years old, in the prime of life, keen, active, interested in everything, and recorded day by day in his journal minute details of events, and especially controversies and disputes, in which he usually gave the arguments of both sides. I have examined this book from beginning to end, and, if it contains anything showing the slightest trace of Holland or Dutch influence, or the slightest trace of any institution, custom, or law established for Dutch reasons, I cannot find it.

So it stands that there is just one solitary passage in Bradford's history giving a Dutch reason for establishing the custom of marriage by magistrate instead of by minister, and this a custom which was not accepted by the American people. As Bradford in this instance gave his reason for the custom, it is fair to conclude that if anything else had been established for a Dutch reason he would have said so, and this conclusion is strengthened when we find that in describing the method of allotting land he gives a reason for it, but instead of being Dutch it is a Roman reason.

I shall quote this passage, but before I do so I wish to say that Winthrop also gives reasons for the establishment of many things, and they are usually drawn from the Old Testament, which was the chief guide of the Massachusetts people in all matters of law and government. It was a rule with the magistrates that when no law could be found applicable to a case it must be decided according to the Word of God. From the Old Testament were drawn their reasons for banishing Anne Hutchinson and Roger Williams, hanging the witches, and persecuting the Quakers. To give a reason for everything they did and give it fully and minutely was one of their most prominent characteristics, and I think that any one who reads the elaborateness of the arguments used in "Winthrop's Journal" and elsewhere must be impressed with the thought that if there had been a Dutch influence at work among these people it would

Dutch Sources

have shown itself unequivocally. Moreover, they were very original in all their methods, and Mr. Campbell is, I think, the first person who has ever charged them with plagiarism.

The passage I wish to quote from Bradford in which the land allotment seems to remind him of Rome is a very important one :

"That they might therefore encrease their tillage to better advantage, they made suite to the Governor to have some portion of land given them for continuance, and not by yearly lotte, for by that means, that which the more industrious had brought into good culture (by much pains) one year, came to leave it the next, and often another might enjoy it ; so as the dressing of their lands were the more sleighted over, and the less profit. Which being well considered, their request was granted. And to every person was given only one acre of land, to them and theirs, *as near the town as might be, and they had no more till the seven years were expired. The reason was, that they might be kept close together both for more safety and defence, and the better improvement of the general employments.* Which condition of theirs did make me often think, of what I had read in Pliny of the Romans first beginnings in Romulus time. How every man contented himself with two acres of land, and had no more assigned them. And chap three. It was thought a great reward to receive at the hands of the people of Rome a pint of corn. And long after, the greatest present given to a Captain that had got a victory over their enemies was as much ground as they could till in one day. And he was not counted a good, but a dangerous man, that would not content himself with seven acres of land. As also how they pound their corn in mortars, as these people were forced to do many years before they could get a mill." (Mass. Hist. Coll., 4th series, vol. iii. 167.)

Now I have quoted this passage not only for the suggestion about Rome which it contains, but because

Evolution of the Constitution

it shows the origin of the towns. "Every person was given only one acre of land," he says, and "as near the town as might be," and "the reason was that they might be kept close together both for more safety and defence and the better improvement of the general employments."

This is the earliest mention of the towns in any Massachusetts writing. The event of the allotment of land of which he speaks happened in 1624, four years after the colony was founded, and he refers to the town as in existence, which of course it was; for when the Pilgrims landed they built a town of log huts, and they dared do nothing else. The barren nature of the country and the immediate hostility of the Indians forbade them to spread out. They must keep together for mutual defence and for their fishing and trade on the sea.

At first they held their land in common, and it was cultivated for the public benefit. But at best their agriculture was merely the cultivation of garden patches. When they passed beyond the communism and garden stage the people still lived in the town and went out to cultivate their lots, which, as Bradford says, were kept as near the town as possible. All other towns in Massachusetts, and, for that matter, in New England, were arranged on the same plan, not because of anything in Holland or Rome, but because it was a necessity.

When we examine "Winthrop's Journal" we find two passages confirming this view. A few days after his arrival with the first ship-load of Puritans that were to begin the second colony, which in the course of years absorbed the Plymouth people, he made an entry as follows:

Dutch Sources

"December 6th, 1630. The Governor and most of the assistants and others met at Roxbury, and there agreed to build a town fortified upon the neck between that and Boston." ("Winthrop's History of New England," Savage's edition, vol. i. p. 38.)

Practical difficulties, such as want of water, prevented the carrying out of this plan, and a few days after we have another entry:

"Dec. 21. We met again at Watertown, and there, upon view, of a place a mile beneath the town, all agreed it a fit place for a fortified town." (*Id.*, vol. i. p. 39.)

In each instance he speaks of a "fortified" town; not a mere straggling settlement, but something more compact, complete, and self-sustaining; the sort of community that every one who landed on that stern coast knew to be a prime necessity.

And so we have both Bradford and Winthrop mentioning the town, referring to it as something which was a matter of course, Bradford giving reasons for keeping all the people close to the town, even when they were cultivating their land, and neither he nor Winthrop referring to Holland in any way whatever. On the contrary, Bradford says that the arrangement about the land reminds him of what he had read of Rome.

In Virginia the natural conditions enabled the reverse plan to be followed. The mildness of the climate and the richness of the soil soon revealed that there was not only a livelihood, but wealth, to be gained by spreading out and cultivating large tracts of land. This was the natural method in all the southern colonies, and, accordingly, the county became the unit of local government instead of the township of New England.

Evolution of the Constitution

The township system would have been an impossibility in the South, where a single farm was often as large as a New England township; and farther south than Virginia several townships could have been put within a single plantation. The county system became an inevitable necessity, and we find it everywhere in the South, becoming of less absolute importance as we go north, until, in Pennsylvania, we have a combination of the two systems,—town and county.

But it is to be observed that the first settlers in Virginia huddled together in Jamestown and held their land in common like the Pilgrim Fathers; and for the same reason. They feared the Indians; and at first they gained their livelihood from the fish in the water and vast quantities of wild fowl along the shores and a few little patches of land, which they cultivated more as gardens than as farms. But as soon as they learned the natural capacity of the country they spread out far and wide. Their energies became absorbed with inland occupations, and they cared little for the sea and ships.

The New Englanders, on the other hand, were obliged to continue as they had begun. They were compelled to devote themselves to the sea more and more or starve. The difficulties with the Indians never ceased, and before long the alliance of the French and Indians made the danger continuous down almost to the time of the Revolution. Town life was therefore a necessity, both for safety and for trade.

As the Massachusetts people advanced into the interior they moved by towns, for the same reasons and

Dutch Sources

with the same caution that they had established towns on the sea-coast. The town was usually set on a hill-top, or on high land. The people went out from it to cultivate their lots, and there was a law that no dwelling in any new plantation should be situated more than a mile from the meeting-house. (Palfrey's "New England," vol. i. p. 434.)

The advancement of the town system into the interior, of course, gave some protection to the sea-coast towns against the Indians, but they continued in their self-governing character because the other conditions remained unchanged and the people were all engaged in trade, commerce, and ship-building. Their agricultural interests were slight, and, from the nature of the soil and climate, incapable of being much enlarged. But commerce, ship-building, and the carrying trade of the world were capable of indefinite expansion, and to these the people devoted their utmost energies, with the result we all know.

That whatever people lived in New England would necessarily be merchants, fishermen, and ship-owners, and therefore townsmen, was clearly foreseen in the earliest times, and the reasons for the origin of the towns which I have advanced receive very strong support from a pamphlet issued in 1622 by the Council for New England, entitled "A Brief Relation of the Discovery and Plantation of New England."

This Council was a company chartered by the Crown, and its full title was "The Council Established at Plymouth, in the County of Devon, for the Planting, Ordering, Ruling, and Governing of New England in

Evolution of the Constitution

America." The Plymouth colony of the Pilgrim Fathers was within its domain, and obtained from it a patent for its land. The Council intended to manage its great domain of New England for profit and the glory and extension of the British Empire, and the pamphlet was intended to describe the country and encourage settlers. It begins with an account of the many voyages of discovery sent out under the auspices of the Council; then follows a description of the climate, animals, and various products, and the last chapter tells of the sort of government the Council intends to enforce. Beginning with praise of monarchical forms, the chapter goes on to show how the people will nevertheless have full representation in making laws. And then comes the following paragraph:

"And there is no less care to be taken for the trade and publique commerce of merchants whose government ought to be within themselves, in respect of the several occasions arising between them, the tradesmen and other the Mechanicks, with whom they have most to do; and who are generally the chief inhabitants of great cities, and towns, in all parts; it is likewise provided, that all the cities in that territory, and other inferior towns where tradesmen are in any numbers, shall be incorporated and made bodies politique, to govern their affairs and people as it shall be found most behoveful for the publique good of the same; according unto the greatness or capacity of them, who shall be made likewise capable to send certain their deputies, or Burgesses to this publique assembly, as members thereof, and who shall have voices equal with any of the rest."

It seems to me that this passage settles the question beyond any reasonable doubt. Here we have a council of persons, many of them noblemen, all of them living

Dutch Sources

in England, in no way connected with Holland, and yet before the New England town system had come into existence they recommended self-governing towns and town representation as part of the government of the country. They give their reasons for it. Merchants and traders must necessarily live in towns, and not only ought they to be allowed to rule themselves in their own local affairs, but their towns should have representation as towns in the legislative assembly of the country.

The passage, it will be observed, recommends two essentials, which afterwards became the characteristic features of the New England town system,—namely, that the towns should be independent, and that they should be represented as towns in the legislature.

If any one has a fancy for fixing upon any one passage or place as the origin of the New England towns, there it is. But I do not like that way of putting it. The New England towns originated in the necessities and circumstances of the country,—necessities and circumstances which the Council, the settlers, and every one saw who became familiar with the land; and it cannot be said that any one man or set of men had the honor of the invention.

The Council of New England saw that the colonists would of course be traders and fishermen, dealing in ships, fish, lumber, and furs; agriculture would be of little importance; and the principal part of the people would live in towns on the sea-coast, some of them large towns; and many of the people would become great merchants. They not only knew this, but they were aware that every one else who thought of going to New

England knew it; and unless they made the government of the country attractive to this merchant class and gave them special privileges, they would not go.

There was nothing new in a town governing itself and becoming a political entity of more or less local independence. The idea is a simple and natural one, springing up instantly when circumstances suggest it as valuable to accomplish a result. History is full of instances, —the Greek towns, Rome, the free cities of the Middle Ages, as well as the towns of Holland. But the Council of New England needed no assistance from such sources any more than did the captains and sailors who visited the New England coast and saw and reported the evident and only way of settling and living upon it.

When we look into the history of the Massachusetts laws relating to the towns we find that the towns existed before any laws were made about them. They sprang up naturally, instantly, and spontaneously wherever a company of settlers pitched upon a tract of land as suitable for their purpose.

Palfrey, in his history of New England, gives us the history of the laws very clearly. The first record is in 1630, when Boston, Charlestown, and Watertown were given their names. The next year each town is required to provide its inhabitants with arms,—a significant requirement in view of the circumstances already mentioned. In 1635 the general court, after saying that "particular towns have many things which concern only themselves," goes on to regulate them in some general matters. In Charlestown it was found that there was "great trouble and charge of the inhabitants by reason

Dutch Sources

of the frequent meeting of the townsmen in general," and because a large body in mass-meeting could not properly transact numerous details; and so it was decided to appoint eleven men to attend to the town's affairs. Other towns, as they grew large, adopted the same plan, and the men chosen for this purpose became gradually known as the selectmen.

By the year 1635 the town system was settled and established, and any one who wishes to prove a Dutch influence must prove it to have been at work before that year,—that is, between the years 1620 and 1635. But there is nothing in the laws or in any other contemporaneous document to show the slightest trace of Dutch feeling. In fact, every step of the development, so far as it can be traced, has all the characteristics of an indigenous growth.

The discussion of the subject would, however, be incomplete without a further consideration of some of Mr. Campbell's arguments. He is not satisfied with the Dutch influence which he supposes was so strong among the people of the Plymouth colony, but attempts to show that the Puritans, who came afterwards and settled in the neighborhood of Boston, were also under that influence.

These Puritans came direct from England and had never been in Holland. They were numerous, powerful, and rapidly filled the country, and there is not a scrap of writing by any one of them to show that they admired Dutch methods or were affected by Dutch influence. But this is a mere trifle for Mr. Campbell, and a few of his clever sentences dispose of it:

Evolution of the Constitution

"Most of the men who founded this colony emigrated from the eastern and southern counties of England, in which, as we have seen, Cromwell raised his army; the counties in which a hundred thousand Netherland refugees had taken up their residence half a century before, and which always had the most intimate relations with the Dutch Republic. All of these men were acquainted with Netherland institutions. Some of them, we know, had passed years in Holland. Governor Dudley, for example, had been a soldier in the Dutch army. The famous clergyman, Hugh Peters, presided over a congregation at Rotterdam from 1623 to 1635, and there were doubtless many others among the rank and file unknown to history who had also lived in that asylum of the persecuted."

This is one of the most charming passages in his book, and, for the boldness and at the same time subtlety of its assumptions, can hardly be equalled in all literature. "Most of the men," he says, "who founded this colony came from the eastern and southern counties of England." That is very likely. A glance at the map shows that this delightfully vague phrase, "the eastern and southern counties," includes fully half of England. In the north England is very narrow, but in the south it spreads out very wide. A majority of the people have always lived in the south of it, and London itself has always been in the southern and eastern counties. In other words, Mr. Campbell says that the Massachusetts Puritans came from those parts of England where the majority of the English people lived; and I suppose it is not worth while to dispute this assertion.

His next assertion is that fifty years before a hundred thousand Netherlanders had taken refuge in those "eastern and southern counties." Well, suppose they had, where is the proof that they infected with their ideas the

Dutch Sources

particular Puritans that came to Massachusetts? Why should they have infected them? They were refugees from their own country because it had become too hot to hold them, and why should they have made a special point of introducing its institutions? How was it that they infected the particular persons who came to Massachusetts, and not the rest of the English people who stayed at home?

As in the absence of direct evidence the whole question is one of assumption only, is it not equally reasonable to assume that a hundred thousand Netherland refugees, scattered through the wide extent of the eastern and southern counties among millions of the hard-headed, insular English people, would have not the slightest influence?

Next, he says that these counties "always had the most intimate relations with the Dutch Republic." But what does this vague expression mean? "Most intimate relations" could hardly have existed between those counties and the Netherlands without England becoming all Dutch or Holland becoming all English. If Mr. Campbell could show that the particular persons who migrated from those counties to Massachusetts had been in Holland or had intimate relations with Holland, whatever that may mean, he might advance his cause. But he makes no such attempt; and his wild assertion that all eastern and southern England was most intimate with Holland, and that any one who came from those parts of England would necessarily establish Dutch institutions wherever he went, is a mere trap for the unwary.

Again, he says "all of these men were acquainted

with Netherland institutions." Hardly all of them; for all sorts and conditions were to be found among the Puritans. He probably means that the leaders and men of education were acquainted with Netherland laws and government. In this sense we can readily admit his assertion, and add to it that they were also well acquainted with the institutions of antiquity, Greek, Roman, and Jewish, and also with the laws and methods of government of France, Spain, and possibly Central Asia and Upper India. Men in all ages and in all nations have often been well acquainted with the laws and usages of other countries. Such an assertion, in the absence of direct, positive evidence of imitation, proves nothing.

But the best comes last. "Some of them," he says, "we know, had passed years in Holland;" and then he goes on to mention two,—Dudley and Hugh Peters. Now, Peters did not reach the colony until 1635, and by that time the town system was firmly established; so he could not have had anything to do with it; and, as he remained in the colony only six years, his after-influence could not have been very great. So it comes to this, that, after asserting that "some of them had passed years in Holland," he has one person to make his assertion good,—one out of more than ten thousand. Dudley had a great task in converting that remnant; and if he really performed it, all the other great men of the earth should sink into insignificance.

But Mr. Campbell is always equal to any emergency, and, after giving his two solitary instances, he adds, "and there were doubtless many others among the rank

Dutch Sources

and file unknown to history who had also lived in that asylum of the persecuted." Could anything be more complete than this? The less evidence you have, and the more utterly ignorant you are of the existence of a fact, the more surely you can prove it. Just confess your ignorance, offer no proof whatever, and add, "but there were doubtless"—whatever you want.

Wishing to be entirely candid with Mr. Campbell, I have looked all through Winthrop's journal to see if I could find any support for this "doubtless there were others," and I succeeded in finding one person, Captain David Patrick, who had served in the Dutch army. As he came out with Winthrop and the first settlers, he will replace Hugh Peters, and Mr. Campbell will still have two persons to introduce Dutch influence.

Patrick had been brought out to help drill the militia, and even if he did not establish the town system it would, I should think, be open to Mr. Campbell to assert that "possibly," or "probably," or "doubtless," he introduced the Dutch military system, which would, of course, spread from Massachusetts to the whole United States. This would explain at once the wonderful success of the Continental army in the Revolution. Trenton, Saratoga, and Yorktown would no longer be mysterious successes; and, as Patrick introduced his system in the North, we could the more easily understand the triumph of the North over the South in the civil war.

Patrick, however, was not congenial to the Puritans. They could not altogether approve of his morals; and after many difficulties, and becoming "proud and vicious," as Winthrop tells us, he fled to the Dutch at

New York, where he was murdered by one of those liberal people. (Winthrop's "New England," vol. ii. p. 151.)

Mr. Campbell's book gives the impression that the Plymouth people were very much enamoured of Holland, and if this were so it might help out his presumptions and inferences. But let us see what Bradford says on this point.

He begins his history by telling us that his people were very unwilling to leave England. They were persecuted for their religion; but they would have remained if they could. Like many others, they loved their country none the less because they were persecuted. What they desired was to convert their country to their own way of thinking. They believed that their religion was the true English religion.

"But to go into a country they knew not (but by hearsay), where they must learn a new language, and get their living they knew not how, it being a dear place, and subject to the miseries of war, it was by many thought an adventure almost desperate, a case intolerable, and a misery worse than death." (Mass. Hist. Col., 4th series, vol. iii. p. 11.)

Arrived in Holland, they had religious liberty, it is true, but in other respects they did not prosper. They were ground down by the most wretched poverty, and such was the "hardness of the place and country" that their friends in England would not join them. That is to say, the English dissenters and Puritans, who were bitterly persecuted in England, preferred to remain in their own country and endure the persecution rather

Dutch Sources

than subject themselves to the miseries and privations of Holland.

This does not comport very well with the impression we gather from Mr. Campbell's book, that the whole mass of English dissenters not only knew all about Holland, but admired its methods and customs, and were running to and fro all the time and on "the most intimate relations." When we come down to actual evidence on the subject, those who knew all about the Netherlands were not so very well pleased with what they knew, and those who really were on "the most intimate relations" with that country were very glad to get away from it.

"In the agitation of their thoughts, and much discourse of things here about, at length they began to incline to this conclusion, of removal to some other place. Not out of any new-fangledness, or other such like giddy humor, by which men are oftentimes transported to their great hurt and danger, but for sundry weighty and solid reasons; some of the chief of which I will here briefly touch. And first, they saw and found by experience the hardness of the place and country to be such, as few in comparison would come to them, and fewer that would bide it out, and continue with them. For many that came to them, and many more that desired to be with them, could not endure that great labor and hard fare, with other inconveniences which they underwent and were contented with.

* * * * * * *

"Yea, some preferred and chose the prisons in England, rather than this liberty in Holland, with these afflictions. But it was thought that if a better and easier place of living could be had, it would draw many, and take away these discouragements. Yea, their pastor would often say, that many of those who both wrote and preached now against them, if they were in a place where they might have liberty and live comfortably, they would then practise as they did.

* * * * * * *

"And therefore according to the divine proverb that a wise man seeth the plague when it cometh, and hideth himself, Prov. 22, 3, so they like skilful and beaten soldiers were fearful either to be entrapped or surrounded by their enemies, so as they should neither be able to fight nor fly; and therefore thought it better to dislodge betimes to some place of better advantage and less danger, if any such could be found.

* * * * * * *

"For many of their children that were of the best dispositions and gracious inclinations having learned to bear the yoke in their youth and willing to bear part of their parents' burden, were often times, so oppressed with their heavy labors, that though their minds were free and willing, yet their bodies bowed under the weight of the same, and became decrepid in their early youth; the vigor of nature being consumed in the very bud as it were. But that which was more lamentable, and of all sorrows most heavy to be borne, was that many of their children, by these occasions and the great licentiousness of youth in that country and the manifold temptations of the place, were drawn away by evil examples into extravagant and dangerous courses. . . . . So that they saw their posterity would be in danger to degenerate and be corrupted. . . . . They lived here but as men in exile and in poor condition."

These passages, it seems to me, make the situation very clear. The great mass of the English dissenters, though persecuted and unable to make England altogether the country they wished it to be, preferred nevertheless to remain and endure these evils and wait for better times, like the sturdy hearts of oak they were. A small company of them, however, after many misgivings, went to try life in Holland; and, though they

Dutch Sources

were not persecuted, their experiment was in other respects a failure.

What they wanted was England without persecution; and they decided that the way to realize that ideal as nearly as possible was to go out on some of the wilderness land that belonged to England on the North American continent. They could have gone to one of the Dutch possessions, and were strongly urged to do it. Indeed, it would have been easier and more profitable for them. But they preferred the harder way beneath the English flag.

Besides Bradford, there is another excellent authority on these points,—Edward Winslow, who had been in Holland, and who came out on the Mayflower with the Pilgrims, and was afterwards their governor. Among his writings there is a pamphlet called "A Brief Narrative," in which he gives the reasons for leaving Holland so clearly and to the point that comment is unnecessary:

"But our reverend pastor, Mr. John Robinson, of late memory, and our grave elder, Mr. William Brewster (now at rest with the Lord,) considering, amongst many other inconveniences, how hard the country was where we lived, how many spent their estate in it, and were forced to return for England, how grievous to live from under the protection of the State of England, how like we were to lose our language and our name of English, how little good we did or were like to do to the Dutch in reforming the sabbath, how unable there to give such education to our children as we ourselves had received, etc., they, I say, out of their Christian care of the flock of Christ committed to them, conceived, if God would be pleased to discover some place to us (though in America) and give us so much favor with the King and State of

Evolution of the Constitution

England as to have their protection there, where we might enjoy the like liberty, and where, the Lord favoring our endeavors by his blessing, we might exemplarily show our tender countrymen by our example, no less burdened than ourselves, where they might live and comfortably subsist, and enjoy the like liberties with us, being freed from anti-christian bondage, keep their name and nation, and not only be a means to enlarge the dominions of our State, but the church of Christ also, if the Lord have a people amongst the nations whither he should bring us etc. hereby in their great wisdoms they thought we might more glorify God, do more good to our country, better provide for our posterity, and live to be more refreshed by our labors, than ever we could do in Holland, where we were." (Young's "Chronicles of the Pilgrim Fathers," p. 381.)

For many years after the Plymouth people were settled in Massachusetts the Dutch occupied the country about two hundred miles southwest of them, at New York. Dutch vessels were frequently working their way through Long Island Sound and up the Connecticut River, exploring the country with the hope of annexing it. They were very pleasant and friendly towards the Plymouth people, with a view of including them within the settlement at New York and having the whole of New England as a part of the Dutch colony. But we find that Bradford and his people withstood them, and distinctly warned the Dutch governor not to trespass within the bounds of New England. Winslow even went so far as to present a petition to the Lords Commissioners for Plantations in England asking for authority to resist the encroachments of both the Dutch and the French. (Mass. Hist. Coll., 4th series, vol. iii. p. 225, note, p. 328.)

As to the Puritans at Boston, they also had no par-

Dutch Sources

ticular liking for the Dutch at New York, and there are a number of passages in Winthrop's journal that show it. Judging from these, the Puritans had no sympathy with the Dutch religion, and regarded the Dutch colony merely as a place to which their heretics and exiles fled. A man or woman who was not moral enough or orthodox enough to live in Massachusetts went to the Hollanders at New York:

"They lay windbound sometime at Aquiday; then as they passed Hellgate between Long Island and the Dutch, their pinnace was bilged upon the rocks, so as she was near foundered before they could run on next shore. The Dutch governor gave them slender entertainment; but Mr. Allerton of New Haven, being there, took great pains and care for them." (Winthrop's "New England," Savage's edition, vol. ii. p. 96.)

"The lady Moodye, a wise and anciently religious woman, being taken with the error of denying baptism to infants, was dealt withal by many of the elders and others, and admonished by the church of Salem (whereof she was a member) but persisting still and to avoid further trouble etc. she removed to the Dutch against the advice of all her friends. Many others, infected with anabaptism, removed thither also, she was after excommunicated." (*Id.*, p. 123.)

"These people" (Mrs. Hutchinson and some others who had been banished for heresy) "had cast off ordinances and churches, and now at last their own people, and for larger accommodation had subjected themselves to the Dutch." (*Id.*, p. 136.)

"Other affairs were transacted by the commissioners of the United Colonies (*i.e.*, the New England Union of 1643) as writing letters to the Swedish Governor in Delaware River, concerning foul injuries offered by him to Mr. Lamberton and those people from New Haven who had planted there, and also to the Dutch Governor about the injuries his agent there had also offered and done to them as burning down their trading house, joining with the Swedes against them, etc." (*Id.*, p. 140.)

Evolution of the Constitution

"The United Colonies having made strict orders to restrain all trade of powder and guns to the Indians, by occasion whereof the greatest part of the beaver trade was drawn to the French and Dutch, by whom the Indians were constantly furnished with those things, though they also made profession of like restraint, but connived at the practice, so as our means of returns for English commodities were grown very short." (*Id.*, p. 311. See also pp. 314, 315, 324, 327.)

"About this time we had intelligence of an observable hand of God against the Dutch at New Netherlands, which though it were sadly to be lamented in regard of the calamity, yet there appeared in it so much of God in favor to his poor people here, and displeasure towards such as have opposed and injured them, as is not to be passed by without due observation and acknowledgment." (*Id.*, p. 316.)

The last quotation refers to the drowning of sixty Dutchmen in a shipwreck, among whom was Kieft, who had once been governor at New York. Other passages of similar import might be cited, but it is needless to multiply them.

The next source of Dutch influence after Massachusetts was, Mr. Campbell tells us, in New York. Of course, every one knows that the Dutch were there for about forty years before the English conquest, and when the assertion is made that these Dutch had the town system, freedom of religion and of the press, recording of deeds, equal inheritance of land, and various other valuable customs, most persons are ready to infer that these things spread thence to the whole United States.

But let us examine these assertions, which are made in Mr. Campbell's usual liberal manner, without citing any authority whatever. The Dutch had towns, of course. People have had towns everywhere, and, as the Dutch

Dutch Sources

at New York were principally traders and the Indians were very hostile, it was absolutely necessary that they should live in towns and have them fortified. But were these towns self-governing, and did they send representatives to the legislature, after the manner of the Massachusetts system? The most superficial glance at the history of New York shows that the Dutch towns never sent representatives to the legislature, for the very good reason that during the Dutch dominion there was no legislature in the colony.

This is the first check one receives after reading Mr. Campbell's extravagant eulogies. The Dutch, the authors of all our American liberty and institutions, had not, it seems, progressed so far among themselves as to have representative government in their own colony. Now the English colonies—those that were owned by feudal proprietors as well as those whose charters were granted by kings—had representative government from the beginning. But in Dutch New York it was not established, and could not be established, although the people rebelled and clamored for it.

There was no self-government in the Dutch colony at large, and no self-government in the towns. These towns were mere ordinary towns, and had none of the peculiar characteristics of the New England system. In some of these Dutch towns on Long Island English people from New England had settled, and they demanded local self-government for themselves. It was granted to pacify them and avoid offence to New England:

> " It is a suggestive fact that the first town court erected by the Dutch was one for the benefit of the English residents of Hemp-

stead, Long Island, a place then within New Netherland. In 1644 Kieft granted land to Robert Fordham, John Strickland, and other persons of English origin, then in allegiance to the States-General, with corporate powers including the right to nominate magistrates for the governor's selection, and to establish laws by ordinances with the consent of the inhabitants. . . . So extraordinary a grant of self-government at this early period was intended to placate the border English." (Fowler's "Introduction to Laws and Acts of New York." Published by Grolier Club, p. 23.)

The Dutch notion of municipal government was, as Bancroft puts it (History of the United States, vol. ii. p. 305, ed. 1846), that "the city had privileges, not the citizens." Citizenship was a mere commercial privilege, not a political enfranchisement. The Dutch in New York learned all they knew of the self-government of towns from the New Englanders. Indeed, so far as they learned any lessons at all in liberty they came from the same source. When the people on one occasion clamored for representative government they were incited by New England influence, and Stuyvesant, the governor, in rebuking them, said: "Will you set your names to the visionary notions of the New England men?" (Bancroft, vol. ii. pp. 306, 307.)

He was supported in his rebuke by the West India Company, which declared that the demand for representation was "contrary to the maxims of every enlightened government. Have no regard to the consent of the people, and let them no longer indulge the visionary dream that taxes can be imposed only with their consent." These New York Dutch were so far from introducing into America any liberty of their own that they were planning to copy English liberty and were listening

Dutch Sources

complacently to proposals of submitting themselves to English jurisdiction. All this is commonplace New York history, which Mr. Campbell could easily have discovered.

Mr. Campbell has much to say about freedom of religion and the absence of an established church in America, and much abuse for the English established church and English persecution. We cannot possibly, he says, have derived our religious liberty and separation of church and state from Great Britain. It must have been introduced among us by the Dutch. Possibly so. But O'Callaghan's volume of the Dutch laws and ordinances in New York does not give one that impression:

"Whereas we daily find that many vagabonds, Quakers and other Fugitives are, without the previous knowledge and consent of the Director General and council, conveyed, brought and landed in this government, and sojourn and remain in the respective villages of this Province, without those bringing them giving notice thereof, or such persons addressing themselves to the government and showing whence they come, as they ought to do, or that they have taken the oath of fidelity the same as other inhabitants; the Director General and Council, therefore, do hereby order and command all skippers, sloop captains and others, whomsoever they may be, not to convey, or bring, much less to land within this government, any such vagabonds, Quakers and other Fugitives, whether men or women, unless they have first addressed themselves to the government, have given information thereof and asked and obtained consent, on pain &c." (O'Callaghan's "Laws and Ordinances of New Netherland," p. 439.)

"The sheriff and Magistrates shall, each in his quality, take care that the Reformed Christian Religion be maintained in conformity to the Synod of Dordrecht, without permitting any other sects attempting anything contrary thereto." (*Id.*, p. 476.)

Evolution of the Constitution

Under these liberal Dutchmen in New York, Roman Catholics, Baptists, Quakers, and Jews were ostracized and refused the right to hold public worship. The Lutherans, after a struggle, secured a minister for themselves, and the English Presbyterians and Congregationalists were allowed their ministers because it was important to please them. Whatever religious liberty existed in New York was due to the English and the Lutherans, and not to the Dutch. (O'Callaghan's Laws, etc., vi.)

The truth is that the Dutch rule in New York was a stifling monopoly of the most arbitrary kind. The land was granted in large fiefs to patroons with the intention of creating a privileged class and aristocracy. Stuyvesant undertook to enforce religious uniformity and relentlessly persecuted the Lutherans and the Quakers, and, as a matter of fact, religious liberty was established in the colony when the English took it in 1664. At the same time representative government appeared.

Mr. Campbell seems to think that fair and honorable treatment of the Indians was a Dutch idea. If it was, the Indians were very ungrateful, for they slaughtered the Dutch without mercy. Every town and village had to be fortified, and at times they almost chased the Dutchmen out of the country. There was one episode in particular which shows the Dutch idea of honor, and, as it is given very concisely by Mr. Lodge in his history of the colonies, I shall quote his words:

"The Mohawks, armed by the Dutch, swept down from the north, driving the river tribes before them. The fugitives sought refuge in the Dutch settlement and were well received, especially by De Vries, who sought to give them every protection; but the helpless condition of his former enemies only aroused Kieft to fury. Two or three of the 'twelve,' who had been dissolved, met and presented a petition to the governor that the Indians should be attacked. . . . The wretched fugitives, surprised by their supposed protectors, were butchered in the dead of a winter night without mercy; and the bloody soldiers returned in the morning to Manhattan, where they were warmly welcomed by Kieft." (Lodge's "History of the Colonies," p. 289.)

In fact, the Dutch rule in New York was so illiberal and impolitic that settlers were kept away from the colony, and it never flourished. It was founded about the same time as New England, and had greater advantages and resources; but in 1664, when it was surrendered to the English, it had only seven thousand inhabitants against over a hundred thousand in New England.

The last place where the Dutch influence is supposed to have entered was Pennsylvania; but Mr. Campbell's argument on this point is scattered in many parts of his book. In the chapter on the Scotch-Irish he says (vol. ii. p. 470) that Pennsylvania and Delaware had a large Dutch population; and this absolutely untrue statement is one of those which appear all through the work, and gradually give the ordinary reader an impression favorable to the author's argument.

There never was a large Dutch population either in Delaware or in Pennsylvania. The Dutch had a few trading stations on the Delaware River and Bay at the same time that they occupied New York; but they never settled the country, or even attempted to settle it. The Swedes came and far outnumbered the Dutch; then the English came when they captured New York;

and at the time Penn and the Quakers arrived, in 1682, all the Dutch, Swedes, and English living on the whole length of the river were less than three thousand. Most of these were Swedes and English, and the Dutch amounted to nothing. They established no institutions of any kind; for any customs they or the Swedes had on the Delaware were swept out of existence by the English and the country put under English law.

Besides this make-weight assertion, Mr. Campbell says that Penn had travelled considerably in Holland, that his mother was a Dutchwoman, and that the Quakers resembled in doctrine the Mennonites of Holland. Now, it is undoubtedly true that Penn had travelled in Holland. He had travelled, however, much more in Germany He and his Quakers encouraged all the German peace sects that resembled the Quakers in religion to come to Pennsylvania, but none came from Holland except a few scattered individuals.

A large number of Germans, however, came; but they established no German form of government as part of the constitution of Pennsylvania, and no one has ever asserted that they did. This goes to show that the presence in a country of a large body of foreigners does not necessarily lead to the establishment of the institutions of the country from which the foreigners come.

If Penn was so familiar with Holland, and if people always imitate the foreign country with which they are familiar, we should expect to find a great deal that is Dutch in Pennsylvania. In fact, Pennsylvania seems to be a much better place for Mr. Campbell to introduce his Netherland influence than New England. But the

Dutch Sources

first thing that strikes us is that Penn did not introduce, nor attempt to introduce, the New England town system, or any system of towns like that in Holland. On the contrary, he introduced the English county system. In after-years the township system was partly introduced as the result of experience and convenience, so that Pennsylvania has a cross between the two, because the nature of the land, climate, and civilization makes the combination the best method, as the county alone is the best method farther south and the town alone farther north. So in this important instance Penn and his people adopted what seemed most suited to their circumstances, and were not looking over the world for something to imitate.

Let us go a step farther. Penn's agent in Holland was Benjamin Furly, an Englishman from Colchester, who at the age of twenty-five went to Holland and in the course of years became a rich and prosperous merchant at Rotterdam. He was a patron of letters, a collector of rare books, a writer of some little celebrity, and very much interested in the Quakers. His house was the resort of learned and distinguished men, and he was a great friend of the philosopher Locke. He interested himself to get German immigrants for Penn's colony, and Penn consulted him on all sorts of matters.

He consulted him about the best sort of constitution for Pennsylvania, and prepared one which contained a good many Dutch ideas, no doubt suggested by Furly. If this constitution had been adopted it would have been a strong point for Mr. Campbell. But it was rejected and abandoned by Penn himself, and in the place of it he prepared another which was adopted; and this also he submitted to Furly. We have Furly's criticisms on it, complaining, in rather strong language, that Penn had repudiated all his Dutch suggestions, and hinting that no good would come of it.

These criticisms of Furly's and the whole subject of his influence over Penn have been recently very carefully investigated by Mr. Julius Sachse in the *Pennsylvania Magazine of History* (vol. xix. p. 277). Penn resisted and rejected the Dutch influence, and all that Furly could persuade him to put in his constitution was a clause allowing the alien Germans greater privileges than were accorded to them in the other colonies.

Furly himself had an opinion about the liberality of Holland which is worth quoting. Among the people who called upon him to see his rare books and hear his opinions on various subjects was Zacharias von Uffenbach, who has left us in his memoirs an account of the visit:

"When I reminded him that in Holland Religious liberty prevailed, he denied emphatically that this assumption was true, and he became quite excited over the procedure of the local magistrates against the so-called English New-prophets.

"He admitted that he not only harbored their tenets, and had printed their writings with a preface of his own, but had defended them as well before the Magistrates and endeavored to shield and protect them, yet notwithstanding all his efforts these innocent people had been expelled from the country." (Penna. Mag. of History, vol. xix. p. 294.)

So, after all, there was not in Holland that absolute and complete religious liberty which Mr. Campbell would have us suppose, and which, he says, was copied

Dutch Sources

in America. There was, no doubt, more freedom in Holland in this respect than in some other countries of Europe. They were all working at the problem, each in its own way. Religious liberty was gradually developing in England, and there was a strong party there in its favor; Voltaire and his friends were fighting for it in France; and the Mennonites, Baptists, and other sects were its ardent advocates in Germany. Holland had rather more of it than some countries, partly because she found that toleration increased her population and commerce.

Each country's struggle for the great principle was encouraged by any success it attained in other nations. Its success in Holland helped its success in England, and what was gained for it in England was an additional encouragement in Holland. The sects that advocated it in Germany had an influence on English thought, and in the reign of Queen Anne, England, in her turn, helped these struggling German sects by delivering more than thirty thousand of them from persecution and settling them in Ireland and America.

In New York, the Dutch, as we have seen, allowed religious liberty to the New England Congregationalists because they feared them, and to the Lutherans because they demanded it; but Jews, Roman Catholics, Baptists, and Quakers they persecuted without mercy. In Holland they granted freedom to many religions to which they had no objection or which they thought it was advisable to encourage, but against others which they did not like they were very severe.

The only way by which the invention of religious

liberty can be traced to one source is by fixing on a favorite source and ignoring all the others. Religious liberty sprang up all over Europe as the result of the revival of learning, the invention of the printing-press, and the progress of the Reformation. There was no country that had not some measure of it, and in each country there were sects, parties, and individuals that had more of it and others that had less of it. Of the people who came from England to America, some, like the Massachusetts Puritans, had none of it, and others, like the Pennsylvania Quakers, had a great deal of it.

Mr. Campbell's argument, that everything advanced and liberal that the Quakers introduced into Pennsylvania must have come from Holland, because the Holland Mennonites were similar in doctrine to the Quakers, is a mere assumption. The Mennonites were a sect as numerous in Germany as in Holland, and many of these German Mennonites settled in Pennsylvania by the encouragement of Penn and his people, but there were very few Hollanders among them. The German Mennonites were a peace sect, like the Quakers, and extremely liberal in their views. They were part of a great movement of religious thought which spread all over the Continent and England in the sixteenth and seventeenth centuries, producing the Quakers and Baptists in England, the Mennonites, Tunkers, Schwenkfelders, Pietists, and a host of other small sects in Germany, and similar sects in Holland, France, and Italy. In Italy the movement gained such ascendency under the leadership of Molinos, the Quietist, that it had to be stopped by the severest measures of the Jesuits and the Inquisition.

Dutch Sources

It is impossible, therefore, to say that Penn and the Pennsylvania Quakers obtained even their religious ideas from Holland alone. In fact, if we start to trace their origin on the Continent, we shall be utterly unable to confine it to any one locality, except by Mr. Campbell's convenient method of exclusion.

He gives instances of laws introduced by Penn which, he says, were copied from Holland, and among these the law requiring every child over the age of twelve to be taught a trade, the law giving one-third of the estate of a murderer to the next of kin of his victim, and the law requiring that before marriage the parents or guardians of the parties should be consulted.

In the case of the law requiring every child to learn a trade the resemblance is very far-fetched. The law in Pennsylvania applied to all children, rich and poor, and was simply an attempt to enforce by statute a practice the Quakers attempted to enforce by their church discipline, of teaching all their children some trade, no matter what were their circumstances in life. But the Holland law, as Mr. Campbell gives it, applied only to the children who became a charge on the public because their parents were too poor to support them (vol. ii. p. 465). There is, therefore, no real resemblance; and even if there was it would not avail Mr. Campbell, for this law was never enforced in Pennsylvania, and has not been adopted in the United States, and even the Quakers themselves soon gave up all attempts to carry it out by their discipline. So if this was an attempt to introduce a Dutch law, it signally failed.

The law giving one-third of the estate of a murderer

to the next of kin of his victim was somewhat like a law of Holland compelling any one who caused the death of another, even by negligence, to pay an annuity to the widow and children. A lawyer would say that the two were by no means alike. But, waiving that, this attempt to introduce a Dutch law also failed. The law was not continued in Pennsylvania, and has not been adopted by the country at large.

The law requiring that before marriage the parents and guardians of the parties should be consulted was another failure. It was abandoned in Pennsylvania, and is not a law of the United States.

In our whole investigation of this subject we have been able to find only one custom introduced into this country for which there is direct and positive evidence of its Dutch origin. This was the custom of marriage before a magistrate, to the exclusion of marriage by a minister of religion, which, as we have shown, Bradford says was taken from Holland by the Pilgrim Fathers. It prevailed for a time in Massachusetts, but has never been accepted by our people. The one instance, therefore, where there is positive proof of Dutch imitation resulted in a failure to establish the imitation, and the three other instances where there is slight or possible evidence of imitation also resulted in failure to establish. This comports with the general principle of my argument in this volume, that our institutions are the growth of natural circumstances and conditions, and are not plagiarisms. Institutions or laws purely exotic or purely imitative usually fail.

Mr. Campbell's extension of the Dutch influence after

Dutch Sources

its establishment in New England, New York, and Pennsylvania is most interesting. Our self-governing States, he says, grew out of the Dutch self-governing towns. He seems to forget that the colonies were all self-governing, even those which, like Virginia, had no township system whatever, and after the Revolution each colony, both South and North, became a self-governing State. Indeed, the vigor with which State rights and State sovereignty were maintained in the Southern States, where Mr. Campbell says there was no Dutch influence, would indicate that there may have been a Netherland influence there which he has overlooked.

Connecticut, he says, was started by "a little detachment from Plymouth, carrying Dutch ideas. . . . Some of its members having doubtless lived in Holland, sailed up the Connecticut River and established a settlement at Windsor." (Vol. ii. p. 416.) Here is that "doubtless" again which he always uses when he has no evidence for an assertion. Afterwards he is able to discover that, when other towns in Connecticut were settled, there was one man among them, Thomas Hooker, who had lived for a time in Holland. Accordingly, when these Connecticut people drew up their fundamental orders on a piece of paper it was the first American written constitution; and, as the Netherland Union of Utrecht was in writing, it must have suggested this Connecticut document, which afterwards, of course, suggested the reducing to writing of the Constitution of the United States.

He forgets that the Massachusetts charter, from which, as we have shown, these fundamental orders of Con-

Evolution of the Constitution

necticut were taken, was also written on a piece of paper or parchment, as was every other charter creating an English colony in America. Whenever a form of government, not having grown up by custom, has to be put in force immediately, or, having grown up by custom, has to be formulated for any purpose, it is natural and even necessary to state it in writing. There is nothing wonderful about it; and most people who can read and write have wit enough to do it.

Our system of recording deeds and mortgages, which Mr. Campbell mentions so often as copied from Holland, might also have been copied from Egypt, where he admits it once prevailed. But the colonists did not have to go so far even as Holland to imitate it, because certain deeds, called deeds of bargain and sale, were recorded in England by the statute of Henry VIII., c. 16. Mr. Campbell seems to have been totally unaware of this. It may not have been mentioned in Carnegie's "Triumphant Democracy," or in the magazine articles he consulted, and he wastes pages and pages of rhetoric on the importance of this gift from Holland.

The recording of deeds is one of those convenient devices which have been known from time immemorial. No one nation can claim the credit of its invention, especially as it is a rather obvious method of accomplishing certain results. But some nations have adopted it, some have not, and some have adopted it only in part. The Pilgrim Fathers, who had lived in Holland, did not introduce it in Massachusetts; but the Puritans, who had never lived in Holland, introduced it, and it was

Dutch Sources

introduced by the English proprietors of both East Jersey and West Jersey in their frames of government.

Along with the recording of deeds, Mr. Campbell has much to say about the equal inheritance of land, which, he insists, was introduced into this country from Holland, as opposed to the system of primogeniture which prevailed in England. In this matter also he wastes many pages of rhetoric on the dreadful evils of primogeniture, which would be crippling and suffocating us to-day if it had not been for Holland.

His mistake here is one which almost any law-student could correct. Before the Norman conquest there was no primogeniture in England, and land descended to children in equal proportions. The Normans introduced the feudal system, and with it primogeniture, which was absolutely essential to the military character of that system. The old Saxon system of equal inheritance, however, survived in the county of Kent; and most of the charters which created the English colonies in America recited that the land should be held on the same tenure as prevailed in "his Majesty's Manor of East Greenwich and County of Kent." This was done because the feudal land tenures and primogeniture would be unsuited to a wilderness country, where there was no aristocracy nor any of the conditions which supported primogeniture in England.

In Massachusetts, where Mr. Campbell supposes the Dutch influence was so strong, the land was expressly held as "of East Greenwich" both in the Plymouth colony and among the Puritans (Winthrop's "New England," vol. ii. p. 301; Palfrey's "New England," p. 20);

and when New York was taken from the Dutch by the English, this same tenure of "East Greenwich and the County of Kent" was introduced.

It may be well, also, to say something of Mr. Campbell's statement that the common- or free-school system of New England was copied from Holland. The importance of free schools has always been obvious, and there were free schools in the Middle Ages. In the Reformation they were recommended in several countries of Europe. Luther advocated them, and, with Melanchthon, drew up the Saxon school system. They were gradually developed in Germany up to 1618; several German states had compulsory education laws, and John Knox had urged their adoption in Scotland in 1560.

In New England they were a gradual native growth. The first schools were not free, but were kept up by the people as best they could from contributions and payments for tuition. Even the famous law which directed each township of fifty householders to have a schoolteacher provided that his "wages shall be paid by the parents or masters of such children, or by the inhabitants in general by way of a supply." The Puritans finally worked out a general free-school system because they were enthusiastic believers in education and learning, and their religion was of a sort that required much erudition and intellectual keenness. They established the free schools in the same spirit which led them to establish Harvard College. But if we are looking for the first free school in America we shall find it in 1621 at Charles City, Virginia,—a part of the country

Dutch Sources

which Mr. Campbell assures us was entirely free from Dutch influence.

It would be useless to follow up all his extraordinary statements of the effect of Dutch influence. They are simply the ingenuity of a brilliant mind carried away by a mere theory. But I shall call attention to one or two points where he has attempted to show Dutch imitation in the development of the Federal government. Finding that in the States-General of the Netherlands each province had only one vote, and that when the Continental Congress assembled at the outbreak of the Revolution each colony had only one vote, he says that one was imitated from the other.

This question whether the colonies should each be represented according to its population, or whether each should have only one vote in any union that was formed, was, as we have shown in previous chapters, an old problem that had been discussed in the plans of union proposed previous to the Revolution and solved in different ways. The general opinion seems to have leaned in favor of representation in proportion to population, but every one felt that the statistics of population were so inaccurate that it would be unsafe to adopt this plan. When the Continental Congress first assembled in Philadelphia, in September, 1774, the subject was debated, and John Adams gives the debate in his diary, with the speeches of the different members. (Adams's Works, vol. ii. p. 366.)

In the whole of this debate there is not a word about the Netherlands. On the contrary, the general feeling was evidently in favor of representation by population, but it was thought impracticable to adopt it without more accurate information. A resolution was finally passed which gives the reason for allowing each colony only a single vote, and it is certainly not Dutch:

"That in determining questions in this Congress each colony or province shall have one vote; the Congress not being possessed of, or at present able to procure proper materials for ascertaining the importance of each colony." ("Journals of Continental Congress," vol. i. p. 10.)

If there is anything in the Articles of Confederation or the Constitution that was imitated from the Netherlands, the debates would surely disclose it, and also the pamphlets that were published criticising the Constitution when it was before the people for adoption. Mr. Campbell makes no quotations from any of these original authorities to support his assertions. He relies entirely on possibilities and presumptions. I have accordingly examined the debates and pamphlets, to see if there was anything that would support him. I find that the Netherlands are often referred to, and also Rome, Greece, Denmark, Poland, Germany, Spain, England, and Switzerland. The general tone is not one of imitation, but rather of dislike and contempt for all European institutions, and I can find nothing that recommends plagiarism.

"Dr. Rush took notice that the decay of the liberties of the Dutch Republic proceeded from three causes: 1. The perfect unanimity requisite on all occasions. 2. Their obligations to consult their constituents. 3. Their voting by provinces. This last destroyed the equality of representation, and the liberties of Great Britain, also, are sinking from the same defect." (Elliot's Debates, vol. i. p. 77.)

Dutch Sources

Voting by states or provinces was by no means a discovery of the Dutch. Hopkins, who followed Dr. Rush, reminded his hearers that voting by states was practised in Germany and Switzerland as well as in Holland. If the voting by colonies in the Articles of Confederation was an imitation, from which country was it imitated? Wilson, the next member to speak, said,—

"The Germanic body is a burlesque on government, and their practice on any point is a sufficient authority and proof that it is wrong. The greatest imperfection in the constitution of the Belgic confederacy is their voting by provinces." (Elliot's Debates, vol. i. p. 78.)

"Mr. Wilson urged the necessity of two branches; observed that if a proper model was not to be found in other confederacies it was not to be wondered at. The number of them was small and the duration of some at least short. The Amphictyonic and Achæan were formed in the infancy of political science and appear by their history and fate to have contained radical defects. The Swiss and Belgic confederacies were held together not by any vital principle of energy, but by the incumbent pressure of formidable neighboring nations. The German owed its continuance to the influence of the house of Austria. He appealed to our own experience for the defects of our confederacy." (Elliot's Debates, Supplement, vol. v. p. 219.)

Mr. Pinckney. "The people of this country are not only very different from the inhabitants of any state we are acquainted with in the modern world, but I assert that their situation is distinct from either the people of Greece or Rome, or of any states we are acquainted with among the ancients. Can the orders introduced by the institutions of Solon, can they be found in the United States? Can the military habits and manners of Sparta be resembled to ours in habits and manners? Are the distinctions of patrician and plebeian known among us? Can the Helvic or Belgic confederacies, or can the unwieldy, unmeaning body called the Germanic empire, can they be said to possess the same, or a situation like ours?" (*Id.*, p. 236.)

Mr. Madison. "What is the state of things in the lax system of the Dutch confederacy? Holland contains about half the people, supplies about half the money, and, by her influence, silently and indirectly governs the whole republic." (*Id.*, p. 252.)

Mr. Gouverneur Morris. "The United Netherlands are at this time torn in factions. With these examples before our eyes shall we form establishments which must necessarily produce the same effects?" (*Id.*, p. 287.)

When the Constitution was referred to the people for adoption, it was thought so unlike anything in Holland or in any other country of Europe that some of its enemies complained of it. There is an interesting passage on this point in an able pamphlet of the time:

"The enemies of the proposed constitution have deemed it material to show that such a one never existed before. It does not, indeed, agree with definitions in books taken from the Amphictyonic Council, the United Netherlands, or the Helvic Body. They would, therefore, infer that it is wrong. This mode of reasoning deserves not a serious refutation. The convention examined those several constitutions, if such they can be called. It found them either woefully defective as to their own particular object or inapplicable to ours. Peradventure our own Articles of Confederation in theory appear more perfect than any of them." ("Remarks on the Proposed Plan of a Federal Government," by Aristides, p. 13.)

APPENDIX

Constitution of the United States

WE THE PEOPLE of the United States, in Order to form a more perfect Union, establish Justice, insure domestic Tranquility, provide for the common defence, promote the general Welfare, and secure the Blessings of Liberty to ourselves and our Posterity, do ordain and establish this CONSTITUTION for the United States of America.

ARTICLE I.

SECTION 1. All legislative Powers herein granted shall be vested in a Congress of the United States, which shall consist of a Senate and House of Representatives.

SECTION 2. The House of Representatives shall be composed of Members chosen every second Year by the People of the several States, and the Electors in each State shall have the Qualifications requisite for Electors of the most numerous Branch of the State Legislature.

No Person shall be a Representative who shall not have attained to the Age of twenty-five Years, and been seven Years a Citizen of the United States, and who shall not, when elected, be an Inhabitant of that State in which he shall be chosen.

[Representatives and direct Taxes shall be apportioned among the several States which may be included within this Union, according to their respective Numbers, which shall be determined by adding to the whole Number of Free persons, including those bound to Service for a Term of Years, and excluding Indians not taxed, three fifths of all other Persons.]* The actual Enumeration shall be made within three Years after the first Meeting of

---

* The clause included within brackets has been altered by the Fourteenth Amendment, section 2.

Evolution of the Constitution

the Congress of the United States, and within every subsequent Term of ten Years, in such Manner as they shall by Law direct. The Number of Representatives shall not exceed one for every thirty Thousand, but each State shall have at Least one Representative; and until such enumeration shall be made, the State of New Hampshire shall be entitled to chuse three, Massachusetts eight, Rhode Island and Providence Plantations one, Connecticut five, New York six, New Jersey four, Pennsylvania eight, Delaware one, Maryland six, Virginia ten, North Carolina five, South Carolina five, and Georgia three.

When vacancies happen in the Representation from any State, the Executive Authority thereof shall issue Writs of Election to fill such Vacancies.

The House of Representatives shall chuse their Speaker and other Officers; and shall have the sole Power of Impeachment.

SECTION 3. The Senate of the United States shall be composed of two Senators from each State, chosen by the Legislature thereof, for six Years; and each Senator shall have one Vote.

Immediately after they shall be assembled in Consequence of the first Election, they shall be divided as equally as may be into three Classes. The seats of the Senators of the first Class shall be vacated at the Expiration of the second year, of the second Class at the Expiration of the fourth Year, and of the third Class at the Expiration of the sixth Year, so that one-third may be chosen every second Year; and if Vacancies happen by Resignation, or otherwise, during the Recess of the Legislature of any State, the Executive thereof may make temporary Appointments until the next Meeting of the Legislature, which shall then fill such Vacancies.

No Person shall be a Senator who shall not have attained to the Age of thirty Years, and been nine Years a Citizen of the United States, and who shall not, when elected, be an Inhabitant of that State for which he shall be chosen.

The Vice President of the United States shall be President of the Senate, but shall have no Vote, unless they be equally divided.

The Senate shall chuse their other Officers, and also a Presi-

Appendix

dent pro tempore, in the Absence of the Vice President, or when he shall exercise the Office of President of the United States.

The Senate shall have the sole Power to try all Impeachments. When sitting for that Purpose, they shall be on Oath or Affirmation. When the President of the United States is tried, the Chief Justice shall preside : and no Person shall be convicted without the Concurrence of two thirds of the Members present.

Judgment in Cases of Impeachment shall not extend further than to removal from Office, and disqualification to hold and enjoy any Office of honor, Trust or Profit under the United States : but the Party convicted shall nevertheless be liable and subject to Indictment, Trial, Judgment and Punishment, according to Law.

SECTION 4. The Times, Places and manner of holding Elections for Senators and Representatives, shall be prescribed in each State by the Legislature thereof; but the Congress may at any time by Law make or alter such Regulations, except as to the Places of chusing Senators.

The Congress shall assemble at least once in every Year, and such Meeting shall be on the first Monday in December, unless they shall by Law appoint a different Day.

SECTION 5. Each House shall be the Judge of the Elections, Returns and Qualifications of its own Members, and a Majority of each shall constitute a Quorum to do Business; but a smaller Number may adjourn from day to day, and may be authorized to compel the Attendance of absent Members, in such Manner, and under such Penalties as each House may provide.

Each House may determine the Rules of its Proceedings, punish its Members for disorderly Behaviour, and, with the Concurrence of two thirds, expel a Member.

Each House shall keep a Journal of its Proceedings, and from time to time publish the same, excepting such Parts as may in their Judgment require Secrecy; and the Yeas and Nays of the Members of either House on any question shall, at the Desire of one fifth of those present, be entered on the Journal.

Neither House, during the Session of Congress, shall, without the Consent of the other, adjourn for more than three days, nor

Evolution of the Constitution

to any other Place than that in which the two Houses shall be sitting.

SECTION 6. The Senators and Representatives shall receive a Compensation for their services, to be ascertained by Law, and paid out of the Treasury of the United States. They shall in all Cases, except Treason, Felony and Breach of the Peace, be privileged from Arrest during their Attendance at the Session of their respective Houses, and in going to and returning from the same; and for any Speech or Debate in either House, they shall not be questioned in any other Place.

No Senator or Representative shall, during the Time for which he was elected, be appointed to any civil Office under the Authority of the United States, which shall have been created, or the Emoluments whereof shall have been encreased during such time; and no Person holding any Office under the United States, shall be a Member of either House during his Continuance in Office.

SECTION 7. All bills for raising Revenue shall originate in the House of Representatives; but the Senate may propose or concur with Amendments as on other Bills.

Every Bill which shall have passed the House of Representatives and the Senate, shall, before it become a Law, be presented to the President of the United States; if he approve he shall sign it, but if not he shall return it, with his Objections to that House in which it shall have originated, who shall enter the Objections at large on their Journal, and proceed to reconsider it. If after such Reconsideration two thirds of that House shall agree to pass the Bill, it shall be sent, together with the Objections, to the other House, by which it shall likewise be reconsidered, and if approved by two-thirds of that House, it shall become a Law. But in all such Cases the Votes of both Houses shall be determined by yeas and Nays, and the Names of the Persons voting for and against the Bill shall be entered on the Journal of each House respectively. If any Bill shall not be returned by the President within ten Days (Sundays excepted) after it shall have been presented to him, the Same shall be a Law, in like Manner as if he had signed it, unless the Congress by their Adjournment prevent its Return, in which Case it shall not be a Law.

Appendix

Every Order, Resolution, or Vote to which the Concurrence of the Senate and House of Representatives may be necessary (except on a question of Adjournment) shall be presented to the President of the United States; and before the Same shall take Effect, shall be approved by him, or being disapproved by him, shall be repassed by two thirds of the Senate and House of Representatives, according to the Rules and Limitations prescribed in the Case of a Bill.

SECTION 8. The Congress shall have Power to lay and collect Taxes, Duties, Imposts and Excises, to pay the Debts and provide for the common Defence and general Welfare of the United States; but all Duties, Imposts and Excises shall be uniform throughout the United States;

To borrow Money on the credit of the United States;

To regulate Commerce with foreign Nations, and among the several States, and with the Indian Tribes;

To establish an uniform Rule of Naturalization, and uniform Laws on the subject of Bankruptcies throughout the United States;

To coin Money, regulate the Value thereof, and of foreign Coin, and fix the Standard of Weights and Measures;

To provide for the Punishment of counterfeiting the Securities and current Coin of the United States;

To establish Post Offices and post Roads;

To promote the Progress of Science and useful Arts, by securing for limited Times to Authors and Inventors the exclusive Right to their respective Writings and Discoveries;

To constitute Tribunals inferior to the supreme Court;

To define and punish Piracies and Felonies committed on the high Seas, and Offences against the Law of Nations;

To declare War, grant Letters of Marque and Reprisal, and make Rules concerning Captures on Land and Water;

To raise and support Armies, but no Appropriation of Money to that Use shall be for a longer Term than two Years;

To provide and maintain a Navy;

To make Rules for the Government and Regulation of the land and naval Forces;

Evolution of the Constitution

To provide for calling forth the Militia to execute the Laws of the Union, suppress Insurrections and repel Invasions;

To provide for organizing, arming, and disciplining, the Militia, and for governing such Part of them as may be employed in the Service of the United States, reserving to the States respectively, the Appointment of the Officers, and the Authority of training the Militia according to the discipline prescribed by Congress;

To exercise exclusive Legislation in all Cases whatsoever, over such District (not exceeding ten Miles square) as may, by Cession of particular States, and the Acceptance of Congress, become the Seat of the Government of the United States, and to exercise like Authority over all Places purchased by the Consent of the Legislature of the State in which the Same shall be, for the Erection of Forts, Magazines, Arsenals, dock-Yards, and other needful Buildings;—And

To make all Laws which shall be necessary and proper for carrying into Execution the foregoing Powers, and all other Powers vested by this Constitution in the Government of the United States, or in any Department or Officer thereof.

SECTION 9. The Migration or Importation of such Persons as any of the States now existing shall think proper to admit, shall not be prohibited by the Congress prior to the Year one thousand eight hundred and eight, but a Tax or duty may be imposed on such Importation, not exceeding ten dollars for each Person.

The Privilege of the Writ of Habeas Corpus shall not be suspended, unless when in Cases of Rebellion or Invasion the public Safety may require it.

No Bill of Attainder or ex post facto Law shall be passed.

No Capitation, or other direct, tax shall be laid, unless in Proportion to the Census or Enumeration herein before directed to be taken.

No Tax or Duty shall be laid on Articles exported from any State.

No Preference shall be given by any Regulation of Commerce or Revenue to the Ports of one State over those of another: nor shall Vessels bound to, or from, one State, be obliged to enter, clear, or pay Duties in another.

Appendix

No Money shall be drawn from the Treasury, but in Consequence of Appropriations made by Law; and a regular Statement and Account of the Receipts and Expenditures of all public Money shall be published from time to time.

No Title of Nobility shall be granted by the United States: And no Person holding any Office of Profit or Trust under them, shall, without the Consent of the Congress, accept of any present, Emolument, Office, or Title, of any kind whatever, from any King, Prince, or foreign State.

SECTION 10. No State shall enter into any Treaty, Alliance, or Confederation; grant Letters of Marque and Reprisal; coin Money; emit Bills of Credit; make any Thing but gold and silver Coin a Tender in Payment of Debts; pass any Bill of Attainder, ex post facto Law, or Law impairing the Obligation of Contracts, or grant any Title of Nobility.

No State shall, without the Consent of the Congress, lay any Imposts or Duties on Imports or Exports, except what may be absolutely necessary for executing it's inspection Laws: and the net Produce of all Duties and Imposts, laid by any State on Imports or Exports, shall be for the Use of the Treasury of the United States; and all such Laws shall be subject to the Revision and Controul of the Congress.

No State shall, without the Consent of Congress, lay any Duty of Tonnage, keep Troops, or Ships of War in time of Peace, enter into any Agreement or Compact with another State, or with a foreign Power, or engage in War, unless actually invaded, or in such imminent Danger as will not admit of delay.

ARTICLE II.

SECTION 1. The executive Power shall be vested in a President of the United States of America. He shall hold his Office during the Term of four Years, and, together with the Vice President, chosen for the same Term, be elected, as follows

Each State shall appoint, in such Manner as the Legislature thereof may direct, a Number of Electors, equal to the whole Number of Senators and Representatives to which the State may be entitled in the Congress: but no Senator or Representative,

Evolution of the Constitution

or Person holding an Office of Trust or Profit under the United States, shall be appointed an Elector.

[The electors shall meet in their respective States, and vote by ballot for two persons, of whom one at least shall not be an inhabitant of the same State with themselves. And they shall make a list of all the persons voted for, and of the number of votes for each; which list they shall sign and certify, and transmit sealed to the seat of the Government of the United States, directed to the President of the Senate. The President of the Senate shall, in the presence of the Senate and House of Representatives, open all the certificates, and the votes shall then be counted. The person having the greatest number of votes shall be the President, if such number be a majority of the whole number of electors appointed; and if there be more than one who have such majority, and have an equal number of votes, then the House of Representatives shall immediately chuse by ballot one of them for President; and if no person have a majority, then from the five highest on the list the said House shall in like manner chuse the President. But in chusing the President, the votes shall be taken by States, the representation from each State having one vote; a quorum for this purpose shall consist of a member or members from two-thirds of the States, and a majority of all the States shall be necessary to a choice. In every case, after the choice of the President, the person having the greatest number of votes of the electors shall be the Vice President. But if there should remain two or more who have equal votes, the Senate shall chuse from them by ballot the Vice President.]*

The Congress may determine the Time of chusing the Electors, and the Day on which they shall give their Votes; which Day shall be the same throughout the United States.

No person except a natural born Citizen, or a Citizen of the United States, at the time of the Adoption of this Constitution, shall be eligible to the Office of President; neither shall any Person be eligible to that office who shall not have attained to the

---

*The clause included within brackets has been superseded by the Twelfth Amendment.

Appendix

Age of thirty five Years, and been fourteen Years a Resident within the United States.

In Case of the Removal of the President from Office, or of his Death, Resignation or Inability to discharge the Powers and Duties of the said Office, the Same shall devolve on the Vice President, and the Congress may by Law provide for the Case of Removal, Death, Resignation or Inability, both of the President and Vice President, declaring what Officer shall then act as President, and such Officer shall act accordingly, until the Disability be removed, or a President shall be elected.

The President shall, at stated Times, receive for his Services, a Compensation, which shall neither be encreased nor diminished during the Period for which he shall have been elected, and he shall not receive within that Period any other Emolument from the United States, or any of them.

Before he enter on the Execution of his Office, he shall take the following Oath or Affirmation :—"I do solemnly swear (or affirm) that I will faithfully execute the Office of President of the United States, and will to the best of my Ability, preserve, protect and defend the Constitution of the United States."

SECTION 2. The President shall be Commander in Chief of the Army and Navy of the United States, and of the Militia of the several States, when called into the actual Service of the United States; he may require the Opinion, in writing, of the principal Officer in each of the executive Departments, upon any Subject relating to the Duties of their respective Offices, and he shall have Power to grant Reprieves and Pardons for Offences against the United States, except in Cases of Impeachment.

He shall have Power, by and with the Advice and Consent of the Senate, to make Treaties, provided two thirds of the Senators present concur; and he shall nominate, and by and with the Advice and Consent of the Senate, shall appoint Ambassadors, other public Ministers and Consuls, Judges of the supreme Court, and all other Officers of the United States, whose Appointments are not herein otherwise provided for, and which shall be established by Law: but the Congress may by Law vest the Appointment of such inferior Officers, as they think proper, in the President alone, in the Courts of Law, or in the Heads of Departments.

The President shall have Power to fill up all Vacancies that may happen during the recess of the Senate, by granting Commissions which shall expire at the End of their next Session.

SECTION 3. He shall from time to time give to the Congress Information of the state of the Union, and recommend to their Consideration such Measures as he shall judge necessary and expedient; he may, on extraordinary Occasions, convene both Houses, or either of them, and, in Case of Disagreement between them, with Respect to the Time of Adjournment, he may adjourn them to such Time as he shall think proper; he shall receive Ambassadors and other public Ministers; he shall take Care that the Laws be faithfully executed; and shall Commission all the Officers of the United States.

SECTION 4. The President, Vice President and all civil Officers of the United States, shall be removed from Office on Impeachment for, and Conviction of, Treason, Bribery, or other high Crimes and Misdemeanors.

ARTICLE III.

SECTION 1. The judicial Power of the United States, shall be vested in one supreme Court, and in such inferior Courts as the Congress may from time to time ordain and establish. The Judges, both of the supreme and inferior Courts, shall hold their Offices during good Behaviour, and shall, at stated Times, receive for their Services, a Compensation, which shall not be diminished during their Continuance in Office.

SECTION 2. The judicial Power shall extend to all Cases, in Law and Equity, arising under this Constitution, the Laws of the United States, and Treaties made, or which shall be made, under their Authority;—to all Cases affecting Ambassadors, other public Ministers and Consuls;—to all Cases of admiralty and maritime Jurisdiction;—to Controversies to which the United States shall be a Party;—to Controversies between two or more States; —between a State and Citizens of another State;—between Citi-

Appendix

zens of different States,—between Citizens of the same State claiming Lands under Grants of different States, and between a State, or the Citizens thereof, and foreign States, Citizens or Subjects.

In all Cases affecting Ambassadors, other public Ministers and Consuls, and those in which a State shall be Party, the supreme Court shall have original Jurisdiction. In all the other Cases before mentioned, the supreme Court shall have appellate Jurisdiction, both as to Law and Fact, with such Exceptions, and under such Regulations as the Congress shall make.

The Trial of all Crimes, except in Cases of Impeachment, shall be by Jury; and such Trial shall be held in the State where the said Crimes shall have been committed; but when not committed within any State, the Trial shall be at such Place or Places as the Congress may by Law have directed.

SECTION 3. Treason against the United States, shall consist only in levying War against them, or in adhering to their Enemies, giving them Aid and Comfort. No Person shall be convicted of Treason unless on the Testimony of two Witnesses to the same overt Act, or on Confession in open Court.

The Congress shall have Power to declare the Punishment of Treason, but no Attainder of Treason shall work Corruption of Blood, or Forfeiture except during the Life of the Person attainted.

ARTICLE IV.

SECTION 1. Full Faith and Credit shall be given in each State to the public Acts, Records, and judicial Proceedings of every other State. And the Congress may by general Laws prescribe the Manner in which such Acts, Records and Proceedings shall be proved, and the Effect thereof.

SECTION 2. The Citizens of each State shall be entitled to all Privileges and Immunities of Citizens in the several States.

A person charged in any State with Treason, Felony, or other Crime, who shall flee from Justice, and be found in another State, shall on Demand of the executive Authority of the State from which he fled, be delivered up to be removed to the State having Jurisdiction of the Crime.

Evolution of the Constitution

No Person held to Service or Labour in one State, under the Laws thereof, escaping into another, shall, in Consequence of any Law or Regulation therein, be discharged from such Service or Labour, but shall be delivered up on Claim of the Party to whom such Service or Labour may be due.

SECTION 3. New States may be admitted by the Congress into this Union; but no new State shall be formed or erected within the Jurisdiction of any other State; nor any State be formed by the Junction of two or more States, or Parts of States, without the Consent of the Legislatures of the States concerned as well as of the Congress.

The Congress shall have Power to dispose of and make all needful Rules and Regulations respecting the Territory or other Property belonging to the United States; and nothing in this Constitution shall be so construed as to Prejudice any Claims of the United States, or of any particular State.

SECTION 4. The United States shall guarantee to every State in this Union a Republican Form of Government, and shall protect each of them against Invasion; and on Application of the Legislature, or of the Executive (when the Legislature cannot be convened) against domestic Violence.

ARTICLE V.

The Congress, whenever two thirds of both Houses shall deem it necessary, shall propose Amendments to this Constitution, or, on the Application of the Legislatures of two thirds of the several States, shall call a Convention for proposing Amendments, which, in either Case, shall be valid to all Intents and Purposes, as Part of this Constitution, when ratified by the Legislatures of three fourths of the several States, or by Conventions in three fourths thereof, as the one or the other Mode of Ratification may be proposed by the Congress; Provided that no Amendment which may be made prior to the Year One thousand eight hundred and eight shall in any Manner affect the first and fourth Clauses in the Ninth Section of the first Article; and that no State, without its Consent, shall be deprived of its equal Suffrage in the Senate.

Appendix

ARTICLE VI.

All Debts contracted and Engagements entered into, before the Adoption of this Constitution, shall be as valid against the United States under this Constitution, as under the Confederation.

This Constitution, and the Laws of the United States which shall be made in Pursuance thereof; and all Treaties made, or which shall be made, under the Authority of the United States, shall be the supreme Law of the Land; and the Judges in every State shall be bound thereby, any Thing in the Constitution or Laws of any State to the Contrary notwithstanding.

The Senators and Representatives before mentioned, and the Members of the several State Legislatures, and all executive and judicial Officers, both of the United States and of the several States, shall be bound by Oath or Affirmation, to support this Constitution; but no religious Test shall ever be required as a Qualification to any Office or public Trust under the United States.

ARTICLE VII.

The ratification of the Conventions of nine States, shall be sufficient for the Establishment of this Constitution between the States so ratifying the Same.

DONE in Convention by the Unanimous Consent of the States present the Seventeenth Day of September in the Year of our Lord one thousand seven hundred and Eighty seven, and of the Independance of the United States of America the Twelfth In Witness whereof We have hereunto subscribed our Names,

            G°: WASHINGTON—
         Presidt. and Deputy from Virginia

New Hampshire.

JOHN LANGDON,   NICHOLAS GILMAN.

Massachusetts.

NATHANIEL GORHAM,   RUFUS KING.

Connecticut.

WM. SAML. JOHNSON,   ROGER SHERMAN.

Evolution of the Constitution

New York.

ALAXANDER HAMILTON.

New Jersey.

WIL: LIVINGSTON, WM. PATERSON,
DAVID BREARLEY, JONA. DAYTON.

Pennsylvania.

B. FRANKLIN, THOS. FITZSIMONS,
THOMAS MIFFLIN, JARED INGERSOLL,
ROBT. MORRIS, JAMES WILSON,
GEO. CLYMER, GOUV. MORRIS.

Delaware.

GEO. READ, RICHARD BASSETT,
GUNNING BEDFORD, Jun., JACO: BROOM.
JOHN DICKINSON,

Maryland.

JAMES MCHENRY, DAN. CARROLL.
DAN. JENIFER, OF ST. THOMAS,

Virginia.

JOHN BLAIR, JAMES MADISON, Jr.

North Carolina.

WM. BLOUNT, HUGH WILLIAMSON.
RICH'D DOBBS SPEIGHT,

South Carolina.

J. RUTLEDGE, CHARLES PINCKNEY,
CHARLES COTESWORTH PINCKNEY, PIERCE BUTLER.

Georgia.

WILLIAM FEW, ABR. BALDWIN.

Attest: WILLIAM JACKSON, *Secretary.*

Appendix

Amendments

ARTICLE I.

Congress shall make no law respecting an establishment of religion, or prohibiting the free exercise thereof; or abridging the freedom of speech, or of the press; or the right of the people peaceably to assemble, and to petition the Government for a redress of grievances.

ARTICLE II.

A well-regulated Militia, being necessary to the security of a free State, the right of the people to keep and bear Arms, shall not be infringed.

ARTICLE III.

No Soldier shall, in time of peace, be quartered in any house, without the consent of the Owner, nor in time of war, but in a manner to be prescribed by law.

ARTICLE IV.

The right of the people to be secure in their persons, houses, papers, and effects, against unreasonable searches and seizures, shall not be violated, and no Warrants shall issue, but upon probable cause, supported by Oath or affirmation, and particularly describing the place to be searched, and the persons or things to be seized.

ARTICLE V.

No person shall be held to answer for a capital, or otherwise infamous crime, unless on a presentment or indictment of a Grand Jury, except in cases arising in the land or naval forces, or in the Militia, when in actual service in time of War or public danger; nor shall any person be subject for the same offence to be twice put in jeopardy of life or limb; nor shall be compelled in any Criminal Case to be a witness against himself, nor be deprived of life, liberty, or property, without due process of law; nor shall private property be taken for public use, without just compensation.

Evolution of the Constitution

ARTICLE VI.

In all criminal prosecutions, the accused shall enjoy the right to a speedy and public trial, by an impartial jury of the State and district wherein the crime shall have been committed; which district shall have been previously ascertained by law, and to be informed of the nature and cause of the accusation; to be confronted with the witnesses against him; to have compulsory process for obtaining witnesses in his favor, and to have the Assistance of Counsel for his defence.

ARTICLE VII.

In suits at common law, where the value in controversy shall exceed twenty dollars, the right of trial by jury shall be preserved, and no fact tried by a jury shall be otherwise re-examined in any Court of the United States, than according to the rules of the common law.

ARTICLE VIII.

Excessive bail shall not be required, nor excessive fines imposed, nor cruel and unusual punishments inflicted.

ARTICLE IX.

The enumeration in the Constitution, of certain rights, shall not be construed to deny or disparage others retained by the people.

ARTICLE X.

The powers not delegated to the United States by the Constitution, nor prohibited by it to the States, are reserved to the States respectively, or to the people.

ARTICLE XI.

The Judicial power of the United States shall not be construed to extend to any suit in law or equity, commenced or prosecuted against one of the United States by Citizens of another State, or by Citizens or Subjects of any Foreign State.

Appendix

ARTICLE XII.

The Electors shall meet in their respective states, and vote by ballot for President and Vice-President, one of whom, at least, shall not be an inhabitant of the same State with themselves; they shall name in their ballots the person voted for as President, and in distinct ballots the person voted for as Vice-President, and they shall make distinct lists of all persons voted for as President, and of all persons voted for as Vice-President, and of the number of votes for each, which lists they shall sign and certify, and transmit sealed to the seat of the Government of the United States, directed to the President of the Senate;—The President of the Senate shall, in the presence of the Senate and House of Representatives, open all the certificates and the votes shall then be counted;—The person having the greatest number of votes for President, shall be the President, if such number be a majority of the whole number of Electors appointed; and if no person have such majority, then from the persons having the highest numbers not exceeding three on the list of those voted for as President, the House of Representatives shall choose immediately, by ballot, the President. But in choosing the President, the votes shall be taken by states, the representation from each state having one vote; a quorum for this purpose shall consist of a member or members from two-thirds of the states, and a majority of all the states shall be necessary to a choice. And if the House of Representatives shall not choose a President whenever the right of choice shall devolve upon them, before the fourth day of March next following, then the Vice-President shall act as President, as in the case of the death or other constitutional disability of the President. The person having the greatest number of votes as Vice-President, shall be the Vice-President, if such number be a majority of the whole number of Electors appointed, and if no person have a majority, then from the two highest numbers on the list, the Senate shall choose the Vice-President; a quorum for the purpose shall consist of two-thirds of the whole number of Senators, and a majority of the whole number shall be necessary to a choice. But no person constitutionally ineligible to the

Evolution of the Constitution

office of President shall be eligible to that of Vice-President of the United States.

ARTICLE XIII.

SECTION 1. Neither slavery nor involuntary servitude, except as a punishment for crime whereof the party shall have been duly convicted, shall exist within the United States, or any place subject to their jurisdiction.

SECTION 2. Congress shall have power to enforce this article by appropriate legislation.

ARTICLE XIV.

SECTION 1. All persons born or naturalized in the United States, and subject to the jurisdiction thereof, are citizens of the United States and of the State wherein they reside. No State shall make or enforce any law which shall abridge the privileges or immunities of citizens of the United States; nor shall any State deprive any person of life, liberty, or property, without due process of law; nor deny to any person within its jurisdiction the equal protection of the laws.

SECTION 2. Representatives shall be apportioned among the several States according to their respective numbers, counting the whole number of persons in each State, excluding Indians not taxed. But when the right to vote at any election for the choice of electors for President and Vice-President of the United States, Representatives in Congress, the Executive and Judicial officers of a State, or the members of the Legislature thereof, is denied to any of the male inhabitants of such State, being twenty-one years of age, and citizens of the United States, or in any way abridged, except for participation in rebellion, or other crime, the basis of representation therein shall be reduced in the proportion which the number of such male citizens shall bear to the whole number of male citizens twenty-one years of age in such State.

SECTION 3. No person shall be a Senator or Representative in Congress, or elector of President and Vice-President, or hold any office, civil or military, under the United States, or under any State, who, having previously taken an oath, as a member of Congress, or as an officer of the United States, or as a member

Appendix

of any State Legislature, or as an executive or judicial officer of any State, to support the Constitution of the United States, shall have engaged in insurrection or rebellion against the same, or given aid or comfort to the enemies thereof. But Congress may by a vote of two-thirds of each House, remove such disability.

SECTION 4. The validity of the public debt of the United States, authorized by law, including debts incurred for payment of pensions and bounties for services in suppressing insurrection or rebellion, shall not be questioned. But neither the United States nor any State shall assume or pay any debt or obligation incurred in aid of insurrection or rebellion against the United States, or any claim for the loss or emancipation of any slave; but all such debts, obligations and claims shall be held illegal and void.

SECTION 5. The Congress shall have power to enforce, by appropriate legislation, the provisions of this article.

ARTICLE XV.

SECTION 1. The right of citizens of the United States to vote shall not be denied or abridged by the United States or by any State on account of race, color, or previous condition of servitude.

SECTION 2. The Congress shall have power to enforce this article by appropriate legislation.

Index

Absolutism, 105.
Adjournment, 65, 98, 99, 135.
Ambassador, 96, 295.
Amendment, 61, 78, 176, 265, 311.
Andros, Sir Edmund, 222.
Appointing power, 64, 78, 98, 171.
Apportionment of Congress, 100.
Arms, right to bear, 208.
Army, 96, 299.
Arrest, privilege from, 132.
Attainder of treason, 210.

Bail, 205.
Bankruptcy, 311.
Bellomont, Earl of, 228.
Bill of rights, 54.
Blackstone, Commentaries of, 94.
Borrow money, power to, 297.
Boundary disputes, 241.
Bradford, 330.
Bryce, 12, 94.

Campbell, on origin of institutions, 13, 19, 315.
Captures, 294.
Carolinas, 41, 51.
Carson, Hampton L., 217.
Censors, council of, 80.
Census, 267, 273.
College, the, of Philadelphia, 262.
Columbia, District of, 310.
Commander-in-chief, 158, 226.
Commerce, regulation of, 99, 225, 293, 311.

Confederation, Articles of, 242.
Congress, control of, by president, 99; general powers of, 275; presiding officer of, 276; restrictions on, 277.
Connecticut, Fundamental Orders of, 41; charter of, 24, 44; Dutch influence in, 367.
Constitution, sources of the, 19; great age of, 22.
Constitutions, native, 23; of 1776, 23, 25, 70.
Continental Congress, 238.
Contracts, obligation of, 262.
Controversies between states, 305.
Convention, the, of 1787, 255.
Corporations, use of, in America, 119.
Council for Foreign Plantations, 222.
Council, the, for New England, 339.
County, the, in Virginia, 337.
Coxe, Brinton, 185.

Debate, freedom of, 130.
Debts under Confederation, 310.
Deeds, recording of, 319, 368.
Departments, confusion of, 34, 38, 64; separate, 109.
Domestic violence in a state, 310.
Drayton, William Henry, 250.
Du Chaillu, 14.
Dudley, Governor, 346.

Index

Duke of York, grants to, 41.
Dutch, in New York, 352, 354, 359; in New England, 353; their ideas of religious liberty, 357; in Pennsylvania, 359, 365.

East India Company, 93,
East Jersey, Concessions of, 48, 50.
Elections, manner of holding, 311.
Electors of the president, 83, 153.
Embargoes, 78.
Eminent domain, 214.
English sources of the constitution, 90.
Excessive bail and fines, 205.
Execution of the laws, 60, 98, 150, 156, 158.
Executive, 80, 94, 242, 246, 248.
Expenditure of public money, 314.
Export duties, 311.
Ex post facto laws, 82, 210.

Federal power, 249, 251.
Federalism, 215, 217, 219.
Fines, 205.
Foster, on the Constitution, 13.
Franklin, Benjamin, his plans of union, 231, 238, 240.
Free schools, 324.
Freedom of debate, 130.
Freedom of the press, 206.
Furly, Benjamin, 361.

Galloway, Joseph, 238.
Georgia, charter of, 68, 70.
German origin of New England towns, 13.
Gladstone, 11.
Grocers' Company, 28.

Habeas corpus, 212.
Hamilton, his plan of union, 261.
House of representatives, 117.
Hue and cry, 220.
Hutchinson, his plan of union, 235.

Impeachment, 59, 78, 86, 147.
Inconsistent offices, 103.
Indians, origin of, 14.
Indians, treatment of, by the Dutch, 358.
Intercourse among the colonies, 220, 221, 225, 245, 290.
Inventions, 188.

Jeopardy, twice in, 205.
Johnson, Dr. Samuel, his plan of union, 236.
Judiciary, the, 174, 295.
Jury, trial by, 201.

Keith, Sir William, 231.
Kid, Social Evolution, 22.

Liberty, religious, 190.
Locke, John, 51.
Lords of Trade, 222.

Madoc, the Welsh prince, 14.
Marque, letters of, 96, 309.
Martial law, 212.
Maryland, charter of, 40; constitution of, 81.
Massachusetts, constitutional experience of, 20, 25; first charter of, 37; second charter of, 62; rejected constitution of, 86; second constitution of, 88.
Mayflower, agreement on board of, 35.

Index

Measures, standard of, 298.
Meigs, William M., 185.
Mennonites, the, 364.
Merchant adventurers, 29.
Message of president, 85, 97, 170.
Militia, 208.
Money, regulation of the value of, 237, 298.
Money, when to be issued from treasury, 307.
Money-bills, 133.
Montesquieu, Spirit of Laws, 114.

Name of United States, 274.
Nationality, 261, 266, 309.
Naturalization, 189.
Navy, 304.
New England, charter of, 35.
New England towns, 318, 320, 325, 336, 340, 342.
New England union, 219.
New Hampshire, grants of, 41; commission for, 55; first constitution of, 71; rejected constitution of, 87; second constitution of, 88.
New Jersey, constitution of, 77.
New states, 311.
New York, constitution of, 83.
Nobility, titles of, 211.
Non-importation agreements, 238.

Obligation of contracts, 262.

Pardoning power, 96, 167.
Patents, 188.
Paterson's plan of union, 261.
Patrick, David, 347.
Peace, power to declare, 266.
Penn, William, 57, 223, 360.

Pennsylvania, constitutional experience of, 21; charter of, 41; first frame of, 56, 65; charter of privileges of, 65; constitution of, 79.
Peters, Hugh, 346.
Peters, Richard, 235.
Petition, right to, 207.
Pinckney's plan of union, 258.
Post-office, 307.
Presents, 211.
Presiding officer of senate, 129.
Primogeniture, 324, 369.
Prisoner's privilege of counsel and witnesses, 203.
Privilege from arrest, 132.
Privy council, 76, 222.
Procedure of Congress, 143.
Profit, offices of, 211.
Punishments, 205.
Puritans, Dutch influence among, 343.

Quartering of soldiers, 209.
Quorum of Congress, 102.

Raleigh, Sir Walter, his charter, 19, 26, 105.
Randolph's plan, 255.
Religion, freedom of, 190, 324, 357, 362.
Representation, 234, 245, 267, 371.
Representatives, house of, 117.
Republican government in a state, 311.
Rhode Island, charter of, 24, 47; patent for, 44; not in New England union, 221.
Rights, bill of, 54, 62, 67, 81.

Index

Salaries, 313.
Schools, free, 370.
Seizures and searches, 199.
Senate, 18, 63, 72, 73, 75, 100, 123, 129.
Separate departments, 109.
Servants, escape of, 220.
Slavery, 311.
Soldiers, quartering of, 209.
South Carolina, constitution of, 73; second constitution of, 87.
Sovereignty of states, 284.
Speakership of Congress, 143.
Spencer, Herbert, 314.
States, controversies between, 305; restrictions on, 279.
Stevens, on the constitution, 13.
Stone, Frederick D., 217.
Subject, equivalent to citizen, 205.

Taxation, 232, 287.
Taylor on the Constitution, 13.
Territory, 311.
Thayer, on Unconstitutional Law, 185.
Towns of New England, 13, 318, 320, 325, 336, 340, 342.
Treason, 210, 250, 308.
Treaty, power to make a, 306.
Trial by jury, 201.
Twice in jeopardy, 205.

Unconstitutional laws, prevention of, 182.
Union, plans of, 218, 267; plan of Charles II., 222; plan of James II., 222; plan of, in 1690, 223, plan of William Penn, 223; plan of Lords of Trade, 227; D'Avenant's plan, 228; a Virginian's plan, 228; Livingston's plan, 229; Earl of Stair's plan, 229; Coxe's plan, 230; Franklin's plan, in 1754, 231; Peters's plan, 235; Hutchinson's plan, 235; Johnson's plan, 236; Galloway's plan, 238; Franklin's plan, in 1775, 238, 240.

Vacancies in office, 312.
Vermont, constitution of, 86; second constitution of, 89.
Veto power, 17, 84, 95, 161, 234.
Virginia, constitutional experience of, 21; first charter of, 27, 29; second charter of, 30; third charter of, 32; house of burgesses of, 33; charter dissolved, 34; constitution of, 75.
Von Holst, 314.

War, power to declare, 96, 140, 226.
Webster, Noah, 252.
Weights, standard of, 298.
West India Company, 356.
West Jersey, Concessions of, 50, 53.
Winslow, Edward, 351.
Winthrop, Governor, 333, 336.

THE END.

Electrotyped and Printed by J. B. Lippincott Company, Philadelphia, U.S.A.

www.ingramcontent.com/pod-product-compliance
Lightning Source LLC
Chambersburg PA
CBHW051248300426
44114CB00011B/941